# The Politics of Iranian C

Iran has undergone considerable social upheaval since the revolution and this has been reflected in its cinema. Drawing on first-hand interviews and ethnographic research, this book explores how cinema is engaged in the dynamics of social change in contemporary Iran. The author not only discusses the practices of regulation and reception of films from major award-winning directors but also important mainstream filmmakers such as Hatamikia and Tabizi.

Contributing to ethnographic accounts of Iranian governance in the field of culture, the book reveals the complex behind-the-scenes negotiations between filmmakers and the authorities which constitute a major part of the workings of film censorship. The author traces the relationship of Iranian cinema to recent social/political movements in Iran, namely the reformist and the women's movements, and shows how international acclaim has been instrumental in filmmakers' engagement with matters of political importance in Iran.

This book will be a valuable tool for courses on film and media studies, and will provide a significant insight into Iranian cultural politics for students of cultural studies and anthropology, Middle Eastern and Iranian studies.

**Saeed Zeydabadi-Nejad** completed his PhD in Media Studies in 2006 at SOAS, University of London. He currently teaches at the Centre for Media and Film Studies at SOAS and at the Institute of Ismaili Studies.

## Iranian Studies

Edited by Homa Katouzian
*University of Oxford*
*and Mohamad Tavakoli, University of Toronto.*

Since 1967 the International Society for Iranian Studies (ISIS) has been a leading learned society for the advancement of new approaches in the study of Iranian society, history, culture, and literature. The new ISIS Iranian Studies series published by Routledge will provide a venue for the publication of original and innovative scholarly works in all areas of Iranian and Persianate Studies.

1    **Journalism in Iran**
     From mission to profession
     *Hossein Shahidi*

2    **Sadeq Hedayat**
     His work and his wondrous world
     *Homa Katouzian*

3    **Iran in the 21st Century**
     Politics, economics and confrontation
     *Homa Katouzian and Hossein Shahidi*

4    **Media, Culture and Society in Iran**
     Living with globalization and the Islamic state
     *Mehdi Semati*

5    **Modern Persian Literature in Afghanistan**
     Anomalous visions of history and form
     *Wali Ahmadi*

6    **The Politics of Iranian Cinema**
     Film and society in the Islamic Republic
     *Saeed Zeydabadi-Nejad*

# The Politics of Iranian Cinema

Film and society in the Islamic Republic

**Saeed Zeydabadi-Nejad**

Routledge
Taylor & Francis Group

LONDON AND NEW YORK

First published 2010 by Routledge
2 Park Square, Milton Park, Abingdon, Oxon OX14 4RN

Simultaneously published in the USA and Canada
by Routledge
270 Madison Ave, New York, NY 10016

*Routledge is an imprint of the Taylor & Francis Group, an informa business*

© 2010 Saeed Zeydabadi-Nejad

Typeset in Times New Roman by Swales & Willis Ltd, Exeter, Devon
Printed and bound in Great Britain by TJ International Ltd, Padstow, Cornwall

*British Library Cataloguing in Publication Data*
A catalogue record for this book is available
from the British Library

*Library of Congress Cataloging in Publication Data*
Zeydabadi-Nejad, Saeed.
    The politics of Iranian cinema : film and society in the Islamic Republic /
    Saeed Zeydabadi-Nejad.
    p. cm.—(Iranian studies ; 6)
    Based on the author's thesis (doctoral)—School of Oriental and African Studies, 2006.
    Includes bibliographical references and index.
    Includes filmography.
    1. Motion pictures—Social aspects—Iran. 2. Motion pictures—Political aspects—Iran.
    3. Motion picture industry—Government policy—Iran. I. Title.
    PN1993.5.I846Z49 2009
    384'.80955—dc22
    2009014858

ISBN10: 0–415–45536–7 (hbk)
ISBN10: 0–415–45537–5 (pbk)
ISBN10: 0–203–86847–1 (ebk)

ISBN13: 978–0–415–45536–7 (hbk)
ISBN13: 978–0–415–45537–4 (pbk)
ISBN13: 978–0–203–86847–8 (ebk)

**To Emmanuela and Sophia Shirin**
**And to the memory of my parents**

# Contents

*Acknowledgements*                                                          ix
*List of tables*                                                            xi
*List of illustrations*                                                     xii

**1  Introduction**                                                          1

*An overview of media research  3*
*Areas of inquiry  5*
*Theoretical framework  6*
*Chapter outline  28*

**2  State control of Iranian cinema: the shifting 'red lines'**            30

*Introduction  30*
*Cinema and the state before the revolution  31*
*The Islamic revolution and its aftermath  34*
*Conclusion  53*

**3  'Social films'**                                                        55

*Introduction  55*
Marriage of the Blessed *(Makhmalbaf 1989)  56*
Glass Agency *(Hatamikia 1997)  69*
House on the Water *(Farmanara 2001)  76*
The Lizard *(Tabrizi 2004)  90*
*A note on the economics of Iranian cinema  100*
*Conclusion  102*

**4  'Women's films'**                                                      104

*Introduction  104*
*Changes to women's social position in contemporary Iran:*
  *an overview  106*
*Background to women and Iranian cinema  107*

Fifth Reaction *(Milani 2003)  110*
10 *(Kiarostami 2002)  125*
*Conclusion  136*

**5    Transnational circulation and national perceptions: art films in
      the Iranian context**                                              138

*Introduction  138*
*Reactions to the New Wave films (1969–79)  139*
*State authorities and international success  142*
*Art cinema filmmakers  149*
*Women and international success  157*
*Reactions among cinema-goers  158*
*Conclusion  159*

**6    Conclusion**                                                      161


*Notes*                                                                  165
*Bibliography*                                                           172
*Filmography*                                                            182
*Index*                                                                  185

# Acknowledgements

I owe my heartfelt thanks to Iran Heritage Foundation for supporting me with a grant to complete this book.

I would like to express my deep gratitude to Professor Emeritus Richard Tapper and Professor Annabelle Sreberny. Both of them supported and encouraged me throughout the time that they supervised my PhD research, upon which this book is based. Their help was crucial in improving it with stimulating comments and helpful suggestions. Special thanks are due to Richard for doing this even after he had retired from his post at School of Oriental and African Studies. I am indebted to both and not least because their great company made our regular meetings a pleasure to look forward to.

I am very grateful to Professor Michael M.J. Fischer for reading a draft of this book and offering invaluable advice. I would also like to thank Dr Ziba Mir-Hosseini, Professor Laura Mulvey, Dr Lloyd Ridgeon, Dr Jerome Bredt and Dr Christopher Gow for either reading the entire manuscript or large sections of it and making suggestions.

There are very many people in Iran to whom I am indebted for helping me with my PhD research fieldwork. I would like to thank the staff of *Mahnameh-ye sinema'i-ye film*, particularly, 'Ali-Reza Mo'tamedi and Hushang Golmakani for giving me interviews, and Hamid Reza Sadr for putting me in touch with a number of filmmakers. I am grateful to the following filmmakers for interviews with me in spite of their busy time schedules: Mohsen Makhmalbaf, Ebrahim Hatamikia, Bahman Farmanara, Kamal Tabrizi, Tahmineh Milani, Behruz Afkhami, Mania Akbari, Jafar Panahi, Parviz Shahbazi and Manijeh Hekmat. Seyed Mohammad Beheshti (the former head of Farabi Cinema Foundation), Seyfollah Dad (the former cinema deputy of the Ministry of Culture and Islamic Guidance (MCIG)), and Habibollah Kasehsaz (the former head of *Nezarat* section of the MCIG) were generous with their time for interviews and I am much obliged to them. I wish to thank Mohammad-Hassan Tahmasebi and Hossein Mohammadi of the MCIG for providing me with much information. Thanks are due to those in Mashhad and Tehran who spent hours watching and/or discussing films with me. For all film still photographs in this book and for permission to reproduce them I owe special thanks to Rakhshan Bani-Etemad. I am thankful to Hamed Ghofrani for taking some photographs in Iran for this book. I also wish to thank Taylor and Francis for permitting me to include a revised version of my article in the *British Journal of Middle Eastern Studies*, 34 (3): 375–98.

Finally, I owe more than I can express in words to my wife Emmanuela, to whom this work is dedicated.

# Tables

| | | |
|---|---|---|
| 3.1 | Box office ranking for the top ten films in 1368/1989 | 60 |
| 3.2 | Box office ranking for the top ten films in 1377/1998 | 72 |
| 3.3 | Censorship of *House on the Water* | 85 |
| 3.4 | Box office rankings for the top ten films in 1382/2003: *House on the Water* | 86 |
| 4.1 | Box office rankings for the top ten films in 1382/2003: *Fifth Reaction* | 114 |
| 5.1 | The international appearance of Iranian cinema in figures | 141 |
| 5.2 | Mohsen Makhmalbaf's films released between 1989 and 1997 | 158 |
| 5.3 | Rakhshan Bani-Etemad's films between 1989 and 1997 | 159 |
| 5.4 | Abbas Kiarostami and Jafar Panahi's films between 1989 and 1997 | 159 |

# Illustrations

1.1 Cinemas on Azadi Ave in the centre of Tehran; photograph
by the author                                                                 24
2.1 Entrance to what used to be Ferdowsi Cinema in Mashhad
which was destroyed in a fire during the revolution; photograph
by the author                                                                 34
2.2 Cinema Qods (formerly Aria) in Mashhad, burnt down during
the revolution; the cinema was rebuilt shortly afterwards;
photograph by the author                                                      35
3.1 Advertisement for Mohsen Makhmalbaf's *Marriage of the
Blessed* on the cover of *Mahnameh-ye sinema'i-ye film*                        57
3.2 Photograph of the author with Mohsen Makhmalbaf, June 2003                 65
3.3 Advertisement for Ebrahim Hatamikia's *Glass Agency* on the
cover of *Mahnameh-ye sinema'i-ye film*                                        69
3.4 Advertisement pamphlet for *House on the Water*                            78
3.5 Still from Bahman Farmanara's *House on the Water* showing
Sefidbakht at a newspaper stand; he notices that he is
being followed                                                                 80
3.6 Still from Bahman Farmanara's *House on the Water*; Sefidbakht
is murdered in his house                                                       81
3.7 Still from Kamal Tabrizi's *Leili is with Me* showing Sadeq
feeling sorry for himself on the way to the war-front                          91
3.8 Still from Kamal Tabrizi's *The Lizard* showing Reza in his
friend's house before he embarks on the trip to the Iran–
Turkey border                                                                  92
3.9 Still from Kamal Tabrizi's *The Lizard* showing Reza preaching             93
3.10 VCD stand, Central Tehran, September 2008; photograph by
Hamed Ghofrani                                                                 101
3.11 VCD stand, Central Tehran, September 2008; photograph by
Hamed Ghofrani                                                                 102
4.1 Cinema Pars in central Tehran showing *Fifth Reaction*,
May 2003; photograph by the author                                            110
5.1 Still from Jafar Panahi's *The Circle*                                     148
5.2 Still from Rakhshan Bani-Etemad's *May Lady*                               154

# 1 Introduction

On 28 October 2003, after the screening of *Deep Breath* (2003) at the Institute of Contemporary Art (ICA) in London, Parviz Shahbazi, the director of the film, appeared on the stage for a Q and A session with the audience who had packed the hall. Responding to a question, the director claimed that if Iraq had a cinema like Iran, it would not have been invaded. This was an extraordinary claim to make, to say the least. Just over six months after the US-led invasion, the situation in Iraq had not yet got out of control and a follow-up attack on Iran, which was the next in line in the 'axis of evil', was therefore not out of the question. The filmmaker's optimism was perhaps built on the idea that Iranian films had humanized the Iranian people to the West. Therefore they would not be seen as the 'other' whose country the USA or the UK would invade. He was perhaps assuming that there would be resistance to the idea of war on Iran at least by the general public in the West. Obviously, he was unaware of the small size of foreign film audiences in the West. In addition, the fact that Tony Blair took Britain to the Iraq war in spite of massive public opposition was lost on the director who only visited the West occasionally. Whatever the filmmaker's logic, what is most significant about his extraordinary assertion is the close connection that he assumed between cinema and politics. He seemed to take it for granted that films could have great political impact. While it would be surprising to assume such a close link between cinema and politics in most places, in Iran it is not strange.

Politics in Iran has been effectively inseparable from culture in its recent history. In February 1979 at the height of the Iranian revolution, Ayatollah Khomeini, in his first speech in Iran upon return from exile, talked about cinema's capacity to impact society (Algar 1981: 258). Ever since the establishment of the Islamic Republic, handling of cinema has been a grave political matter. In 1979, 1991 and 1998, three different ministers of Culture and Islamic Guidance – namely Mo'adikhah, Khatami and Mohajerani – were strongly attacked because of matters that included their handling of cinema. Mo'adikhah resigned over a film and Mohajerani was impeached. That a government minister could lose his post because of a single film demonstrates the gravity of cinema in Iran.

The 1978–79 Iranian revolution and its aftermath have had a profound effect on the shifting boundaries of what is considered 'political' in Iran and this too has been strongly manifested in Iranian cinema. Following the Iranian revolution, as part of its Islamization policy, the regime sought to control all aspects of culture, not least cinema, so as to ensure that it served the purposes of the ruling establishment. Hence, the regime politicized culture, and cinema in particular. Politicization of Iranian cinema has had much to do with the context of upheaval which over a 30-year period has seen a revolution (1978–79), a war (1980–88) and a strong reformist movement (since 1997).

Less than a decade after the war Iran was in the grip of another transformative socio-political movement which came to be known as reformism. What began with the candidacy of Mohammad Khatami for presidency in 1997 evolved into a sweeping popular movement with high hopes for democratization, civil society and rule of law. Almost in tandem, the women's movement made its presence felt in the 1990s, engaging in vocal criticism in the post-1997 period. The challenge that the reformist movement posed led to a severe backlash from the conservative establishment which frustrated the materialization of the movement's demands. For over seven years after Khatami's election as president, reformist-conservative confrontation dominated national politics.

The revolution, the war and the reformist movement have all been phases of the period of upheaval that Iran has been going through in the last 30 years. This book uses cinema as a prism to look at Iran in this context and in particular to examine its cultural politics. Concentrating on how Iranian cinema has been embroiled in political discussion, this book explores the processes of film reception and examines the role which Iranian cinema has played at this time of ideological rupture. The main areas in focus are state control mechanisms and policies, political films, and the impact of the recent international acclaim of Iranian films on the politics of cinema in Iran.

Pursuing a number of aims and objectives, this book explores cinema as a situated social/political practice rather than seeking to fix the meaning of films. Looking at the negotiations of power and meaning at the level of filmmaking, it seeks to demystify the relationship between filmmakers and state control, which have so far been treated as a binary opposition. Furthermore, recognizing these negotiations as part of the work of accounting for 'reception', the book contributes to reception studies. Currently reception studies only consider the cinema and video audiences as their subject of study. However, both in the West and in Iran, films go through various stages of being 'seen' as scripts, rushes and later as completed films before they are ever released. Drawing on illustrative examples from Iranian cinema, this book argues that the problematic of reception starts much earlier, before the above audiences see the film.

At the level of cinema audiences, the book examines the assumptions and strategies that Iranians use to engage with political films and the pleasures they derive from them. It looks at local/national reactions to the international prominence of Iranian films to explore the ramifications of such global processes in relation to Iranian cinema.

This book is an exploration of the relationship between the cinema and its social/political context. Therefore, unlike much research so far about Iranian cinema, which has focused on 'art films' or festival films, this book does not exclude films that are not recognized as such. Furthermore, there are only few published accounts that have placed Iranian cinema in the context of film reception in Iran. A number of films that have critically engaged with political issues such as social justice, the aftermath of the Iran–Iraq war, the place of the clergy in Iranian society, as well as women's issues, are discussed at some length. These films are commonly referred to in Iran as *film-e ejtema'i* or 'social films'.

Finally, this book is not just about Iranian films from the perspectives of film and media studies. It is also about Iran in general and its political culture specifically. It aims to contribute to ethnographic accounts of Iranian governance in the field of culture, of social and cultural critique, of women's voices against patriarchy, and of transnational cultural politics from domestic perspectives.

This introductory chapter offers an overview of media research in general and how it relates to the present inquiry. It then presents the questions that are explored in the book. Next, it focuses on the theoretical framework of the research upon which the book is based. Finally, it summarizes the other chapters.

This book is based on doctoral research completed in 2006 in the newly established Centre for Media and Film Studies at the School of Oriental and African Studies (SOAS). Fieldwork was conducted in Iran in 2003 and 2004.

## An overview of media research

Since my exploration of Iranian cinema is on a new terrain, I have engaged with a range of theoretical and methodological approaches which have been employed in social research on the media in order to map out my own approach.

The early model, which become known as 'hypodermic' in hindsight, was generated by the Frankfurt School. The theorists conceptualized the media effects on the basis of their knowledge of the complicity of the media with Nazism in Germany. In this model, as opposed to the all-knowing elite, the 'masses' were imagined as an atomized and homogenized group of alienated individuals who were without traditional bonds of locality and were hence left at the mercy of industrialism. The pessimism that intellectuals of the Frankfurt School felt at the time was reflected in their gloomy predictions about 'mass society' and 'mass culture'. Therefore, they maintained that messages of the media were 'injected' into the uncritical masses and thus ensured the dominance of the ruling class. At around the time of WWII, when members of Frankfurt School went into exile in the USA, they predicted the rise of totalitarianism under the influence of the 'culture industry' in the USA, the main proponent of which was Hollywood in its heyday. The philosophical position of the school was not, however, based on empirical research on the production or consumption of media texts.[1]

The theoretical assumptions of the Frankfurt School came under attack in the post-war period. Merton (1946), who worked on war propaganda, argued that the negative effects of media messages were assumed or inferred because little attempt had been made to study the 'actual effects' of such communication. Katz (1959) maintained that individuals who did not have any 'use' for media messages would not 'choose' to accept them. He stated, the 'approach assumes that people's values, their interests . . . associations . . . social roles, are pre-ponent, and that people selectively fashion what they see and hear' (Katz 1959 in Morley and Brunsdon 1999: 119). Thus, instead of the negative effects assumed by the Frankfurt School, this post-war American approach described media as having a benign role in society, capable of fulfilling a diversity of uses and gratifications as instruments of democratization in society (Counihan 1972: 43).

Attention to what people do with the media later re-emerged in the British 'uses and gratification' approach. This was a welcome change from the earlier paradigm of passive audiences upon whom the media had negative effects. Although this approach signalled the return of the agency of the audience, at the same time it had its own inherent problems. First, media messages were presumed to be open to multiple readings, potentially as many as there were audience members. As Hall (1973 in Morley 1980a) argued, 'polysemy must not be confused with pluralism'. Thus, although texts have multiple meanings, which are not equal among themselves, Hall rejected the over-optimistic arguments for the freedom of the audience to make meaning. Second, the 'uses and gratifications' model, like the 'mass society' model before it, imagined audiences as atomized individuals with psychological needs which were to be gratified. This psychological focus came at the expense of social and historical factors, which had been ignored (Morley and Brunsdon 1999: 127).

In a break with what had been done before, Hall's ground-breaking theoretical approach paved the way for new approaches to the study of audiences. In his key article entitled 'Encoding/Decoding', Hall put the emphasis on 'audience interpretations' of media texts (Hall 1980). Accordingly, audiences 'decode' media messages from three distinct positions. First, they could accept the 'preferred meaning' of a media text as intended by its producers. Second, they could negotiate the meaning of the text, accepting certain elements while rejecting others. Third, they could adopt an 'oppositional reading' of the text, rejecting what the producers intended.

Although the model has since been criticized for a number of reasons (Morley 1980b: 172; Hall 1989: 273, Staiger 2000: 31–32), at the time it paved the way for empirical research on audiences by David Morley and Charlotte Brunsdon who carried out their seminal ethnographic research on the reception of the TV programme *Nationwide* (Brunsdon and Morley 1978; Morley 1980a). In what has been termed the ethnographic turn, numerous other ethnographic inquiries have been carried out in cultural studies generally, focused on TV audiences.

Within film studies, ethnography has generally been a marginal pursuit while research on film texts has dominated. This is because, in film theory, 'spectators' have commonly been taken to be inscribed in the film text. As Jenkins explains:

> Film theory's abstract generalizations about spectatorship often depend upon essentialized assumptions about 'archetypal' exhibition practices; theorists compare the experience of watching a movie in a darkened theatre to a dream state, or contrast the focused gaze of the film-goer with the distracted gaze of the television viewer.
>
> (Jenkins 2000: 172)

Bennett (1983) has criticized this approach suggesting that a large gap remains between such an imagined spectator and the real readers of the media texts, who are subject to a particular history and live in social formations. The conditions of watching films are also socially and culturally contingent. For example, in Iran neither is the cinema totally dark nor do people watch films in silence. Since the 1980s, under the influence of cultural studies, audience studies have begun to appear in film studies as well.

In film studies, while 'in the 1970s theory psychoanalysed the pleasures of the cinematic situation . . . in the 1980s and 1990s analysts became more interested in socially differentiated forms of spectatorship' (Stam 2000: 229). Researchers such as Dyer (1986), Walkerdine (1999), Bobo (1988, 1995) and Stacey (1994, 1999) have researched audience responses to Hollywood films and their stars. Nevertheless, such research on cinema reception is rare and in general limited to Western contexts.[2] As regards Iranian cinema, while no publication has been dedicated solely to ethnographic research on the subject, some have included ethnographic observations and interviews.

Having considered the above approaches to the study of the media, I did not find any which would be directly adaptable to my research project. Film studies research on audiences is mainly focused on Western audience perceptions of Hollywood stars and hence is far removed from the reception of Iranian films in Iran. The media studies approaches discussed earlier, in spite of the welcome turn to ethnography, are generally based on rather static models of communication of meaning from production to reception. In the case of Iranian cinema the construction of meaning is a dynamic process involving the censors, the filmmakers, and audiences in the post-revolutionary context. Hence, taking on elements of the above studies, I have devised my own approach, the theoretical underpinnings of which I discuss later.

## Areas of inquiry

Iranian cinema has been a significant social/political institution, which has caused much debate within the country. In order to explore the role of cinema in Iran, I began with interrelated questions about: the significance of the institution of cinema in contemporary Iran, the negotiation of meaning in the processes of film regulation and reception, and finally the implications of the international prominence of Iranian cinema in discourses of Iranian identity.

As mentioned earlier, three ministers of Culture and Islamic Guidance have been strongly criticized in relation to their handling of cinema in the post-revolution period. One of these ministers had to resign in direct relation to a film and another was impeached (see Chapter 2). My aim has been to study how cinema is implicated in the contemporary cultural/political debates in the country, taking into account the complexity of the factors involved.

Since I am not convinced that the Iranian censors are tricked by the use of metaphor, allegory and symbolism as some have claimed, I explore the state control of Iranian cinema to demonstrate the openings and opportunities that have existed for filmmakers. I focus on the processes of negotiation that take place between filmmakers and the authorities in charge of regulating filmmaking practices. I aim to demystify how films critical of post-revolutionary predicaments get made and receive government permits. I explore the negotiation of meaning that happens around the watching of Iranian films, which is particularly significant to study in relation to Iranian cinema as a social practice. Since women's issues have been recurrent themes in numerous films, the viewers' negotiations of gender in discussions about these films have also been a focus of my inquiry.

In Iran there has been a range of contradictory reactions to the phenomenal acclaim of Iranian films around the world. Some of the conservative elite, who wish to fix the Iranian identity as first and foremost Muslim, have condemned the films for their secular representations. Some middle class Iranians, worried about a presumed orientalizing Western 'other' watching these films, consider the films embarrassing for their perceived focus on the urban or rural poor. They disavow these images, with which they do not identify. Such contradictory interpretations necessitate an examination of the factors involved in identity discourse about the films.

Answering the above questions requires careful theoretical and methodological framing which I will now outline.

## Theoretical framework

Like all cultural expressions in Iran, cinema cannot be considered in isolation from the ideology of the Iranian regime. The post-revolution regime has made a conscious effort to 'Islamize' Iran in order to create a society made up of 'good Muslims' (Higgins and Ghaffari 1994: 20; Milani 1994: 200). The process has involved efforts that range from re-writing school history books in order to put emphasis on Islam's role in Iranian history, to installing people with religious credentials in government posts, regardless of their qualifications. As for cinema, Ayatollah Khomeini declared that it had to be used as a tool by 'educating the people' (Algar 1981: 258) and similar to all art it should be in the service of Islam.[3] Therefore, akin to all aspects of social/cultural life, cinema has become entangled in 'Islamic' ideology. In order to examine the politics of Iranian cinema, it is necessary to explore the concept of ideology and its articulation through hegemony.

### *Ideology*

The concept of ideology was introduced by Marx and Engels. Although it is still used by cultural theorists such as Hall, its meaning has been somewhat modified. The notion of ideology has been basically used in two different senses. The first meaning, which is most widely associated with ideology, is the 'false consciousness' of 'the masses'. Marx and Engels used this sense of the term in *German ideology*, referring to it as an upside down worldview of 'the masses' which is contrary to their class interests (Marx and Engels 1998: 47). According to this concept, 'the masses' are deceived by the bourgeoisie into perceiving as the norm the exploitative relations of production which privilege the bourgeoisie. The acceptance of the way of thinking of the bourgeoisie by the working class would thus perpetuate class inequality. In this sense of the word, ideology is unitary as the bourgeois ideology which is also adopted by other social classes. This pejorative conception of ideology privileges the researcher's position as the one with 'true consciousness', knowing what lies behind the taken-for-granted norms. The validity of such a claim is questionable since the researcher would have to prove that he/she knows 'the truth', thus turning his/her position to something similar to that of a religious authority rather than an academic researcher.

Ideology was also used in a different sense by Marx, referring this time to a set of ideas that arise from the economic conditions of every class within society according to their material interests (Marx 1845 in Williams 1976: 156). This sense of the word is rather neutral and allows for the possibility of a multiplicity of class ideologies, and consequently of the masses' consciousness of their disadvantaged position and struggle for social change. However different these two senses of the word may be, what they have in common is their basis in material conditions as the determinant of class-based ideology. This model, known as the 'base-superstructure model', means that the material conditions at the base determine the ideology as part of the superstructure. This notion has been criticized for reducing social factors to economic ones, failing to acknowledge others.

Gramsci, however, redefined the concept of ideology, suggesting that it consists of two levels: a higher-level philosophy, and 'common sense'. At the higher level it is a 'conception of the world, . . . which becomes a cultural movement, a "religion", a "faith", that has produced a form of practical activity' (Gramsci 1971: 328). He states that there is not one philosophy but multiple philosophies that contest each other in every society. These philosophies attempt to constitute the society, fixing the identity of its members. Laclau maintains that the 'ideological' is 'the will to "totality" attempting to create a closure or fixation of meaning out of the infinite play of differences within society' (1990: 92). This 'will' has been expressed by the Iranian state's attempt at suturing Iranian society through the 'Islamization' of post-revolutionary Iran, endeavouring to fix the identities of the people first and foremost as Muslims. The efforts of the Islamic regime were to a degree a reaction to ideological work of the Pahlavi regime which was aimed at redefining Iran as a secular society (Abrahamian 1982). In this vein, state authorities in Iran have attempted to use social institutions, including 'the education system, the family, the legal system, the political system, the trade unions, the media, and the culture', which Althusser refers to as Ideological State Apparatuses (ISAs) (1971: 136–37). However, their degree of success has depended on the second level of ideology or 'common sense'. According to Gramsci, ideology has a more felt sense in everyday life, which he refers to as 'common sense'. This is the popular philosophy of life which is an uncritical worldview formed historically, upon which each philosophical current leaves behind a sediment. Therefore, it is necessarily 'fragmentary, disjointed and episodic' made up of very contradictory elements from 'Stone Age' ideas to scientific ones (Gramsci 1971: 324). There is obviously a gap between the two levels of ideology, but what could bridge this gap is hegemony.

Hegemony is created when a social group or class under the leadership of some of its members unites, forming what Gramsci calls a 'historical bloc' (1971: 182). Then the social group extends its ideological discourse to encompass the interests of other marginal groups, therefore creating solidarity among these disparate groups. This leadership is only possible when they have won over the 'common sense' of the other groups. The instances of winning the consent of the society are momentary and do not last. Consequently the consent has to be won over and over again to prove the viability of the leadership.

Gramsci attempts to shift the concept of ideology beyond economic determinism, highlighting the importance of attention to the historical specificity of determining factors in any particular case. Although he acknowledges the importance of economic conditions in belief systems, he does not take them for granted as determining social action (1971: 163–64). He explains that the material conditions 'create a terrain more favourable to the dissemination of certain modes of thought, and certain ways of posing and resolving questions involving the entire subsequent development of national life' (1971: 184). As Hall puts it, this is a move away from economic determinism 'in the last instance' (1996: 45). However, Laclau and Mouffe point out that Gramsci still maintains that the historical bloc is necessarily made up of members of the same class (1985: 109). They refute this by suggesting that what joins the dominant group together is the momentary fixing of meaning which is the result of the same articulatory practices that attempt to constitute the dominated groups. They define articulation as 'any practice establishing a relation among elements such that their identity is modified as a result of the articulatory practice' (1985: 105). Thus, articulation instils a structured system of differences that defines the articulated as well as the articulator, constituting both 'us' and 'them'. This eliminates the theoretical necessity of class as a binding factor.

The Iranian revolution and post-revolutionary period best exemplify the concept of hegemony in practice. The effectiveness of the hegemonic leadership of the revolution by Ayatollah Khomeini was partly due to his appeal to the common sense of the religious majority of the population. His hegemony continued after the revolution and was aided by the establishment of the Islamic state which backed up the Ayatollah's rule by repression. As Althusser asserts, the state takes advantage of Repressive State Apparatus (RSA) such as 'the government, the administration, the army, the police, the courts, the prisons, etc', which function 'by violence at least ultimately (since repression, e.g. administrative repression, may take non-physical forms)' (1971: 136). The Islamic state used repression unrestrictedly in its first decade particularly during the 1980–88 Iran–Iraq war, which was a useful excuse for the silencing of internal opposition.

While the coercive powers of the state continued to operate, although rather less severely than they had in the past, the hegemonic leadership of Ayatollah Khomeini was not replicated by other leaders after his death in 1989. In the hegemonic vacuum after Khomeini, there was an opening for negotiation, debate and critique of post-revolutionary society (see Chapter 2).

In the post-Khomeini era the frictions among the political elite, which Khomeini had previously kept under control, surfaced. The political elite gradually split into two opposing camps, which later became known as conservatives and reformists. While the conservatives have insisted on tight control by the regime, as was the case under Khomeini, the reformists, who have stimulated a social movement for change, have criticized the old approach, putting emphasis on issues such as freedom of speech, democratization and social justice, which had earlier been part of the 1978–79 revolutionary ideals. In this context, films such as Makhmalbaf's controversial *Marriage of the Blessed* (1989) lent their voice to the critique of the postwar predicaments and were supported by reformists (see Chapter 3).

The critique of ideological perspectives has been a significant factor in the evolution of the Islamic state. As Gramsci states, ideologies cannot replace each other totally; rather it is through critique of what has already been accepted that new forms of thinking or consciousness can be advanced. He states:

> What matters is the criticism to which such an ideological complex is subjected by the first representatives of the new historical phase. This criticism makes possible a process of differentiation and change in the relative weight that the elements of the old ideologies used to possess. What was previously secondary and subordinate . . . becomes the nucleus of a new ideological and theoretical complex. The old collective will dissolve into its contradictory elements since the subordinate ones develop socially.
>
> (Gramsci 1971: 195)

In the post-Khomeini period, the push for the reformation of Iranian politics and society gradually gained popularity. The role that Iranian cinema has played in relation to the reformist movement is an important question which I address in Chapter 3. The involvement of the media in social movements and resistance to hegemonic/repressive powers is a topic that has been addressed in theories of 'radical media', a concept to which I now turn.

### *Radical media*

Downing defines radical media as those which 'express an alternative vision to hegemonic policies, priorities, and perspectives' (2001: v). According to him, what such media, which range from graffiti to Internet sites, have in common is that 'they break somebody's rules, although rarely all of them in every respect' (2001: xi). Although this is a broad definition, its inclusiveness is important in order to be able to address the practices and reception of anti-hegemonic media, about which, as Downing points out, there is shortage of research (Downing 2003: 642). Others such as Atton (2002) refer to such media as 'alternative media'. Downing (2001) and O'Sullivan (1994) consider the main aim of these media to be social change. Thus, particularly for Downing (1984, 2001), the relationship between radical media and consciousness-raising in relation to social movements is of particular importance.

Arato and Cohen (1992) suggest three models for classifying social movements: the model of the rioting mob, the more organized and focused model of organized action such as sit-ins and demonstrations, and finally the model of New Social Movements such as the environmentalist and feminist movements. Although drawn from Western examples, this classification has relevance for social movements in Iran which have elements of all three models. Under Khatami, there were many demonstrations in support of the ideals of democratization, rule of law and civil society, all of which had been part of the slogans of the reformists. At times, in a number of cities, particularly in Tehran, these demonstrations ended in confrontation with hardline vigilantes in mob-like clashes. Furthermore, a number of prominent women politicians, activists, journalists and filmmakers addressed legal discrimination based on gender, and participated in raising awareness. Iranian cinema has been implicated in both the reformist and women's movements,[4] partly at the level of raising consciousness.

Downing (1984) had earlier assumed a clear delineation between radical and mainstream media – that is, between those that use alternative sources of funding and channels of distribution and those that use mainstream channels controlled by hegemonic/repressive powers. However, he has since abandoned this binary opposition in favour of considering hybrid forms which are politically progressive but use mainstream financial sources and circulation channels. Atton (2002: 151–52) also celebrates the overlap between the two in a version of Bhabha's (1990) 'third space' of hybridity. Given their larger audience compared to small-scale 'pure' forms, hybrid media are more likely to have a significant impact.

Radical/alternative media framework is relevant to my research because I am dealing with 'social films' which have become controversial for going against the hegemonic/repressive order. In addition, many Iranian filmmakers have aligned themselves with the reformist and the women's movements. Because the relationship between social movements and the media has been addressed by Downing's theory of radical media, it is relevant to my research.

## Art and radical media

Artistic expressions such as cinema are important to the project of radical media. This is because, rather than only imparting counter-information, they have the potential to 'stimulate alternative dialogue' among audiences (Downing 2001: 63). Art forms inspired by the realities of life, which are recognizable as such by those looking at them, can stimulate a dialogue of sorts between the artist and the viewer through the art work and among the viewers themselves. This is helped by ambiguities in works of art that stimulate such dialogue among viewers. In Iran, ambiguities in films help propel interpretations among viewers who are used to such elements in Iranian poetry.

Indirect communication is very familiar for Iranians, who have an ancient tradition of poetry with strong symbolism and allegorical references. Iranians generally do not take things at 'face value' or *zahir* and often look for hidden layers of meaning or *batin*. This multilayered engagement has its roots in Persian mystical poetry. The poetic tradition developed in a hostile cultural and political environment which forced Iranian mystics to use indirect communication in order to ensure transmission of their thoughts and beliefs. A well-known poem by Rumi speaks of the seed and the skin: one has to break through the skin (*zahir*) to get to the seed (*batin*). The tradition of layered meanings was adopted by *she'r-e no* or the New Poetry that developed in the twentieth century. Like its predecessors, the New Poetry has managed to make political criticism during the oppressive conditions under the Shah. In the 1970s, sessions of poetry reading by dissident poets were popular among the secular opposition to the Pahlavi regime and the tape recordings of these sessions circulated in Iran (Sreberny-Mohammadi and Mohammadi 1994: 104).

The New Poetry has influenced Iranian cinema (Dabashi 1995; Makhmalbaf 1997). In traditional poetry, there is a relatively restricted range of symbols, with stock meanings; with the New Poetry the range is wider, including everyday life, and the meanings are more varied and subtle. With such a background in indirect communication of meaning, now at times Iranian filmmakers use a similar approach in their work.

The better-educated Iranian viewers, who engage with poetry, apply similar skills to reading cinematic texts. An integral part of the experience of watching such films is the critical discussion and negotiation of these meanings that happens both during and after watching the films.

## *Cofabulation*

In his work about theatre, Brecht discusses audience involvement with meaning making. He advocates theatrical communication strategies which would get the audience involved in the performance rather than have them absorb the narrative in a passive way. The example he invokes is that of sports spectators who constantly remark on the game, rather than remaining detached. The mainstream theatre practice which he denounces is the 'obsession with coercing the spectator into a one-dimensional dynamic where he is prevented from looking left or right, up or down'. Rather Brecht advocates the spectators coming to their own conclusions by 'creating in their own mind other ways of behaviour and situations, and, following the events, holding them up to comparison with those presented by the theatre. Thus the audience itself becomes a storyteller' (Brecht 1967: 1145, 924 cited in Mueller 1989: 65). Brecht favours audience involvement in the making of the play, in what he calls 'cofabulation', in such a way that the 'spectators were free to agree with, disagree with, or change any of the parts presented on stage' (Mueller 1989: 94).

Similar to the theatre practice that Brecht had in mind, I found that Iranians who watch films not only comment to each other while watching, they also at times clap or verbalize loud and often collective exclamations (see, for example, Chapter 3 about *The Lizard*). Filmmakers are aware of this practice, and this feedback loop influences them in their future work (see, for example, my discussion of Milani's work in Chapter 4).

Importantly, awareness of film censorship makes Iranians extra-vigilant towards political 'messages' in 'social films'. This is because the controversies around films have predisposed audiences to consider them 'political' and hence they try to discern the oppositional aspect(s) of the films. As my research shows, those who watch the films are extra vigilant to retrieve what the censored parts of films may have been. In addition, at times they try to 'edit the films' for themselves rejecting some parts of the films, hence the notion of 'cofabulation' is relevant to understanding how Iranians engage with the films (see, for example, Chapter 3 about *House on the Water*).

### Liminality and 'cultural performances'

The engagement of artists and their audiences with 'cultural performances' is particularly significant at 'liminal' moments of social crisis. Based on Turner (1984), I have taken liminality to mean the period of destabilization that occurs with rapid social change. He argues that at times of crisis, such as war or revolution, the society as a whole goes through a liminal phase 'betwixt-and-between' what was and what will be (Turner 1984: 21). This phase provides an opportunity to step out of everyday routines and reflect on them from a detached position. Reflection can take the form of a 'cultural performance' that itself has a transforming effect on those creating it. Turner defines these performances as 'modes of exhibition or presentation – such as ritual, carnival, theatre, and film – as commentaries, critiques on, or as celebrations of, different dimensions of human relatedness' (1984: 19). According to him, the performances are conducted in the phase of redress, when the society seeks to find a way to 'stabilize the destabilized cosmos' through pulling 'meaning from the tangle of action' (Turner 1990: 17). Thus cultural performances are, 'a metacommentary, implicit or explicit, witting or unwitting, on the major social dramas of social context (wars, revolutions, scandals, institutional changes)' (1990: 16). Of course, in this commentary, the voice of the creator of the work looms large. As for this creative role, Turner takes it as 'the supreme honesty of the creative artist who, in his presentation . . . reserves to himself the privilege of seeing straight what all cultures build crooked' (1984: 40).

The Iranian revolution of 1978–79, followed by the 1980–88 Iran–Iraq war, contributed to the social and political instability in the country which has shown no sign of abating since then. With this backdrop, Iranian films' critical commentary on the predicaments of the country can be considered in relation to Turner's theory about the role of cultural performances. This raises the question of how filmmakers and audiences engage in generation of meaning in relation to the politics of Iranian films. Are the films meant and received as metacommentaries about Iranian society? Is the 'honesty' of the creator of the work taken for granted, as Turner presumes? In other words, are audiences critical of 'social films' as well? In this book I address these questions.

### The public sphere

Based on his research on eighteenth-century London tea-houses, Habermas (1989) introduced the concept of the public sphere in relation to bourgeois discussions about political and social matters. According to him, until then such discussions happened in the exclusive domain of royal courts. The bourgeois public sphere was a realm of free speech and critique of the monarchy, in an atmosphere of rational exchange of ideas.

Fraser (1992) and Sreberny and Zoonen (2000) maintain that, rather than talking about the public sphere in the singular, research must focus on the plurality of such publics. Fraser (1992) suggests the existence of 'counter public spheres' which stand in contrast to the official hegemonic public. Discussing women's movements, Sreberny and Zoonen (2000: 8–9) argue for tripartite 'counter publics': the women politicians who fight at the level of changing policies, the activists who promote awareness of the women's cause and the weak public of the ordinary women and men supporters of the women's movement.

The concept is of particular relevance to my research on 'women's films' or films focused on women's issues to do with patriarchy which I discuss in Chapter 4. I argue that the women filmmakers' role is akin to the activists at the second level of 'counter publics' in Sreberny and Zoonen's model above for seeking to raise feminist consciousness.

## *Media and resistance*

The relevance of the project of radical media does not end with ebbs in social movements such as reformism in Iran, but is relevant to resistance when the momentum of the movement wanes. Downing points out:

> A model of media influence that maintains a constant tight close-up on immediate consequences will fail to register accurately the significant long-term resonance of radical alternative media, especially if yoked only to the consideration of the moment-by-moment of social movement at their height of activity . . . [T]his sense of the longer term is crucial for understanding all media.
>
> (Downing 2001: 31)

Part of the relevance of radical media is the stimulation of resistance. In Chapters 3 and 4, I examine how films are appropriated by Iranians in their discourse of resistance to the hegemony of the Iranian state.

Scott defines 'class resistance' as

> *any* act(s) by member(s) of a subordinate class that is or are *intended* either to mitigate or deny claims (for example, rents, taxes, prestige) made on that class by superordinate classes (for example, landlords, large farmers, the state) or to advance its own claims (for example, work, land, charity, respect) vis-à-vis those super-ordinate classes.
>
> (1985: 290, emphasis in the original)

Although Scott's definition is based on class, it can be extended to include other forms of domination such as patriarchy which are not necessarily based on economics in the first instance. In Iran, the impositions of the ideological regime have met much resistance among filmmakers and cinema audiences. Resistance can take the form of a cultural discourse competing against that of the hegemonic powers. Cultural representations play an essential role in the expressions of resistance through their 'dissenting narratives' (Fox and Starn 1997: 7). For the filmmakers, their constant negotiation of the boundaries of censorship is a major instance of resistance to the regime (see Chapters 2 to 5). Negotiation of oppositional readings of intended and unintended 'messages' in film is one way for audiences to resist the impositions of the regime (see Chapters 3 and 4). In this sense, resistance is not considered as a single act of revolt or 'locus of great refusal' (Foucault 1981: 96), but as a plurality of experiences that are manifested in individual or collective practices. Because of their symbolizing counter-hegemonic power, these practices often heighten the individual or collective sense of dignity. Scott (1985: 34) suggests that everyday forms of cultural resistance are often more effective than short-lived armed uprisings.

*Cinema and resistance*

Socially critical cinema as resistance has its roots in the Italian Neorealist cinema of the 1940s, a style that has been adopted by present Iranian filmmakers. For the Neorealist filmmakers everyday life became the subject of film. They created a realistic vision by grounding their representations in local space, time and social issues (Cook 1981: 39). However, because of its political undercurrent, that cinema came under attack by the Italian administration and was soon completely stopped.

Later, in the context of Latin American struggles against neo-colonialism in the 1960s, Solanas and Getino set out the theory of Third Cinema in a manifesto for political filmmaking in the region. Solanas and Getino's theory was the most influential among the several manifestos for revolutionary filmmaking in Latin America. According to the theoreticians, in general films can be divided into three types: First, Second and Third Cinemas. First Cinema is Hollywood and other mainstream cinemas modelled on Hollywood. Second Cinema is 'art cinema' (festival films), which according to them was aimed at the elite and did not engage with the rest of society. Third Cinema was socially critical of the neo-colonial circumstances from a counter-hegemonic, nationalist perspective. Solanas and Getino believed in 'making films that the system cannot assimilate and which are foreign to its needs, or making films that directly and explicitly set out to fight the system' (1976: 52). Accordingly, cinema is anti-hegemonic either when it cannot be co-opted by the hegemonic forces, or if it directly sets out to fight them.

The films that Solanas and Getino created themselves, which had a clear anti-state agenda, were shown to activists in clandestine screenings. These screenings were occasions for political discussions generated around the themes in the films (Solanas and Getino 1976: 62).

The theoreticians themselves and others modified the original polemical conception of Third Cinema. Getino, for example, suggested that the original formulation was due to the filmmakers universalizing from specific conditions which Solanas and Getino faced at the time (Getino 1986: 101). That Second Cinema films could have a political agenda was later accepted. Solanas himself, for example, has since made films such as *South* (1988), which has been received well at 'art film' festivals.

Others elsewhere in the world have also adopted the Third Cinema agenda, where some filmmakers have exposed the many layers of the socio-historical formations of their societies, rather than opting for a simplistic notion of a homogeneous national identity. Filmmakers have revealed 'divisions and stratifications within a national formation, ranging from regional dialects to class and political antagonism' (Willemen 1989: 4).

Some researchers have considered resistance in media practices in terms of a relationship to the sources of economic and political power. Atton (2002: 153–56) based on Melucci (1995) and Cox (1997) suggests that radical/alternative media must be 'free spaces' (1995) independent from determination by the 'logics of power and economics' (1997). Thus, state influence under repressive regimes, or capitalist interests in the West, and a combination of the two in most cases, are considered inimical to the project of radical media.

The questions I pose in relation to Iranian cinema concern whether the cinema should necessarily fulfil the criteria set out above by Atton as well as the original theory of Third Cinema to be politically engaged. Examining the case of Iranian cinema makes me wonder about the very stark binaries and oppositions set up by Atton and the original theory of Third Cinema. This is because the Iranian state has been far from monolithic and has been subject to fierce confrontation between political factions particularly since 1997 (see Chapter 2). Filmmakers with a critical outlook have at times been helped by reformist authorities but restricted by their conservative opponents. This split character of the state does not fit with the above stark binaries. Hence their generalizations require reconsideration. In Chapter 3, I examine the issues raised here in more detail.

## Gender and cinema

Some of the 'social films' deal with women's issues. In Iran some refer to these films as *filmha-ye zananeh* or 'women's films'. These films are significant in terms of their negotiation of gender roles in defiance of patriarchy, and subsequently their role in the raising of gender consciousness. Since under the Islamic Republic patriarchy has been institutionalized in Iran, 'women's films' have particular political significance (see Chapter 4). In the making and reception of such films, the very notion of 'gender' is at stake. Zoonen argues that, rather than a fixed essence, gender can be thought of as 'a particular discourse, that is a set of overlapping and often contradictory cultural descriptions and prescriptions referring to sexual difference, which arises from and regulates particular economic, social, political, technological and other non-discursive contexts' (1994: 33).

Gender discourse is never straightforward or total but ambiguous and contradictory, a site of conflict and contestation, partly owing to the material implications which Zoonen points out above. In Iran these contradictions play out at various levels in film regulation and reception in which gender is an issue.

The relationship between gender and film has been considered from several perspectives. Mulvey suggests that in feminine melodramas, i.e. films about tension in the domestic realm, 'there is a dizzy satisfaction in witnessing the way that sexual difference under patriarchy is fraught, explosive and erupts dramatically into violence within its own private stamping ground, the family'(1987: 75). She adds that the strength of these films is 'the amount of dust the story raises along the way, a cloud of over-determined irreconcilables which put up a resistance to being neatly settled in the last five minutes' (1987: 76). Thus, in spite of ideological endings, the articulation of gender conflict within film narratives enables women who watch them to take pleasure. Mulvey's remarks are relevant to some Iranian films about women, such as Milani's *Fifth Reaction* (2003) and Kiarostami's *10* (2002) (see Chapter 4).

Female characters in films have been considered as possible role models for female audiences. Discussing female action heroes, Inness argues that characters which break established stereotypes are important for offering a more powerful vision of womanhood and as 'new models for female comportment' (2004: 15). Ang suggests that female audience members at times weigh up the circumstances of the characters on the screen as if they were their own, regardless of how unpleasant those circumstances might be. This is because, when talking about films, 'there is no punishment for whatever [character's] identity one takes up, no matter how headstrong or destructive; there will be no retribution, no defeat will ensue' (Ang 1990: 86).

Butler argues that gender also has a 'performative' role: the repetition of a particular enactment of gender roles results in their becoming normalized. Accordingly, a patriarchal discourse of gender is the result of normative conduct which perpetuates male dominance. In contrast, Butler highlights the possibility of women's agency in counter-hegemonic performance of gender, the repetition of which is a subversive strategy (Butler 1990: 147). This is because such repetition is constitutive of identity. Here (gender) identity is not an essence but is 'actively constructed, chosen, created and performed by people in their daily lives' (Roseneil and Seymoure 1999: 5). Speech acts which defy male hegemony have such a potential if they are normalized through reflexivity and repetition.

Whether reflexive engagement with the media occurs outside feminist circles has been questioned. Skeggs suggests that self-reflection is part of 'the project of the self as a Western bourgeois project' and is irrelevant to other contexts, '[M]any post-modern theories and theories of performativity assume that people can traverse the boundaries in which they are located, and many feminists have assumed that all have equal access to ways of being, be it feminist, gendered, sexed, etc.' (1997: 163). Skeggs warns researchers against projecting their own notions onto those they research. Butler herself is not over-optimistic. She maintained that while some repetitions are 'effectively disruptive, truly troubling', others 'become domesticated', reinforcing male dominance (Butler 1990: 139).

Considering all of this, I pose the following set of interrelated questions: Have 'women's films' been the subject of interest in Iran at all, or do they only matter in

Western commentary? How are the regulation processes to do with these films any different from other 'social films'? How have the male leaders/supporters of the reformist movement related to 'women's films'? How do Iranian women engage with these films? Do they use the opportunity of watching and/or discussing films as a moment for self-reflection, and do these instances strengthen patriarchy? How are the films appropriated by women in their negotiations of gender with men? How is the cinema space used by women after the revolution? In relation to the women's movement in Iran, where does cinema fit in the context of Sreberny and Zoonen's (2000) tripartite 'counter publics' model above? These questions are addressed in Chapter 4.

### *Films in transnational circuitry and national identity*

Several Iranian films, including many of those about women's issues, have been shown at film festivals around the world. A number of these films have won major awards. Farahmand has argued that the international acclaim has led to Iranian cinema becoming apolitical (2002). Naficy has claimed that the Iranian art films have become independent of Iranian tastes (2002: 54). The consequences of the international renown particularly in terms of the practices and the politics of Iranian cinema require close consideration.

In today's global 'mediascape' (Appadurai 1991), films traverse state boundaries in multiple directions. While there has been much interest in global flows and how media representations enter the global mediascape, the consequence of news or commentary about these media travelling back to the local/national places of origin has not been given much attention. In Chapter 5, examining the discourses around Iranian cinema, I address this gap in the literature.

Once films enter the transnational circuitry of 'world cinema', they are generally classified together under the label of the nation-state producing the film – for example, Iranian cinema, Chinese cinema, etc.[5] Thus filmmakers' fictions become 'Iranian films', representing Iran as a society and/or a nation-state. However, do they get classified neatly as the cinema of a nation-state?

As Cheah (1998: 22) suggests, global movements have loosened the hyphen between nation and state. Iranian films and diaspora have both been on the move and neither have an easy relationship to Iran as a nation-state. Although the films are taken to be Iranian, they are not understood to represent the Iranian state. Most festival catalogues advertise the films as appearing *despite* the repressive state rather than *because of* it.

The relationship of Iranian diaspora and Iranian cinema has not been free of tension either. Most of the estimated two million strong Iranian diaspora do not associate themselves with the Islamic Republic, yet they still identify themselves as Iranians.[6] Iranians abroad are also divided in their stance towards Iranian films shown in the West. While some promote the films, others disavow them as showing an image of Iran which they reject.[7] This highlights the complexities of the concept of identity.

Sreberny states that identity is 'the conscious awareness by members of a group and implies some degree of reflection, articulation, emotional connection, the sharing of commonalties and differing from others' (2002: 297). Identities are multiple, contextual, shifting and negotiated. Any individual could have a number of social bonds that impact their social identities. Laclau points out that, 'the identity and homogeneity of social agents was an illusion, that any social subject is essentially decentred, that his/her identity is nothing but the unstable articulation of constantly changing positionalities' (1990: 92).

Identity is about unstable boundaries and ways of including 'us' to the exclusion of 'others'. These boundaries are drawn and redrawn, changing the groupings and those who are included and excluded. As mentioned earlier, Butler argues in the case of gender that repeated performance of behaviour results in its normalization and hence is constitutive of identity (1990: 147). Finally, as Stokes suggests, 'the content, boundaries and practical implications of the group identity' are contested issues (1997: 10). This is because 'who I am now determines what I can and cannot do, can and cannot have, can and cannot be' (Linnekin and Poyer 1990: 13). Such implications demonstrate the political significance of identity.

Since Iranian films have crossed national boundaries and have represented Iran outside the country, they have become tangled in the discourses of identity. This is owing to concerns in Iran about how the country is imagined by non-Iranians who watch these films. Awareness of negative stereotypical images of the country in the West plays a significant role here. Some Iranians are concerned whether the films reinforce or challenge such negative stereotypes.

Concerns with *the other's* perception of *self* is neither necessarily unfounded nor limited to Iranians. Arora notes that stereotypical and one-dimensional representations are generally the ones that are most easily read by mainstream Western audiences (1994: 303). Writing about Celtic cinema, McArthur (1994) argues that the old stereotypes of uncivilized and uncultured Celts still persist in Britain today and warns filmmakers against pandering to such perceptions.

Marks suggests that films in transnational circuitry acquire new meanings because,

> as well as bearing meanings to the audience, [films] receive impressions from the people who have seen them. [This process] builds up these impressions like a palimpsest and passes them on to other audiences. The very circulation of a film among different viewers is like a series of skin contacts that leaves mutual traces.
>
> (Marks 2000: xii)

Accordingly, by virtue of going to international festivals, films are imbued with the perceptions of *the other* who watches them and hence acquire new meanings. Once films are shown abroad, they are perceived differently in the country of origin than they would have been otherwise. In the course of my research I came across many instances of viewers discussing Iranian cinema in the light of their international exposure.

In Chapter 5, I focus on the implications of the international prominence of Iranian cinema in the discourses of identity in Iran, addressing questions such as:

Has the international acclaim led to apoliticality of Iranian cinema as Farahmand argues? What are the claims made about art films (festival films), by whom and to what ends? How and why do the reactions to the international prominence of Iranian films before and after the revolution differ from each other?

### *Ethnography and the problem of reception studies*

Since Brunsdon and Morley's (1978) groundbreaking work on the TV programme *Nationwide*, ethnography has generally been the most common way of approaching audience research. The 'ethnographic turn' meant a shift in thinking about audiences, from passive recipients of dominant discourses via the media, to a focus on 'active audience' participation in the process of construction of meaning. Ethnography has been defined as an attempt to get 'close to those studied as a way of understanding what their experiences and activities mean to them' (Emerson and Shaw 1995: 12). In classic anthropology, ethnography entails an extended period of stay in the 'field' to gain access to the everyday lives of the subjects of study. In media research it involves attention to the audience interpretation of media texts while paying particular attention to the context of interpretation (Livingstone 1998).

Ethnography has been criticized for tending to focus on micro-narratives while failing to address adequately macro-level questions of power relations (Ang 1996; Corner 1991; Curran 1990). For example, Fiske (1989) has been attacked for celebrating 'semiotic democracy' for audiences while allowing the macro-narratives of the power of media institutions to slip the agenda. Morley (1997) warns against the romanticization of consumer freedoms which leads to forgetting the original objective of reception studies that has been to tackle the question of cultural power.

Another inherent problem of reception studies, which has persisted during the turn to ethnography, is about where 'reception' begins. Traditionally the object of study has only begun with the finished products' public release when a paying public (or non-paying one in the case of television, the Internet and bootleg videos) access already produced content. However, as I show below in the case of Iranian cinema, the film 'text' (from script to the finished film) has already been (re)viewed several times by the authorities. The negotiations taking place between the film-makers and the authorities are very significant and must be studied as part of the reception problematic. Only if we do so will the full complexities of the reception as an object of study surface.

'Audience' has been a challenging concept itself. There is little doubt that attention to media reception has shaken the assumed hypodermic power of the media on homogenized passive masses. Instead it has made visible the hitherto marginalized and devalued audiences who are now understood to engage with media messages. Although everyone acknowledges that there are people out there who watch films, listen to the radio and read the papers, how to define them as a collectivity is a theoretical and empirical problem for researchers. Hartley (2002: 11) suggests that the audience may be imagined theoretically, empirically or politically, but in all cases audience is a construction that serves the purpose of the imagining institution, which in terms of academic inquiry refers to the researcher.

Difficulties with the conceptualization of audience(s), as Bird notes, have arisen because we cannot 'isolate the role of the media in culture, because the media are firmly anchored into the web of culture, although articulated by individuals in different ways' (2003: 3). However, she cautions against abandoning the 'audience' in despair:

> Even as we acknowledge the importance of global and national economic and political forces in constructing the 'mediascapes' in which we live, we don't all need to become political economists . . . we need to move beyond the audience as a theoretically definable construct, but we should not be abandoning the goal of understanding real people, living real lives in which media play an ever-increasing, if certainly problematic role.
>
> (Bird 2003: 190)

Having the difficulties of conceptualizing 'reception' and the 'audience' in mind, I devised my research focus and methodology accordingly.

### My approach to the study of Iranian cinema

Conscious of the above-mentioned debates and issues, I concentrated on issues of political importance to do with Iranian cinema which seem to matter beyond film as just a means of entertainment. Owing to my awareness of Iranian cinema's involvement in social movements in Iran, I made this involvement as well as the discourses of identity around the films the subject of my inquiry. Since these topics involved powerful institutions within the Islamic republic, their examination exposes the macro-level relations of power.

It is a truism that researchers start their academic inquiries with pre-conceptions. Mine were grounded in my having engaged with Iranian cinema until the early 1990s in Iran before leaving the country to live outside. From that experience I knew about the relevance of Iranian cinema as a social practice which had not so far been adequately reflected in academic writing. I also had first-hand experience of the socio-political context of post-revolution Iran. Nevertheless, I wanted to explore the particularities of engagements with Iranian films at the time of research, many years after I had settled in the West. I was ready and eager to find out how things had changed over the years, and how this was reflected in the discourses around Iranian cinema.

In addition, I was aware of the implications of the international success of the film in the discourses of identity in Iran and among the diaspora. I have been personally involved with Iranian cinema as a means of 'looking back' at my country of origin. Ever since I settled outside Iran, I have watched Iranian films, discussed them with Iranians and non-Iranians, and promoted as well as taught Iranian cinema in the West.

An inquiry that would take the above contexts into account necessitated a 'multi-sited ethnography' (Marcus 1998).[8] Increasingly, anthropologists have accepted that the boundedness of cultures and societies has been dissolving. Appadurai (1991) suggests that the imaginations of people are not limited to local alternatives suggesting that owing to global cultural processes today, one should study transnational 'mediascapes'. While Appadurai does not suggest how mediascapes are to be studied, Marcus suggests 'multi-sited' ethnography as a solution. This means

> literally moving over discontinuous realms of social space in order to describe and interpret cultural formations that can only be understood this way. Now they must understand the operations of institutions [. . .] as much as the modalities of everyday life lived in communities and domestic spaces, which have been the most usual sites of anthropological study.
>
> (Marcus 1998: 240)

Such ethnography is bound to discard some of its classic goals such as holistic representation, or the portrayal of the cultural/social system as a totality. Multi-sited ethnography is designed around chains, paths, threads, conjunctions of locations where, through his/her physical presence, the ethnographer follows an explicit logic of association or connection among the sites. Such construction of the space which the ethnographer traverses requires him/her to 'follow the people' (e.g. focusing on an ethnic group 'at home' and in diaspora), 'follow the thing' (e.g. an object of art from the artist to the market), 'follow the metaphor', 'follow the plot, story, or allegory', etc. (Marcus 1998: 90–98).

My research attempts a contextualized and nuanced reading of Iranian films, moving from the processes of film regulation and the filmmakers' negotiations through them, to 'audiences' and to forces working on both, as a move 'beyond audiences' (Abu-Lughod 2000). Therefore, I consider reception of Iranian cinema from the level of the authorities viewing of films and the negotiations involved. Hence, I follow 'the life of a film'.

### *'Insider' research*

I begin with my analysis of audience reactions to films from my own experiences of engaging with films in Iran in 1989 (in Chapter 3) and end up discussing my engagement with films since I began living in the West (in Chapter 5). Thus my role as an 'insider' ethnographer is significant to my research.

In anthropology there is a debate about the objectivity of 'insider research' or the practice of ethnography 'at home'. Traditionally, anthropology has been the Western academics' study of the non-Western other. Over the history of anthropology, however, the distance between the anthropologists and their informants has been decreasing, with increasing numbers of anthropologists studying their own societies. This phenomenon has created a debate concerning issues that include familiarity with the field and objectivity (Weston 1997).

A number of arguments have been raised against insider research. Stephenson and Greer (1981) allege that the 'insider' is much too familiar with his/her culture to question taken-for-granted norms. In contrast, the 'outsider' would detect implicit cultural patterns, thanks to an initial 'culture shock' that entices curiosity. The indigenous ethnographer is said to be too involved with the issues he/she attempts to study and is therefore unable to research them objectively.

In defence, the advocates of 'insider' research maintain that the lived experiences of the 'insider', his/her linguistic competence as well as knowledge of literary tradition give substantial advantages (Nakane 1983: 54). Furthermore, the fact that, when writing up, the 'insider' is back in the academic environment, with enough distance from the field, facilitates his/her role as the 'impersonal analyst' (Srinivas 1966: 157).

Considering the debate, it seems that the arguments for and against 'insider' research presume a clear delineation between 'inside' and 'outside'. However, such boundaries are increasingly porous because of the growing interconnectedness of societies around the globe and the increasing movement of images, commodities, and people across boundaries separating nations or states (Appadurai 1991: 197). In the same manner, the indigenous researcher, such as myself, who is trained in the West, may be able to inhabit and understand both cultures equally well as an 'epistemological amphibian'[9] (Aguilar 1981: 20). The acceptability of multiple identities that can be deployed in different contexts means moving beyond notions of a single identity tied to a single society.

I argue that 'insiderness' and 'outsiderness' are relative concepts. Such relativity denotes that, with respect to any given culture, researchers may be considered 'insiders' or 'outsiders' according to the intimacy of their knowledge and the degree to which they are accepted within those societies; they are all part of the same continuum. Furthermore, contrary to reifying viewpoints, 'insiders' (like 'outsiders') do not necessarily share the same perspectives. This lack of homogeneity may not be only related to distinguishable factors such as gender or social class. This is particularly true in the case of societies of countries like Iran where there are a range of voices and insights from within.

The debate about 'insiderness' underlines that, in studying one's own society, the researcher has to be conscious of certain issues, such as multiple audiences and cultural chauvinism. 'Insiders' are writing not only for other academics but for the subjects of their study. Because of these multiple audiences, researchers are also held accountable by intellectuals from their own culture (Abu-Lughod 1991: 142). This accountability may be a source of enrichment for the researcher through the added incentive to research more extensively. As for objectivity, the 'insider' has to subdue cultural chauvinism, just as an 'outsider' must overcome ethnocentricity (Aguilar 1981: 25). Value judgements should be avoided while the researcher should take care not to project their personal perspectives onto the subjects of their study. This requires researchers to be vigilant when they produce ethnographic texts. Clifford notes that the ethnographer's work begins, 'not with participant observation, or with cultural texts (suitable for interpretation), but with writing, the making of texts' (1986: 2). As in the field, the ethnographers' presence is 'visible' in their writing, where they engage in construction of texts. Their representations tell their readers not only about their research but about the ethnographers, their biases and historical context. Therefore, ethnographic writing must be reflexive, exposing the ethnographer's biases (Scholte 1972; Watson 1987; Marcus 1994).

My study constitutes a critique of present-day Iranian society. I broadly support the reformist and women's movements in the country, noting that both movements are heterogeneous in terms of their supporters and objectives. I share the ideals of the movements for democratization, social freedom and feminist social change. Since I held similar views to the reformists and feminists, this created empathy with those who shared these views. This sort of politically committed sharing of knowledge and establishment of rapport is referred to by Marcus as 'circumstantial activism' (1998: 98). Thus, this book is about interrogating not just other Iranians' engagement with cinema, but also my own.

### *Field research*

This book is based on field research which consisted of a total of eight months in Iran on three different trips between January 2003 and April 2004. In that period I conducted research in Tehran, the capital, and in Mashhad, my hometown and Iran's second-largest city.

My reason for the choice of the sites was twofold. First of all, Tehran is the hub of film activity in Iran where all major filmmakers live and the Ministry of Culture and Islamic Guidance (MCIG) is located. In addition, the Fajr International Film Festival (FIFF), which is Iran's major film festival, takes place in Tehran. Staying in Tehran afforded me the opportunity to meet and interview a number of filmmakers, cinema authorities and others involved in cinema.[10] I chose Mashhad because of my already existing network of contacts there, which I used to find people willing to participate in the study.

In Tehran there are 75 cinemas and in Mashhad 19, while at the time of writing the total number in Iran is 305. There is also a very large number of video shops in both cities where VCD (video CD) and DVD copies of films are available.[11]

Once in Iran, I used 'snowballing' in order to meet people to interview. I used this method not only for meeting authorities, filmmakers and other cinema-related people, but also for cinema-goers. On numerous occasions in Iran, I watched films in the company of others, in cinema and on video, and discussed them afterwards. Those people I watched and/or discussed the films with, whom I shall call my informants, were all pre-existing groups, the members of which knew each other well. I call them 'interpretive groups', following Fish's concept of 'interpretive communities' who used the concept in relation to communities of literary scholars (1980: 303–75). The members of these communities share basic assumptions about the literature and about the nature of the meaning making process as well as its goals. All participants in interpretive groups do not necessarily agree about the meaning. Nevertheless, certain strategies and assumptions about the process of meaning making can be teased out. For my research, the fact that the group members knew each other was also important for my attempt to access normally-occurring conversations about films. This would not be the same working with a focus group brought together by the researcher. My informants ranged in age from 20 to 45; all of them

*Figure 1.1* Cinemas on Azadi Ave in the centre of Tehran; photograph by the author.

had some university education and were middle class by their own definition. I would try to meet the group before the discussion or, if I could not, I would allow enough time to establish rapport with them before watching and/or discussing films.

The films I watched and discussed with these various groups were those that they wanted to watch. In the case of the older films (discussed in Chapter 3), to avoid artificial situations, I did not ask them to watch a film which they had seen before. Rather, the discussion was based on their recollections of the films. Not all interviews or group discussions were recorded. At times I realized that taking out the tape recorder would disrupt a discussion which was taking place already. Some did not wish their voices to be recorded. In addition, in one case (Chapter 3, *The Lizard*) the discussion took place on a long walk and then in a car, which prevented me from audio taping. My approach was to get people talking about a film and try not to interrupt if the conversation was going in the general direction I wanted. The informality of talking like this made the discussions closer to ordinarily occurring ones among people who usually watch the films together. The objective was to get them to talk about what they considered important in the films. Discussions of six of the films, namely *Marriage of the Blessed* (Makhmalbaf 1989), *Glass Agency* (Hatamikia 1997), *House on the Water* (Farmanara 2001), *The Lizard* (Tabrizi 2004), *Fifth Reaction* (Milani 2003) and *10* (Kiarostami 2002), are analysed in detail in Chapters 3 and 4.

In terms of discussing 'women's films' (Chapter 4), as a man, my access to women-only groups was limited. Hence, I rarely managed to discuss the films with women without the company of other men, and therefore the discussion groups consisted of members of both sexes. Although this may be a limitation in one sense, since negotiations of gender do occur between men and women, here the discussions afforded me the opportunity to witness gender discourse in the process of making meaning about films. In the discussions, I believe my presence and their knowledge of my feminist perspective perhaps had a bearing in encouraging my female informants to feel free to articulate their similar opinions.

The people I watched and/or discussed the films with were educated middle-class women and men. By focusing on middle-class educated women, who were either working or would work in the future, I am not suggesting that these women are the only ones who are challenging patriarchy in Iran. My own late mother, who was neither working outside the house nor educated, was a very strong-minded woman and had carved out a big share of power in my own family. She was not the exception either, and there were many strong women in her generation. However, women of the next generation(s) have been able to go further, thanks to their education and a degree of financial independence.

The interviews conducted were variously semi-structured, unstructured and open-ended. The semi-structured interviews were those with filmmakers, cinema authorities and critics. There were a number of unstructured, open-ended and informal interviews in the context of participant observation. The open-endedness of the interviews allowed the interviewees to talk about what they thought was relevant.

All interviews and group discussions happened in places where those I talked to felt comfortable. They were either at people's houses, in their offices or at times in cafés or restaurants. Apart from some filmmakers and authorities with whom formal arrangement had to be made, I established rapport with the interviewees before the interview. As for formal interviews with filmmakers and authorities, I was generally introduced to them by someone whom I had already interviewed. This was particularly important because of political sensitivities in Iran. With two exceptions – one from the censorship section of the MCIG and the other a manager there – interviewees did not mind my recording of the interviews.

In the following chapters only relevant sections of interviews and group discussions are quoted. Often my discussions with the respondents were wide ranging and beyond the scope of this book.

In the analysis of the group discussions and one-on-one interviews, I have understood the discourse as fragments of narratives. This was a key point, as the transcripts of data appear incomplete and disjointed (Lewis 1991). In understanding the data as part of wider discursive frameworks, I had to make links and try to piece together not just what was said but also what was implied. Audience discourses about the films which I have recounted in this thesis are exemplary and not representative of how the Iranian middle class read particular films. Through discourse analysis, I have sought to examine the shared assumptions, the interpretive strategies and the pleasures involved in their engagement with the politics of the films.

Furthermore, I have considered the way in which people's discourse embodies wider social processes, conceptualizations, and ways of thinking (Barker and Brooks 1998: 115).

My presence obviously had a bearing on the socially situated discourses between the interviewees and me. As mentioned earlier, my own bias in favour of the reformist and the women's movements also had a bearing on my research in encouraging those I interviewed to also articulate such opinions. Therefore, I do not claim to have done value-free research, but at the same time I maintain that all research is influenced by values held by researchers.

My aim has been to see how my informants draw on films to resist the ideological impositions of the Islamic republic, and how the discourses of the filmmakers and audiences engaged with the social movements in Iran. I also wanted to see how the discourse around film was implicated in the continuing construction of national identity, and finally, how such films which are critical of the status quo are made in Iran in spite of the state's ideological control.

Other data used in the research include unpublished documents as well as box office figures obtained from the MCIG, articles in newspapers and magazines as well as web postings. Although my research is qualitative, some quantitative data – i.e. box office figures – have been used to broaden the picture.

### My presence in the field and Iran's political atmosphere

Generally throughout the research period I found it easy to establish rapport with those I came into contact with, including the authorities. There were a number of reasons for this. Although I have lived abroad for several years, my Persian is very fluent and I do not have to resort to using English words, as Iranian expatriates often do. Also, that I had come to Iran to do my research was seen as an act of patriotism which was considered favourably. The fact that I lived in the West was also an advantage because many wished to have a friend who lived in the West. Many were (and still are) asking me about procedures to get university admission and/or student/migrant visas. Others needed books and other material that are published in the west, which I took with me or sent to them. I have also tried to promote some filmmakers' work in the UK. This reciprocity has been important in establishing and maintaining my relationships in Iran.

Although coming from the West was generally an advantage for me, at other times it was a disadvantage because of the current political atmosphere. In 2003/4 there was a continuing struggle between the reformists and the conservatives, in which the conservatives tended to look for pretexts for attacking the reformists. One such pretext was to charge reformists and secular forces with espionage. President Bush's inclusion of Iran in the 'axis of evil' had also complicated matters. The Americans claimed to want to influence Iranian politics directly through support for opposition forces, including financial help. This has played into the hands of the conservatives, who are happy to condemn any acts of opposition to themselves as 'sleeping with the enemy'. In this charged atmosphere, since I was coming from the UK (the USA's closest ally) and wanted to research contentious issues raised in cinema, I had to be cautious. I was told by several people in Iran not to draw attention to myself.

It was essential to establish trust for people to agree to having their voice recorded at interviews – or to interview them at all. I would assure people that I was the only one who would listen to the interview recordings, and that I would be transcribing them myself. Generally this was enough, but when they did not want to be recorded, I just took notes. I would turn off the tape recorder if people wished to say something off the record. On a few occasions I was asked to erase a certain comment from the tape.

In general, I approached the authorities with third-party introductions. I learned the hard way about the importance of this. When I approached Tahmasebi, the manager of the Centre for Research and Study of Cinema at the MCIG, he treated me with much suspicion and scepticism, even though I showed him a letter from my supervisor about my research. The encounter made me feel very uncomfortable. Surprisingly, however, Tahmasebi seemed like a different person the next time I met him and treated me excellently. Not only did he provide me with much of the box office figures and the yearly cinema directives which I had asked for, but on two occasions he gave me unrecorded interviews. Later I realized that in the course of our first meeting I had mentioned having already contacted the editors of *Mahnameh-ye sinema'i-ye film* (henceforth *Mahnameh*), Iran's renowned cinema periodical. Tahmasebi had apparently got in touch with them and verified this, and their recommendation had helped. From then on, I did not go to see anyone without an introduction.

Third party introductions, however, were not always a guarantee of trouble-free contact. I once mentioned to an employee of the MCIG whom I had befriended that I wanted to know about the closure of two cinema periodicals by the judiciary. While I was in his office he called a friend of his in the press section of the MCIG and passed me the phone to ask my question. When I did so, his friend, whom I had met previously, sounded abrupt and unfriendly and told me that he had no idea about such matters. I was surprised by his behaviour. Later, he informed us that the telephones of the reformist-controlled press section were tapped. I was worried that I might have attracted undue attention to myself. To my relief, however, no trouble ensued. The lesson I learned was that I must be extra vigilant and not trust others' judgement blindly.

### The choice and analysis of films

The films which I discuss in detail in Chapters 3 and 4 are 'social films', i.e. films about social/political issues such as social justice and the place of the clergy in the Iranian society, which have been controversial. The main reason for the controversies has been the conservatives' reactions to the films, because of their engagement with sensitive social issues. The press coverage of the controversies, as well as word-of-mouth news and rumours about them, make the films topical for discussion. This highlights cinema's role as a significant social practice beyond simply a form of entertainment.

Apart from the two films discussed in Chapter 3, namely *Marriage of The Blessed* and *Glass Agency*, which were screened before I went to Iran for research, the others were made or shown during the course of my research. In Chapter 4, I discuss 'women's films' separately. Other films such as Makhmalbaf's *Time of Love* (1991) and *Nights of Zayandehrud* (1991), Mirbaqeri's *Snowman* (1995) and Afkhami's *Hemlock* (2000) could have been included in these chapters. However, since many whom I talked to mentioned the films in Chapters 3 and 4 as particularly important, I have focused on these. Furthermore, many of the issues raised in the films which I have omitted have been covered in my analysis in the two chapters.

In my inquiry about the films, I have interrogated the films' narratives in order to relate them to the controversies that they caused in Iran, the references by the film-makers whom I interviewed, and the discussions of the films by the cinema-goers to whom I talked. The discussions of the films in the thesis are informed by the polysemic possibilities in the film texts that open them up to multiple readings. Rather than to fix the meaning of the films, I have sought to explore them as a situated social practice.

Owing to the importance that the Iranian authorities have placed on filmmakers in the post-revolution cinema, interviewing filmmakers has been an important part of my inquiry. While the cinema before the revolution was star based, in the post-revolution period, the new cinema authorities put the focus mainly on directors and secondly on script-writers as the creative forces in cinema. The change was reflected in the relative prominence of the names of directors and actors in film posters, and in the directors' and scriptwriters' earnings. Filmmakers' presence has been enhanced extra-textually through their writings (Makhmalbaf, for example, is also a prolific writer) and media interviews or live question-and-answer sessions (as with Milani, see Chapter 4). As a result, many filmmakers such as Milani, Makhmalbaf, Hatamikia, and Tabrizi have become household names. In addition, as can be seen in Chapters 3 to 5, people discuss films in relation to their directors, their previous films and extra-textual information about them. In my interviews with the filmmakers I had the following main motives: I wanted to find out about the negotiations of meaning at the level of regulatory process in Iran and how these are informed by the filmmakers' social/political commitments.

## Chapter outline

In Chapter 2, I discuss the state control of Iranian cinema, and notably the issue of censorship. Some have described Iranian film censorship as impenetrable, and others as easily manipulated. Unsatisfied with either of these two descriptions, I attempt to unravel some of the complexities of the state control of Iranian cinema against the backdrop of post-revolutionary political developments. I also contrast the controls exerted on cinema with the press and state broadcasting.

Chapter 3 investigates 'social films'. The four films discussed – namely *Marriage of the Blessed, Glass Agency, House on the Water* and *The Lizard* – were produced between 1989 and 2004, and cover some of the most controversial issues of their times, such as the aftermath of the Iran–Iraq war, social justice, the social position of the clergy. As a multi-sited ethnography requires, I have 'followed the film' from its makers to the people who watch it in its social/political context. Turner's theory of liminality and cultural performances as well as Downing's theory of 'radical media' have been useful in my interrogation of the material.

In Chapter 4, I focus on 'women's films'. Although Iranian cinema is famous for films about gender issues, there has been little analysis of how these films are considered in Iran and their relation to the women's movement. Chapter 4 examines the dynamics of negotiations of gender in the reception of the films.

Chapter 5 explores the issues and debates regarding the international acclaim of Iranian cinema. Representations of Iran outside the country are relevant to Iranians' sense of identity.

Chapter 6 is the conclusion to the thesis and suggests where future work can build on my research.

# 2 State control of Iranian cinema

## The shifting 'red lines'

## Introduction

The apparent contradiction between strict state control of filmmaking in Iran, on the one hand, and a large number of socially/politically critical films, on the other, has created much interest in censorship in Iranian cinema. Some researchers suggest that filmmakers evade censorship by means of symbolism, metaphor and allegory. Devictor calls these the 'tricks' that filmmakers play on the censors (2002: 71). Naficy (2001a) and Rahimieh (2002), among others, highlight instances of filmmakers' use of indirect means to bypass censorship. Conversely, Ghazian (2002) claims that the censorship of Iranian cinema is a united, impenetrable ideological machine. None of the two explanations is entirely satisfactory. If the censors were fooled by the filmmakers' use of indirect devices, then they would not ban so many films by experienced filmmakers. And if the censorship barrier was impenetrable, the previously banned films would not be released at all. We need to look again at the control framework and the way it has operated.

In this chapter, I explore the censorship's attempt at controlling the political content of Iranian films. I argue that neither is the censorship process impenetrable nor are the authorities so easily fooled as has been suggested. Rather, there are complex negotiations at work, which have not been examined fully thus far. I demonstrate that the censorship code is not clearly defined and there is no unitary censorship mechanism. This presents filmmakers with opportunities to get past the barrier. My argument is based on interviews with major cinema authorities, including some from the censorship section of the Ministry of Culture and Islamic Guidance (the MCIG) as well some cinema experts. In relation to state control, I examine the unique position of Iranian cinema in contrast to the broadcast media and the press.

I focus on the dynamics of the state control of cinema in Iran, starting from the pre-revolution period. This brief foray into pre-revolution cinema is to highlight the state's relationship to cinema in that period as well as to lay the ground for the examination of the religious figures' reaction to cinema. Next, against the backdrop of post-revolution Iranian politics which has had a profound effect on Iranian cinema, I highlight the dynamics of the shifting boundaries of filmmaking in the country. This chapter also sets the scene for the next three.

## Cinema and the state before the revolution[1]

From its very beginning, Iranian cinema has had a tight relationship with the state. The first footage ever shot by an Iranian was of a trip by the Iranian monarch Mozafferoddin Shah to Belgium in 1900. The court photographer, Mirza Ebrahim Khan Akkas-bashi, from then on chronicled the trips of the king. These films were only shown at the royal court. Under the Qajar dynasty, the use of film for state propaganda or as a medium in need of control was not feasible, because only a handful of cinema halls were ever built at the time and film was far from a popular form of entertainment (Omid 1998: 20–61).

Under the Pahlavi dynasty (1926–79), however, the situation gradually changed. The main agenda of the Pahlavi regime was that of Western-style modernization. Pursuing this goal, the rulers sought to weaken traditional lifestyles and the religious leadership. During the Pahlavi period, policies of modernization were implemented with an iron fist, without much regard for public opinion. Obviously, the modernization drive did not extend to the regime itself which remained an undemocratic traditional monarchy.

The first ever Persian-language talkie, *The Lor Girl* (1933), which was in fact filmed in India, was made to accord with the state doctrine of modernization. The film paid lip service to state policies under the first Pahlavi monarch, Reza Shah (1925–41). *The Lor Girl* is about Golnar, a young woman who supports herself working in a café as a dancer. A group of bandits take her hostage but Jafar, a government detective, frees her. Chased by the bandits, the two escape Iran and live in India for years but when they hear about the modernization of their country under Reza Shah, they go back to the country. The ending, with the return to Iran, was added by the producers in order to appeal to the new regime and gain its backing. The newspaper advertisement for the film announced, 'in this film the predicaments of Iran previously and the rapid advancements of the country under his just and powerful majesty Pahlavi are shown' (Omid 1998: 160). Under the first Pahlavi monarch, however, like in the Qajar era, film did not become a form of mass entertainment and therefore was of limited use or importance to the regime.

The second Pahlavi monarch, Mohammad Reza Shah or the Shah, followed his father's vision of modernization. Less powerful than his father, he faced a number of crises during his reign (Abrahamian 1982). Most notably, prime minister Mosaddeq led a popular political movement which resulted in the Shah almost losing the throne. However, a CIA-led coup restored his power in 1953. In the post-coup era, the regime relied on a combination of propaganda and coercion. Since its formation in 1957, SAVAK, the Shah's brutal secret police, controlled or physically stopped expressions of free thought. State propaganda portrayed the Shah as the captain who would lead the nation through the stormy waters of social change to the heights of a 'Great Civilization' that would match the Achaemenid Dynasty's splendour of 25 centuries ago.

State propaganda tried to portray a modern image of Iran to the world as well as fostering such aspirations in Iran. Film and television became major vehicles in this project. Most of the state-sponsored documentaries produced during the Shah's era, which were shown by mobile cinemas around the country, highlighted the achievements of the Pahlavi dynasty in modernizing the country (Issari 1989: 164–98). At the time, cinemas and television were inundated with Hollywood films and locally produced programmes which conformed to the state's modernizing ideology. However, there was practically no state support for local production of fiction films, which relied on box office earnings.

### Film-e farsi *(literally Persian film)*

The commercial films made under the Pahlavi regime have been collectively referred to as *film-e farsi*. Many have discussed *film-e farsi* as a pejorative term of reference for the popular melodramatic cinema which often featured song and dance routines in imitation of Indian cinema (Golestan 1995: 80–81; Tapper 2002: 13). However, the label has a longer history, dating back to the beginnings of Iranian talkies which were called *film-e nategh-e farsi* (literally Persian film with sound). That was to distinguish them from the foreign talkies in the original languages (Omid 1998: 66–71). Gradually the title seems to have been shortened to *film-e farsi*. The appearance of films in Persian was a source of nationalist pride among the producers and cinema-goers. They were popular not only because of the language spoken in them but also for showing Iranian locations (or appearing to show them, as was the case with *The Lor Girl*) and being about Iranian lives (Omid 1998: 66–67).

In the absence of state support, until the mid-1960s Iranian cinema was generally in a constant state of financial crisis. In 1965, however, with the amazing box office success of *Croesus' Treasure* (Yasemi 1965), the fortunes of Iranian cinema seemed to be about to change. This was a melodramatic feel-good film about a poor but happy-go-lucky hero called 'Ali Bigham (Carefree 'Ali) which featured song and dance routines. 'Ali rescues a rich man who was about to commit suicide. He later finds out that the man was his father who had deserted him and his mother long ago. After the initial rejections, 'Ali and his mother accept him back into the family.

The film's success led to the rise of *film abgushti* (*abgusht* is common man's stew), a new cycle of Iranian films which would, like *Croesus' Treasure,* famously include a scene with the protagonist eating *abgusht* (Mehrabi 1984: 111). The immense popularity of *Croesus' Treasure* resulted in a large number of new cinemas being built around the country (Golestan 1995: 81). Local production also grew significantly during the same period (Omid 1998: 411). Films of this type were noted for their on-screen resolution of class differences, sometimes through the poor hero marrying into a rich family, or somehow finding out that he was rich by birth. Thus, while highlighting the moral superiority of the poor, the legitimacy of the riches of the modern affluent classes was reaffirmed, hence complying with state ideology.

### Sinema-ye motefavet *(alternative cinema)*

From the late 1950s a number of socially conscious films, both documentary and fiction, were made, many of them by intellectuals including writers and poets who had earlier produced realist literary work and the New Poetry. While in Iran the film movement was named *sinema-ye motefavet* or Alternative Cinema, in the West it became known as the Iranian New Wave.

Social realism in these films had its roots in realism in Iranian modern literature, which had began in the early 1900s. Since then many realist stories were written with pointed social/political critique. Jamalzadeh's *Once upon a Time* and Hedayat's *The Blind Owl* were predecessors of Afghani's *Mrs Ahu's Husband and* Sa'edi's *The Mourners of Bayal.* The development in prose was contemporaneous with the emergence of a new form of poetry called *she'r-e no* or the New Poetry. In the works of poets such as Shamlu, Farrokhzad and Akhavan-Sales, unlike the generally philosophical pre-occupations of traditional poetry, there was more concern with social realities. From the late 1950s onwards, some renowned writers and poets such as Golestan, Farrokhzad and Sa'edi turned their attention to cinema, thanks to its capacity for dynamic representation (Fischer 1984).

The first of the socially realist films, Gaffary's *South of The City* (1958), was about life in the poor suburbs of Tehran. Gradually many more such films were made including: *The House is Black* (Farrokhzad 1964), *Night of the Hunchback* (Ghaffari 1964), *The Brick and the Mirror* (Golestan 1965), *Mrs Ahou's Husband* (Mollapur 1968), *Qeysar* (Kimia'i 1969) and *The Cow* (Mehrju'i 1969). These films were well received by the critics. Dariush (1964: 80 in Omid 1998: 369–70) praises *Night of the Hunchback* as 'the beginning of Iranian cinema'. He adds,

> issues that our society is afflicted with are expressed [in this film] . . . an intellectual critique of different classes of the society has been done . . . something has been said, something essential about you and people like you who belong to this time and this place.
>
> (Omid 1998: 369–70)

These filmmakers were often critical of the cultural/social predicaments of the country. They underscored the social/economic problems that the regime attempted to gloss over with a veneer of modernization. For example, in *The Mongols* (1973) Kimiavi likens the invasion of public spaces in Iran by television with its modern imagery to the invasion of Iran by the Mongols in the 13th century.

### Censorship

Ironically, New Wave films which were generally funded by state-affiliated institutes, were also often banned or censored. Under the Shah, censorship was meant to prevent attempts at undermining state values and aspirations. For example, one of the articles of the 1959 censorship code prohibited 'presentation of ruins, poverty, backwardness and scenes that damage the state's national prestige' (Golmakani 1992: 20). Many films were censored or banned as a result of these restrictions. Gaffary's *South of the City* (1958), which was mostly filmed in the poor suburbs of Tehran, was banned and its negative mutilated by the censors (Golestan 1995: 107). Filmed in a poor village in Iran, *The Cow* (Mehrju'i 1969) was famously banned initially and only released when the filmmaker agreed to have a statement added to the beginning of the film which said that the story took place before the Pahlavi dynasty.

By the mid-1970s, with state support discontinued, production of these films dwindled to a trickle. In addition, because the New Wave's critique was rather intellectual and not easily digestible, the films generally did not do well at the box office. At the time there were far fewer educated, even literate, people in the country and hence the audience for social realist films was very limited.

## The Islamic revolution and its aftermath

The traditional Shi'ite clergy were deeply opposed to cinema, and this had strong implications for Iranian cinema during and after the revolution. Before the revolution, the clergy believed that Iranian and imported films were a threat to the public morals. This had mainly to do with the representation of women. Many of the *film-e farsi* included women without Islamic dress who sang and danced in cafés. There were also many scenes showing the consumption of alcohol. Some of the clergy perceived their mission to be fighting back against the perceived 'moral decadence and unseemly social filth' that filled the streets and was promoted in film and television (Abrahamian 1982: 474). During the Iranian revolution, 180 out of 436

*Figure 2.1* Entrance to what used to be Ferdowsi Cinema in Mashhad which was destroyed in a fire during the revolution; photograph by the author.

*Figure 2.2* Cinema Qods (formerly Aria) in Mashhad, burnt down during the revolution; the cinema was rebuilt shortly afterwards; photograph by the author.

movie houses, which to the traditional clergy symbolized Western values, were set on fire (see Figures 2.1 and 2.2). In one incident on 10 August 1978, about 300 people died in an inferno in the Rex Cinema in the city of Abadan, and from then until the establishment of the Islamic Republic in early 1979, cinemas remained closed across the country.

As mentioned in Chapter 1, the post-revolution state in Iran is based on Islam as its ideology. Much like the previous regime's modernization drive, the new elite attempted to Islamize the society through the use of what Althusser refers to as Ideological State Apparatuses (ISAs) (1971: 136–37). Thus, the education system and the mass media were used for indoctrination.

The national radio and television, run by the Islamic Republic of Iran Broadcasting (IRIB), came under the strict control of conservatives from early on. The head of the organization is directly appointed by the Supreme Leader.[2] In the absence of private broadcasters, the TV has played a major role as the mouthpiece of the Islamic regime and in particular the powerful conservatives.

Ayatollah Khomeini declared the role of cinema to be a tool for 'educating the people' (Algar 1981: 258) and that, like all art, it was to be put in the service of Islam.[3] Therefore, cinema, which was rejected by the clergy under the previous regime as a Westernizing medium, was legitimized. Going to the movies became an acceptable activity for the Ayatollah's followers. However, at the time there was no guideline as to what constituted an Islamic cinema.

In the absence of filmmakers with Islamic background, some *film-e farsi* directors were the first to make films. Golmakani, chief editor of *Mahnameh*, Iran's best-known film publication, told me:

> The period from 1979 to 1982 was a period of chaos and opportunism. There were no guidelines and no plans so the time was right for opportunists to take advantage. The only criterion was that [the authorities] wanted to have a revolutionary cinema. The foreign films they showed at that time were either revolutionary films such as Z and *Battle of Algiers* or others which were turned into revolutionary films in the dubbing.[4] [Among Iranian films,] one of the first made after the revolution was *Mojahed's Call*. These films were based on the same concept as the pre-revolution action cinema but the filmmakers tried to fit them into the new situation with a revolutionary gloss. So now the action hero was a revolutionary but that was just superficial change and the film was full of action sequences.

For the first few years, there was a chaotic situation. Cinema halls were intermittently closed and reopened, and the affairs of cinema were passed between different ministries. On the one hand, a 'purification' process began as part of the transformation of cinema after the revolution. For example, much of the already available pre-revolution foreign and Iranian stock of films were rejected for having scenes which were 'un-Islamic'. The authorities sought to stop those filmmakers and actors who had been active in pre-revolution cinema from working (Naficy 2002: 33–35).

The purification process was however applied inconsistently. Hojjatolislam Mo'adikhah, who was in charge of the MCIG at the time, believed that those filmmakers who had publicly declared their allegiance to the Islamic regime should be allowed to continue working. His critics were relentless in their condemnation of his leniency, particularly when Mo'adikhah allowed the making and exhibition of *Barzakhiha* in 1982. The film was made by Qaderi, a pre-revolution *film-farsi* director, and featured Fardin and Malak-Moti'i, two major stars of that cinema. The backlash against the film forced Mo'adikhah, who took responsibility for it, to resign (Javedani 2002: 156–57). As the controversy indicated, there were divergent attitudes to what constituted an acceptable cinema in post-revolutionary Iran.

Politically the country was also in a chaotic state during the first few years after the revolution when the country was also at war with Iraq. The first post-revolution government, headed by Bazargan, faced multiple challenges to its authority by numerous conservative-led organizations. Later, the first democratically elected president, Bani-Sadr, was ousted by Ayatollah Khomeini in June 1981. Raja'i, the next president and Bahonar, his prime minister, as well as 73 members of parliament were assassinated by the armed opposition in two separate incidents in June and August of 1981 respectively.

In the ensuing atmosphere of total suppression of internal opposition by the Islamic rulers, which was aided by the fact that the country was at war with Iraq from 1980 to 1988, the print media were reduced to those which reflected the conservative views (Bakhash 1984; Millet 1982). The national radio and television networks became inundated with conservative propaganda and programmes with an overt agenda of Islamization. As for cinema, new authorities were appointed to regulate it in 1982.

### Cinema after 1982

There has been much disagreement among the post-revolution authorities in relation to matters of culture. Luckily for cinema, under prime minister Mir-Hossein Musavi (1980–88), Khatami, a moderate cleric, took over the reins of the MCIG. Khatami put Anvar in charge of the cinema section of the MCIG, as the ministry's Cinema Deputy. The Farabi Cinema Foundation, the executive arm of the MCIG, was then formed and managed by Beheshti. Unlike the earlier cinema authorities, Beheshti and Anvar were both acquainted with cinema and theatre from before the revolution. As Beheshti explained to me in an interview:

> Musavi the prime minister and Abdollah Esfandiari [a high ranking Farabi official] were involved in producing plays in a theatre group called Milad before the revolution in the early 1970s. We were influenced by 'Ali Shari'ati and worked at Hosseinieh Ershad.[5] Two years before the revolution, we started a filmmaking company called *Ayat Film* to produce religious films against the Shah's regime.[6]

After the revolution, when they took over the affairs of cinema, they found the job daunting. Beheshti continued:

> the great revolutionary transformation in Iran had led to an aspiration to transform the culture of the country, and along with that the cultural institution of cinema. Nevertheless, few of the authorities thought this would be possible. So when we took over, many [conservative authorities] would have been happier if we had simply stopped cinema all together. We had an uphill road ahead of us. Nonetheless, because of the trust that prime minister Musavi had in us, he supported us in our pursuit.

The new authorities announced their responsibilities as *hemayat* (support), *hedayat* (guidance) and *nezarat* (literally supervision, but in effect censorship). In their capacity to support, they took numerous measures to revitalize the industry. They subsidized the importation of filmmaking materials; lowered the tax on cinema tickets; made low interest loans for filmmaking. At the same time, many ideologically committed youth were trained as filmmakers by various institutes (see Naficy 2002 for more details). Thus, Iranian cinema awoke from revolutionary hibernation with a rising number of productions. Between 1981 and 1984 the number of films produced annually rose from 12 to 40 (Talebinejad 1998: 54–55).

Hedayat *(guidance)*

The MCIG has been actively 'guiding' Iranian cinema. Naficy describes with approval the moves the MCIG has made in encouraging technical improvements to films through mechanisms such as a rating system (2002: 52). However, the purpose of the rating system was not just to improve the quality of films, and it has also had a major role in support of films with an overt agenda of Islamization. In addition to funding, the awards at the annual Fajr International Film Festival have been another mechanism of guidance by the MCIG.

In 1986, having succeeded in increasing the quantity of films produced, the Beheshti-Anvar team focused their attention on improving the quality of Iranian films. As mentioned in Chapter 1, in a series of moves they made sure that more emphasis was put on the director as the creative force behind the making of a film. This was a clear departure from the star-based *film-e farsi* of the Pahlavi era.

A lasting legacy of the period has been the rating system, which at the time was on a four-category basis, from 'A' to 'D'.[7] An 'A' rated film, for example, would receive preferential treatment such as higher ticket prices, screening during better periods at better cinemas.[8] The rating system was based on the three loosely defined criteria of technical aspects, aesthetics and content. In terms of techniques of filmmaking, for example, simultaneous sound recording was preferred to post-production dubbing. As for aesthetics, innovation and experimentation were encouraged. What constituted better content was determined by 'closeness to the cultural currents' within the Islamic Republic (Anon. 1998: 52) and therefore was not as innocent as Naficy implies in only encouraging 'the production of quality films' (2002: 52).

In general, filmmakers whose ideological commitment to the regime was not questioned and were, hence, referred to as *khodi* or insider were privileged by the MCIG in terms of support over secular filmmakers who were referred to as *gheyr-e khodi* or outsiders. This was endorsed by state authorities such as the Supreme Leader, Ayatollah Khamene'i, who in a meeting with the MCIG authorities said, '[i]f you want cinema to grow, you have to provide opportunity to insider filmmakers.'[9]

Another mechanism for 'guidance' is the annual set of directives published by the MCIG in the *daftarcheh-ye sinema'i* or Cinema Booklet which outlines some of the conditions for extra funding/privileges for the following year. Generally the directives have pledged support for films that explicitly conform to the regime ideology.

Filmha-ye dini *(religious films)*[10]

According to directions given by Ayatollah Khomeini, cinema was to be put at the service of the regime ideology. Nevertheless, what constitutes 'Islamic' or 'religious' cinema was a matter of dispute. One of the earliest contenders in defining such cinema was the Art Centre of the Islamic Propaganda Organization (henceforth the Art Centre) which is known in Iran as *howzeh-ye honari*. As the name suggests, the organization was created to produce propaganda for the Islamic regime. The cinema section of the Art Centre has been very active in terms of film output.

The Centre was also the place where many of the ideologically committed film-makers such as Makhmalbaf and Majidi learned filmmaking. Since the head of the organization was directly appointed by the Supreme Leader, and it had its own sources of funding and later even technical equipment, the Art Centre became a powerful parallel organization to the MCIG.

The Art Centre's filmmaking section started with films which were intended to teach about religion through film. The early films by the then ultra-religious Makhmalbaf are good examples of this type of films. He was one of the founding members of the Art Centre. His *Nasuh's Repentance* (1983) was meant to warn against the consequences of materialism by depiction the deterioration of the life of a man who is focused on pursuit of wealth in his life. Made during the Iran–Iraq war *Two Sightless Eyes* (1983) features a middle-aged villager called Iman (faith) who wants to go to the war-front but has to take care of certain matters before departure. He pays back the money he owes, and marries off his daughter, but he is stuck with his blind son Nurollah (light of God). His son-in-law and his other son go to the war-front, but Iman cannot. Soon his son-in-law dies and his son returns home wounded. Iman takes his two sons to the holy city of Mashhad to pray for their health. In the end, Nurollah gains his eyesight by miracle.

The film also features several sermons by a clergyman, played by Makhmalbaf, about the importance of faith in life and encouraging participation in the war. With films like *Two Sightless Eyes*, the Art Centre sought to create a 'religious cinema'. Many of these 'religious films' made by the Art Centre have been of the Sacred Defence films (about the Iran–Iraq war).

Beheshti, on the other hand, wanted to get away from the Art Centre's early attempts at religious films. Speaking of the tendency to use film didactically, Beheshti said at the time, 'we cannot teach by force' (Talebinejad 1998: 51). He gave special support to a different type of film, referred to as *filmha-ye erfani* or mystical films which he and Anvar advocated. Many of these films were centred upon the personal discovery and transformation as a result of re-evaluation of one's own life. This preference for 'mystical films' had implications for Iranian films in general. As Golmakani explained to me:

> The cinema authorities at the time wanted filmmakers to make films which were thought provoking. Since both Beheshti and Anvar were into mysticism and philosophy, they started supporting *filmha-ye erfani* (mystical films). Well, of course not everyone appreciates inner beauty in cinema or thought-provoking films. Most of these mystical films did not attract audiences to cinemas.
>
> At the same time, Beheshti and Anvar were against physical beauty taking centre stage in cinema. So if there were good-looking actors and actresses [in the appointed cast of a film], the MCIG would either not allow the filmmaker to use them, or they would warn him/her about this issue. I remember, in a meeting with filmmakers Anvar said that films should also not promote luxury. The examples he gave with disapproval were some films which had used chandeliers in their film sets.

At the same time, foreign films shown in Iran were chosen to match the mystic concerns of these authorities. The two main foreign filmmakers whose films were promoted for their metaphysical themes were Andrei Tarkovsky and Sergei Parajanov. The officials' interest in such films resulted in many imitators trying to copy them. Hassani-Nasab, a critic from *Film Monthly*, said to me:

> I remember a film by Parajanov called *The Colour of Pomegranate* [1999] was shown in cinemas and was highly publicized here. Then, copying that film, a lot of Iranian filmmakers had somebody holding a pomegranate in their hand in a scene that was supposed to make their films mystical.

The support for this category of film would only last while Beheshti and Anvar were in office.

### Nezarat *(supervision)*

The MCIG's policy to 'guide' filmmakers was augmented by 'supervision' which in fact amounted to censorship. In February 1983 the cabinet of Mir-Hossein Musavi approved a filmmaking code according to which the *Nezarat va Namayesh* (Supervision and Exhibition) section of the MCIG[11] was put in charge of censorship of movies and videos. The code stipulated that exhibition permits would not be issued to films that:

- insult directly or indirectly the prophets, imams, the supreme jurisprudent, the leadership council or the qualified jurisprudents
- encourage wickedness, corruption and prostitution
- encourage or teach abuse of harmful and dangerous drugs or professions which are religiously sanctioned against such as smuggling, etc.
- encourage foreign cultural, economic and political influence contrary to the 'neither West nor East' policy of the Islamic Republic of Iran
- express or disclose anything that is against the interests and policies of the country which might be exploited by foreigners.

A sub-clause declared that:

> The *nezarat* committee is responsible to determine the regulations regarding the way women can appear in Iranian and foreign films in a way which would not be at variance with the high position of women, having in mind the shari'a laws. The regulation should be made available to makers of Iranian films and importers of foreign ones.
>
> (Nuri 1996: 191–93)[12]

The filmmaking code is ambiguous and open to interpretation. For example, whether or not a film has encouraged 'wickedness' could be a debatable matter; and so could whether a film has encouraged foreign cultural influence in the country.

As for how women were to be represented in cinema, the code also remained unclear. For example, what constitutes appropriate Islamic dress for women was not defined. Much was thus left to those who put the code into practice. Hence, the limits of freedom of expression in cinema – the 'red lines' as they are referred to in Iran – have been blurred. This has had implications for filmmaking which I will discuss in the text that follows.

At an official level, censorship has comprised a number of stages which have increased or decreased at different periods. At its most extensive, films have had to go through the following sequential stages of vetting in order to receive a screening permit: summary of the plot; the screenplay; approval of the cast and the film crew; make-up test (see below); surveillance of the filmmaking process (to make sure the cast and the crew behave morally); vetting of the completed film and the film trailer. At an unofficial level, reactions to the film at Fajr International Film Festival (FIFF), which is the biggest film event in Iran, are also taken into account.

Every year since 1982, the FIFF has been held in February, coinciding with the anniversary of the revolution. The FIFF has gone through various changes since its inception. For example, until the early 1990s, films had to be shown at the FIFF before they could go on general release. What remains constant at the FIFF is that political considerations play a role in the decisions about awarding prizes to films. While the jury appointed by the MCIG includes some filmmakers, the MCIG keeps a close watch on the granting of the awards. For example, Behruz Afkhami, a renowned filmmaker, told me that in the 10th FIFF (1992), when he was a member of the jury, he and other jury members had decided to give most of the major awards to Beyza'i's *The Travellers* (1992). However, they did not do so owing to an intervention by the MCIG authorities who were worried about a backlash from the conservatives against the MCIG if they gave Beyza'i's film many awards. Beyza'i is part of the Writers' Guild whose members have often been persecuted by hardliner conservatives since the revolution (for more about Beyza'i see Chapter 5).

The FIFF provides the MCIG the chance to gauge reactions to the films before allowing their public release. Hossein Mohammadi, a middle-ranking employee of the censorship section, told me that at the same time as the festival, state authorities such as members of parliament and the judiciary were invited to the MCIG to see the films in private screenings. If these authorities object to a film, the MCIG will not give it a screening permit. This is to avoid fuelling hostile reactions against the MCIG that might be triggered by the film's eventual release.

## Cinema after 1989

After Ayatollah Khomeini's death in 1989, which followed the end of the Iran–Iraq war a year earlier, the coercive powers of the state continued to operate, although rather less severely than they had in the past. There was also an opening for negotiation, debate and critique of post-revolutionary society. This was facilitated by Rafsanjani who was elected as president later that year. Under this pragmatic clergyman, a process of cultural and economical openness began. Rafsanjani declared the post-war era to be the 'reconstruction period'; he tried to reduce the role of the state in the economy and allowed a degree of openness to market forces. As for the MCIG, Khatami remained at his post as the minister and so did those in charge of cinema, but they were allowed to relax some of the earlier limitations. For example, filmmakers no longer needed to gain the approval of the MCIG for their screen-plays.[13] Some previously banned films were released. From this time onwards, filmmakers had some room to breathe, thanks also to the ongoing debate about culture and cinema.

The authorities of the MCIG, including Farabi, were often engaged in negotiations with filmmakers which determined the direction that a particular film and filmmaking in general took. About that period, Beheshti told me:

> We would talk about [the filmmakers'] scripts, we would see their films and discuss them. We would discuss changes to their films. Our discussion was cultural and technical rather than political. In fact these relationships developed so much that even now, when I have been away from cinema for about a decade, I still spend a quarter of my time with filmmakers.

In the absence of a blueprint, cinema under the Islamic Republic took shape in part in the course of such discussion. Although Beheshti downplays the political dimension of these discussions, it was significant (see my interview with Makhmalbaf in Chapter 3). Then, as now, politics and culture in Iran are inseparable.

Negotiations took place over the content of mystic cinema, leading the way for the inclusion of the previously forbidden theme of 'love' in Iranian cinema. The representation of 'love of God' in mystical cinema, ironically, paved the way for the appearance of the theme of 'earthly love' between man and woman. Esfandiyari, a high-ranking official at Farabi, and a close ally of Beheshti, explains:

> We were interested in . . . any concept which was of the same essence as religion, such as earthly love, and spiritual love. [. . .] Earthly love is a symbol of real love and when it deepens it is not separate from [real love]. This is the surface and when it deepens it becomes [real love]. We were wondering how to express these concepts. People today are thirsty for such concepts [. . .]
>
> Some [conservatives] were suspicious, like, God bless his soul, Avini (documentary maker and film expert at the Art Centre). We used to have heated discussions. Avini at the beginning had an antagonistic attitude towards the film *In the Alleys of Love* (Sina'i 1992), which he said should be called '[In the] alleys of desire'. He said [sarcastically], 'bravo, now you are going into such things'. Gradually, however, his perspective changed. As it happens, those 'alleys of desire' are the beginning of alleys of love. One is a symbol of the other.

> (Anon. 2001a: 46–47)[14]

With such negotiations, previously forbidden themes were legitimized. The presence of authorities who are ready to engage in such dialogues has been an important contributing factor to the evolution of post-revolution cinema.

A key figure who has made a major contribution to these processes of change is Hojjatolislam Zamm, former director of the Art Centre. Like many other Islamic authorities Zamm gradually became more open-minded in his outlook. From the mid 1990s, Zamm initiated an annual conference entitled, 'Religion from the Perspective of Cinema'. Through the interactions at the conference not only did many clerical participants become familiar with the history of the interface between cinema and religion outside Iran, they also became better educated about cinema in general.

One of the unlikely places where the Art Centre looked for representations of religion was Hollywood cinema. Foreign films, and in particular Hollywood films, were shown at the Art Centre, where they were discussed in relation to religion. These sessions were open to people who were not necessarily involved with cinema. Neda, a 30 year-old university graduate who regularly attended the screenings in the Art Centre, told me:

> The films they showed were uncensored so they were very popular and it was very difficult to get a pass to the screenings at the Art Centre. I used a connection for that. [After we watched the films] we would sometimes discuss them in relation to religion. For example, one of the films I saw there was *Ghost* (Zuker 1990). We discussed the metaphysical side of the film and how it shows the afterlife.

Such eclectic considerations of religious themes in cinema at the Art Centre paved the way for the emergence of films which appeared later exploring the themes in unorthodox ways. *The Lizard* (Tabrizi 2004) is one example which I discuss in detail in Chapter 3.

### Censorship after 1989

In spite of such positive developments, in the post-Khomeini era censorship did not disappear but was not applied as strictly as before. Its application can be considered under four categories: political expediency, moral reasons, the censors' tastes, and private party law suits against films.

#### Censorship based on political expediency

Political expediency has been the main factor in film censorship in Iran in the post-1989 period. If a film was deemed to be touching upon any politically sensitive issue at the time, it was not allowed to be made and/or shown. Beheshti called these sensitive issues, *davayer-e moltaheb* or 'hot zones' which were 'serious social issues and [those which] were related to the revolution and contemporary problems' (quoted in Sadr 2002b: 261). When I asked Beheshti about this issue, he explained:

> Our main mission was to protect the totality of Iranian cinema; therefore we tried to keep it away from political turmoil. We feared that if cinema got

involved in politics, we would face suppression [of cinema as it was] and its replacement by propaganda [favoured by the conservatives]. We tried very hard to keep cinema far from these issues so that it would keep its cultural aspects.

Beheshti's paternalistic attitude had several reasons. To a degree, I believe it shows his genuine concern about cinema as a whole coming under question, as a result of some films entering politically sensitive areas. The powerful conservatives, who generally have a restrictive view of culture, are more than willing to shut the doors to any liberal-minded expression in the arts. On the other hand, Beheshti and others also feared putting their own position at risk of attack by the conservatives.

One filmmaker who did enter these 'hot zones' was Makhmalbaf in his *Marriage of the Blessed* (1989). This film, which I examine in detail in Chapter 3, is a sharp critique of post-war Iran from the perspective of an idealist war veteran.

### Political factions and their impact on cinema

Although political factions have existed in Iran since the early 1980s, under Khomeini's leadership their disputes were resolved through the charismatic leader's arbitration. This has no longer been the case since his death.

The political faction which has mainly been in charge of matters of culture in the Islamic republic is the culturally tolerant *chap-e modern* or modern left, so named because they consist of generally well-educated religious individuals who are concerned with ideals of social equality. They were in power in the 1980–88 period and one of their affiliates, Musavi, was prime minister. Mohammad Khatami and many others who came to be known as reformists after 1997 are also from the same faction. Allies of the modern left in matters of culture have been the *rast-e modern* or modern right. As Siavoshi states, the two modern factions believe in *feqh-e puya* or dynamic jurisprudence and assert that the survival of the Islamic regime depends on the adaptability and flexibility of the religious leaders (1997: 514). Although the modern right faction have a similar outlook with respect to matters of culture, unlike the modern left faction they are not concerned with social justice. Hence, the right faction supports minimal intervention by the state in matters of economics, leaving them to market forces. The modern right took power with the rise of Rafsanjani to the presidency in 1989.

Under Rafsanjani, Khatami stayed at his job until he was pressured to resign in 1992 by the conservatives, partly over two films by Makhmalbaf, partly because of the degree of press freedom Khatami had allowed, as well as his leniency towards the use of satellite television, which the conservatives referred to as a 'Western cultural threat'. After his departure, to appease the conservatives, Rafsanjani appointed their affiliates to the MCIG.

The conservatives, who tend to be culturally intolerant, are made up of two factions, *chap-e sonnati* or the traditional left and *rast-e sonnati* or the traditional right. The two factions believe in *feqh-e sonnati* or traditional jurisprudence, based on a stagnant exegesis of Islam, and are also afraid of cultural change (Siavoshi 1997:

513). Like the modern groups above, the conservatives are divergent in their outlook towards matters of economics. While the traditional left believe in state control of the economy, the traditional right believe in the free market approach.

Until Ahmadinejad's presidency, apart from a short period after the revolution, members of the ruling elite always belonged to one of the four aforementioned political factions.[15] At different periods, when a faction's members have been in positions of power, members of rival factions have generally been moved to rather less significant jobs. However, the powerful judiciary and the Guardian Council, the members of which are directly appointed by the Supreme leader Ayatollah Khamene'i, have generally consisted of conservatives, leaving the modern factions, particularly the modern left, vulnerable.

The conservatives have often attacked the reformists for their handling of matters of culture, particularly cinema. Part of the reason for this seems to be that among the conservatives there is a genuine lack of understanding about the modern medium of cinema. They are generally in favour of films such as Makhmalbaf's early works or the Sacred Defence films about the Iran–Iraq war.[16] On the other hand, their political concerns play a major part in shaping their reactions. In general the conservatives do not miss any opportunity to attack their reformist rivals, and cinema has often provided them with the excuse for an offensive. When it suits their political agenda, they claim that conspiracies must be at work. The discourse of 'cultural invasion by the West' and 'the enemy's plots' has often been mobilized to attack the reformists (see also Chapter 5 about the international success of Iranian cinema).

Contrary to what is generally assumed, the reformists have not always been wholehearted supporters of artistic freedoms either. They have often put their own political survival ahead of their concerns for artistic freedom. Thus, numerous films have been temporarily or permanently banned for reasons of political expediency. Mohammadi (censorship section, MCIG) told me that, if there was a period of tension between the conservatives and the reformists, the reformists in the MCIG would not allow the screening of a film that they decided might be attacked by the conservatives.

In some rare cases, however, filmmakers have benefited from the clash between the reformists and the conservatives. Kasehsaz, former head of the censorship section, told me that the reformists pushed for the release of *Women's Prison* (Hekmat 2002) in 2002, because they thought it could help their case against the conservative-run judiciary.[17] At the time, several prominent reformists had been imprisoned by the judiciary, and the maltreatment and torture of political prisoners were topical. Since *Women's Prison* hinted at such maltreatment in prisons, reformist MPs pushed for its release.

### Censorship based on moral issues

In their puritanical discourse, the conservatives highlight the danger of moral corruption in cinema. This is mainly to do with the representation of women and on sexuality, which have been problematic particularly since 1979. Soon after the revolution the then ultra-religious Makhmalbaf advised filmmakers not to use women at all or to give them peripheral roles, for fear of moral dangers. Just as women are 'supposed to' behave in post-revolutionary Iran, in films female characters have had to appear modest in appearance and behaviour.[18] In front of the camera, women's bodies should be covered apart from the face, hands and feet. They can only appear wearing either a headscarf and loose clothes or a *chador*.[19] Although this is no longer the case, for years filmmakers were required to refrain from close-ups of young women who were deemed attractive. The so-called 'make-up test' was to make sure that little or no make-up was used on actresses. Direct eye contact between characters of the opposite sex on film was discouraged. In sum, there has been an attempt to desexualize the representation of women and on-screen relationships between couples.[20]

Although women's representation has been generally caught up in the discourse of morality, often the reason for the censorship of films focused on women has been the patriarchal attitude of the censors. Milani, director of *Two Women* (1998), told me in an interview that she was prevented from making that film for five years because the censors claimed that her film would make women *por-ru* (shameless and challenging). They also said that the behaviour of the male protagonist, who imprisons his wife out of anxiety about her possible contact with other men, was normal. According to them, Milani had 'unjustly criticized the man in her film'.[21] Milani was only allowed to make her film in 1998, when the reformists removed the necessity for approval of a screenplay before making a film.

Scenes suggestive of sexuality can also be censored. A film called *Letters of the Wind* (Amini 2002) met with this fate. Kasehsaz, the former head of the censorship section, who made the final decision regarding the censorship of the film, discussed the case with me. *Letters of the Wind* is about a soldier training in an army camp in Tehran. The soldier often listens to monologues by a girl on his personal tape-player. Kasehsaz said to me:

> After seeing the film, I said to Amini [the director], 'I cannot allow two or three scenes in this film. I would not allow my family to see such a film either. I am not concerned what everyone else thinks.' There was one particular scene where all the soldiers were lying down [on their bunk beds] and passing the walkman [sic] to each other. As each one was listening to the walkman [with the girl's voice playing on it], he would cover himself with the blanket and then he would pass the walkman to the next person. And the next one would do the same and pass it on. Well, the soldiers [sexually] satisfied themselves with this. I said, 'you cannot have a scene like this and I will have to cut it.'

When I saw the uncensored version of the film on a bootleg VCD, there was no hint of the soldiers masturbating while holding the personal tape recorder under the blanket. Each soldier would pull the blanket over themselves and almost immediately pass the tape player to the next person. Although a metaphoric reading of the scene would be that the soldiers all went to bed with the girl, this was not Kasehsaz's concern. His interpretation shows the conservative authorities' acute sensitivity about sexuality.

Another example was related to me by Mohammadi concerning a particular film which included a scene showing a woman's bare foot. Discussing the censorship of that film, one of the clergymen in charge commented that the scene had to be censored because it would have excited the male viewers. This is in spite of the fact that covering of a woman's foot is not necessary as part of Islamic dress code in real life.

### Censorship based on taste and pragmatic considerations

Some instances of censorship appear to be largely due to the censors' taste. For example, Mohammadi told me that they reject some scripts because 'some of these filmmakers don't know how to write a good script'. He added, 'After so many years of working in the censorship section we know what a good script should be like.' This is in spite of the fact that he had no education relating to cinema (or art), nor any experience in filmmaking. This applies to most people who are involved in censorship (see Chapter 3, my interview with Tabrizi).

Some other decisions are based on purely pragmatic considerations by the MCIG. Tahmasebi, manager of the Centre for Research and Study of Cinema at the MCIG, told me that one of the reasons for the rejection of screenplays at the MCIG was shortage of resources such as funding and equipment. In terms of equipment, he said that until recently there were only five 35mm cameras available in Iran. The figure had increased to eight at the time of the interview. According to Tahmasebi, such shortages result in attempts to keep the number of approved scripts low. For example, if too many screenplays of a certain genre, such as family melodrama, were submitted to the MCIG in one year, they would reject some in order to try to spread the resources. He explained that they would otherwise have to fund and support films which would probably not be screened.

### Censorship based on law suits

At times a (generally influential conservative) person or organization unhappy with their claimed portrayal in a film files a law suit against a film. The matter is then often handled by the judiciary (see Chapter 3 about the censorship of *House on the Water*, 2001). The judge handling the matter then generally demands that the MCIG make the necessary changes to the film. To deal with the judiciary, under the reformists the MCIG has employed legal experts.

### *1992 and the end of a brief period of relative freedom*

With the departure of Khatami in 1992 not only did censorship become somewhat stricter but also subsidies to filmmakers were removed. The government's cutting of subsidies caused a doubling of production costs. However, to keep cinema afloat, Khatami's replacement Larijani brought large sums of money into the film industry. Furthermore, Farabi introduced new measures such as insurance for investment in films, buying the video and TV rights of films beforehand to stimulate film production (Dorostkar 2000: 38). The measures worked to keep the production levels steady.

Under Larijani, Beheshti and Anvar continued working. However, they had to tread carefully. As Beheshti explained to me:

> In those years, because cinema was so politicized, the politicians were weighing cinema in political scales. So we had to be more cautious. We continued like that until Mirsalim replaced Larijani [as the minister of culture] and if Mirsalim had not fired us, we would have continued under him as well.

The appointment of Mirsalim was the beginning of a difficult period for the filmmakers.

### 1994–97 and the introduction of a new censorship code

In May 1994, Mirsalim, a conservative politician, was appointed as the new Minister of Culture. Initially, the cinema managers under him were a mix of moderates and conservatives, which was a blessing for the filmmakers. For example, Makhmalbaf explained to me that he made the two films *Salam Cinema* and *Gabbeh* in 1995 and 1996 respectively by negotiating with a more moderate official in power. Makhmalbaf explained to me:

> I don't believe that one should see the authorities as black and white. One cannot say that every official in this regime is bad and their opponents are all good. In cinema, sometimes the person in charge was strict and his deputy was sympathetic, and vice versa. We always found loopholes which we went through like water through a crack.

The situation changed drastically when Zarghami was appointed as Cinema Deputy in 1996 and introduced a draconian code which prohibited:[22]

- giving the negative characters in films names which have Islamic roots (page 74)
- wearing of tight clothes by women (76)
- showing more than the face or the hands above the wrist of women (76)
- multiplicity of the costumes worn by characters in a film, which can lead to the culture of consumerism (77)
- using clothes which could create a new trend in wearing Western clothes (77)
- close-up of women's faces (79)
- body contact between men and women (79)
- use of abusive language (81)
- negative portrayal of the personnel of the armed forces, the police, the revolutionary guards, people's *Basij*[23] (84–85)
- use of music which is similar to famous songs, both foreign and Iranian (84)
- scenes in which somebody is attacked with a weapon (91)
- smoking of cigarettes and pipes (92)
- sympathetic portrayal of criminals (92)
- the winning of bad against good, cruel against humane, unethical against ethical behaviour, whether it is [shown in the film] directly or indirectly (92).

The 95-page document included many more specific restrictions than the cinema code of 1982, which had been passed by the government at the time of Khatami at the MCIG. Unfortunately, during this period, those in office at the MCIG were all hard-line conservatives, leaving no room for negotiation.

Understandably, working under such conditions was extremely difficult, if not impossible. Thus, in that period many filmmakers felt dejected: Makhmalbaf migrated to Canada, Beyza'i left for France and Hatamikia considered giving up filmmaking altogether.[24]

## Cinema after 1997

When the reformist candidate Khatami was elected as president in 1997 by a land-slide majority, there was much optimism in Iran. He won the election on a ticket promising rule of law, creation of civil society, establishment of democracy, and with a campaign slogan of 'Iran for all Iranians'. Khatami's inclusive articulation of Iranians was a major re-imagining of 'the nation'. As Laclau and Mouffe (1985: 105) suggest, as a result of articulation new relations are established among articulated elements thus modifying their identities. Some who had previously been excluded from the nation were thus afforded a degree of inclusion. Khatami's suturing of Iranians of all backgrounds earned him enormous popular backing which was to prove the biggest challenge that the conservative forces had experienced until then.

The powerful conservatives responded by stifling the reformist moves and by repression. A number of reformists such as Abdollah Nuri, Akbar Ganji and Gholam-Hossein Karbaschi were imprisoned, and many reformist periodicals such as *Tus*, *Khordad* and *Neshat* were banned. There were a number of major crises including extra-judicial killings of intellectuals and violent suppression of student protests. Nevertheless, the reformists' period in government resulted in the introduction of a number of unprecedented democratic changes.

The MCIG was entrusted to Mohajerani, a well-educated and open-minded politician from the modern right faction. Under Mohajerani, the press was given a degree of freedom unprecedented since the early 1980s. A director called Seyfollah Dad became the Cinema Deputy. Filmmakers, who generally supported Khatami's election campaign, had high expectations. Dad introduced sweeping changes with major effects on Iranian cinema.

## New directions under Dad

Following Khatami, Dad declared that the earlier nepotism, under the labels of *khodi* (insiders) and *gheyr-e khodi* (outsiders), would no longer be applied to include and exclude filmmakers from opportunities to make films. Dad abandoned the criterion of film content in the rating of films. Earlier, if a film's content was deemed to be in line with the cultural policies of the Islamic Republic, it would receive a better rating and hence would enjoy certain privileges such as better funding. Under Dad such discrimination was removed and therefore films were only rated according to their aesthetics. The move worked against many filmmakers who were used to receiving subsidies, and turned them against the reformists, particularly Dad. Many of New Wave filmmakers veterans like Farmanara, who had not previously been allowed to make films, or others like Taqva'i and Beyza'i, who were rarely given the opportunity, were able to resume their careers.

One of the major changes Dad (a sociology graduate) introduced was the use of survey statistics about audiences' tastes to decide the allocation of resources to filmmakers.[25] In the wake of Khatami's popular backing in the elections, in the discourse of reform, popularity became a yardstick. Soon after coming to office, Dad released the results of a survey about cinema that showed Sacred Defence films (about the Iran–Iraq war), which had thus far enjoyed considerable state support, were popular neither with the public nor even with state authorities. The survey showed that only 4% of the ministers and their families, 8% of the MPs and their families and 3.6% of the general public liked Sacred Defence films. On the other hand, the three groups' interest in 'political and social films' was 32%, 20% and 30.9% respectively (Mohajerani 1999: 302).

Dad made further use of statistical methods. He explained to me:

> We would give the filmmakers statistical information regarding the number of the educated, the youth, etc. I was explaining to them that Iranian cinema means the middle classes. These are people who look up and not down. Once upon a time Fardin[26] was popular because the educated middle class were few. The lower classes on the other hand were more and Fardin belonged to them. Now the number of the educated are perhaps 100 times more than they were before the revolution. At the moment we have two million university students. I told them that these students read books, watch Iranian and foreign films. They are interested in politics and follow the social ills. I was saying, 'these are your customers'. At the FIFF we also introduced an award for the most popular film. So we were trying to make the filmmakers aware of the audiences.

Under Dad the MCIG introduced a new category of *sinema-ye moslehaneh* or 'cinema of reform'. They defined the films as those made with 'reformist intentions' which would focus on social, political and cultural problems.[27] Such films, which (as mentioned earlier) are popularly known 'social films' and in particular 'women's films', have generally been very popular in Iran (see, for example, Chapter 3, Table 3.1).

*Changes to censorship*

Under Dad, censorship eased. Some of the films which had been banned earlier, such as *Snowman* (Mirbaqeri 1995), were now released. That film had been banned for depiction of transvestism. At the same time, Dad proposed that in order to limit the role of arbitrary decisions in relation to film censorship, a cinema law should be passed which would make the judiciary the arbiter in charge of holding filmmakers accountable in law. He explained to me:

> I was telling the filmmakers that things were as they were at the MCIG because Khatami, Mohajerani and I were in office at the moment. If we had a set of laws in relation to cinema, you would not have to depend on who is in office. The 'red lines' would become clear cut. Also there would not be any need for a permit system. The filmmakers could go and make their films, but if they did something which breaks the cinema law, they would be called to the court. I prefer the filmmaker to go to the court, and not to the censorship committee, because then there is a law for the judge to go by. The taste of the censors would no longer play a part in decision making.

Dad produced a draft of the laws, against which many filmmakers voiced their opinion. When Dad tried to pass the laws in the parliament, the filmmaker and reformist MP Afkhami opposed the motion. Considering the judiciary's persecution of some Iranian journalists, for whom press laws exist, Afkhami's opposition was of course justified. Afkhami told me that the reason he opposed the motion in the parliament was that he would much rather deal with the censors at the MCIG than with the judiciary. He added that this was because if one failed in negotiation with the censors, one would not end up in jail. The strong opposition resulted in Dad abandoning the idea.

### The role of cinema guilds

Another organization which has at times entered the debate has been the House of Cinema, which is made up of professional guilds for those active in the industry, such as editors, sound-technicians, etc. After the appointment of Dad, more agency was given to the guilds. With the promise of civil society, Dad was trying to reduce the role of the MCIG in cinema and to put some of the responsibility on the shoulders of civil society institutions. For example, the exhibition of films, which used to be decided by the MCIG, was delegated to the House of Cinema.

At times, the House of Cinema has intervened in matters such as censorship. Davudi, then head of the House of Cinema, told me about his intervention in support of a screening permit for a film called *Deep Breath* (Shahbazi 2003). Davudi agreed to take responsibility for the film in case the conservatives raised any objection after its screening. Nevertheless, the power of the House of Cinema is very limited. Tahmasebi told me that since the guilds were not allowed to go on strike, they remained ultimately under the control of the MCIG.

### Impeachment of Mohajerani

Mohajerani's liberal attitude to the press and cinema met with much conservative hostility, culminating in his impeachment in 1999. In the impeachment motion, the main target was Mohajerani's granting of press freedoms, but his cinema policies were also criticized. In the section about the arts, the motion condemned Mohajerani for,

- ... ignoring the values and the high position of women from the perspective of the progressive school of Islam as well as trampling over limits and shari'a rules on a large scale (in films such as *Tutia* and *Red*).
- Lack of attention to Sacred Defence (war) filmmakers, which has resulted in the drastic decrease in the number of the films. Stopping the subsidies for this sort of cinema (which is one of the main incentives for the spread and propaganda of the values of the eight years of Sacred Defence and its transfer to the next generation) under insubstantial pretexts such as their lack of popularity.

(Mohajerani 1999: 116–17)

According to Dad, the impeachment had been in preparation for a while. He told me: 'From late 1998 we knew that the conservatives were laying the ground work for the impeachment of Mohajerani. So they were after creating political tension with the MCIG.'

Although the impeachment movement was not successful, Dad claims he had to take a more cautious approach from then on. For example, Dad told me that in order to avoid political strife he was forced to ban Panahi's *The Circle* (2000; see footnote 29 about the film in Chapter 5). Once again, political expediency proved to be more important than freedom of artistic expression. In spite of surviving the impeachment, Mohajerani left the MCIG, and Dad followed soon after.

*Cinema after Dad and Mohajerani: my fieldwork period*

While many filmmakers feared the reversals of cinema policies after the departure of Mohajerani and Dad, in spite of some changes, in many ways the situation did not revert to the pre-1997 period. Mohajerani was replaced by the less confrontational Masjed-Jame'i, and Dad by Pezeshk. Pezeshk was brought in to appease the conservatives because of his good relations with them.

Dad told me that when Pezeshk took over, he advised Pezeshk against his planned changes of policy. Pezeshk, nevertheless, did overturn some of Dad's progressive moves. For example, he brought back the vetting of screenplays. The rating of films became once again related to content and whether the film followed the 'cultural aims of the country'.[28] Nevertheless, the move did not result in the making of a large number of Sacred Defence films.[29] During Pezeshk's time in office there were a few cases of controversies in cinema, including *House on the Water* (Chapter 3) and *10* (Chapter 4).

In February 2003, when I went to Iran to attend the FIFF, at the beginning of the festival Pezeshk was replaced by Heydarian, who had been head of the censorship section of the MCIG between 1982 and 1994. He had since worked as head of a TV channel and was therefore backed by influential conservatives. At the MCIG, I heard many in the cinema circles express worries about cinema becoming as severely controlled as the conservative-run national TV.

According to an insider to cinema circles who did not wish to be named, in a private meeting with filmmakers in 2004, Heydarian emphasized that in films from then on women must wear the veil as strictly as they do on the TV. He also said that he wished filmmakers to stay away from contentious issues. Nevertheless, the highly controversial film *The Lizard* (Chapter 3) was made during his period in office.

### Ahmadinejad's presidency and cinema

Since the election of the conservative president Ahmadinejad in 2005, many have voiced concerns about the direction Iran could take in matters of culture including cinema. In 2005, the newly appointed culture minister, Hossein Saffar-Harandi, announced that from then on distribution and exhibition of films which promoted feminism and secularism were prohibited (Honarkar 2005). However, one year after his appointment he was himself under fire by the more conservative MPs. They asserted that the films produced since his appointment were not significantly different from those in the Khatami era and were not meeting the 'higher values of the Islamic regime'. Some MPs were even considering his impeachment for this reason.[30] When later on the minister personally got involved in the banning of a film called *Santuri* (Mehrju'i 2007), a number of filmmakers and actors wrote an open letter to protest (Dowlatkhah 2008). The minister and his Cinema Deputy, Mohammad Reza Ja'fari Jelveh, did not responded favourably to these protests. According to Azmoudeh (2008), in the 2008 Fajr Festival, films with 'social and critical' themes were excluded. Jamal Shourjeh, a member of the selection committee of the festival, said that part of the reason for exclusion of the films was their point of view (ibid.). Two film periodicals called *Donya-ye tasvir* and *Haft* were also banned in this period. Nevertheless, my recent conversations with filmmakers demonstrates that the situation has not changed drastically under the Ahmadinejad regime. In filmmakers' dealings with the authorities, negotiation is still the order of the day. However, like the 1994–97 period, these negotiations can be more difficult than with the reformist authorities under Khatami.

## Conclusion

The state control of Iranian cinema has so far been understood as monolithic and impenetrable by some and as easily outwitted by others. As I have demonstrated, both positions tend to simplify the complex dynamics which have been at work.

Examination of the shifting and complex framework and application of censorship and its relationship with the political atmosphere of the country shows that in the absence of a clearly defined censorship code or a unitary censorship mechanism, the 'red lines' are blurred and open to negotiation. This sets cinema apart from the press and the heavily controlled national broadcasting. Hence, cinema is in a unique position compared to the other media in the country.

In Chapters 3, 4 and 5, in my interviews with filmmakers, I explore the processes of negotiation of power and meaning that take place between the filmmakers and the authorities.

This chapter and subsequent ones contribute to reception studies of film by demonstrating that the problematic of reception begins much earlier than conventionally considered, that is, when the film is released. As discussed above in Iran, before release, films and their scripts are seen and discussed by those who make decisions about whether or not and with what changes a film is to be released. These negotiations are part of the reception of the film, forming a feedback loop which influences the final form of the film and the decision whether a film is released. In Chapters 3 and 4 I demonstrate how cinema-goers watch/discuss the films in the light of the earlier reception of the films at the level of the authorities.

# 3 'Social films'

## Introduction

Many Iranian filmmakers have explored post-revolution social/political issues in films which are commonly referred to as 'social films'. These issues range from social justice to the place of the clergy in the post-revolution society. As mentioned in Chapter 2, some reformists like Dad particularly encouraged the making of 'social films' with financial incentives. Nevertheless, there has been much adverse reaction to these films and their filmmakers by conservative authorities in the establishment. Often as a result of such reactions, many 'social films' have become controversial. In this chapter, I examine the political aspects of these films.

My analysis of 'social films' is in relation to Downing's theory of radical media as outlined in Chapter 1. Since 'social films' are produced and distributed through the same channels as other Iranian films, I consider them as a hybrid form between radical and mainstream media. Although Downing (2001) and Atton (2002) do not raise this as an issue, in this chapter I argue that researchers should be more cautious in such cases. Because of their reliance on mainstream funding and distribution which are controlled by the state, hybrid media (and in my case 'social films') are more susceptible to its influence. Therefore, researchers have to be careful in their examination of such media.

In this chapter I examine the politics of 'social films' in relation to the reformist movement and their involvement in raising political consciousness. Although all the filmmakers I interviewed and my informants told me that they had supported the movement, at the low point of reformism when I did my fieldwork in 2003 and 2004 none of them showed much enthusiasm with regard to the movement. Part of my inquiry was to investigate whether the fates of 'social films' and the reform movement were directly related to one another.

As mentioned in Chapter 1, social/political upheaval has marked the (post)revolutionary period in Iran. The role that 'cultural performances,' such as film and theatre, can play in such liminal moments has been addressed by Victor Turner (1984, 1986, 1990), who maintains that at liminal junctures of social upheaval 'cultural performances' such as theatre and film are utilized to reflect on the destabilized cosmos in which the society finds itself.

To approach Iranian 'social films' in the light of these theories necessitates to concentrate not only on Iranian audiences but on how the filmmakers deal with hegemonic/repressive powers.

In this chapter I examine how the filmmakers and the cinema-goers in Iran have resisted the regime's attempts at controlling the political content of films. I investigate four 'social films' as nodes of media activity where the discourses of the producers, the controls exerted by the censors and the discourses of audiences intersect. The films are *Marriage of the Blessed* (Makhmalbaf 1989), *Glass Agency* (Hatamikia 1997), *House on the Water* (Farmanara 2001) and *The Lizard* (Tabrizi 2004). I have chosen these films in particular because of their prominence in Iran, which has to do with controversies around them. The four films are examined in chronological order. For each film, I recount the controversy around it, explore the context of the production of the films through interviews with the filmmakers and analyse the reactions to the films at the box office and among the 'interpretive groups' with whom I discussed the films. I also investigate the interpretive assumptions and strategies they employ in meaning-making. Since filmmakers are prominent in Iranian cinema and their films are discussed in relation to them, I briefly discuss their other works and their public personas as intertextual and extra-textual elements. My objective is to explore cinema as a situated social/political practice rather than to fix the meaning of these films. Finally, in a separate note, I examine the economics of 'social films'.

I mentioned in Chapter 1 that reception of films begins much earlier than has so far been acknowledged in media and film studies. To back this argument, I provide evidence from my interviews with filmmakers they have described their negotiation through the state regulatory processes. While in the previous chapter I discussed how censorship operates in more general terms, here I explore specific instances of the restrictions and how filmmakers and audiences deal with them.

## *Marriage of the Blessed* (Makhmalbaf 1989)

When Makhmalbaf was making *Marriage of the Blessed*, the eight-year Iran–Iraq war was about to end (see Figure 3.1). It was released just after the death of Ayatollah Khomeini (June 1989). The film, which was also written by Makhmalbaf, was an unprecedented commentary on the social predicaments of post-revolution Iran ten years after the establishment of the Islamic Republic. For many like myself, the significant transition to the post-war/post-Khomeini period was thus associated with this film. From 1989, under the presidency of Rafsanjani, the 'reconstruction' period began. Contrary to the earlier discourse of support for the *mostaz'afin* (the downtrodden), Rafsanjani, a pragmatic cleric who was part of the mercantile bourgeoisie himself, declared that accumulation of wealth was a legitimate pursuit. Makhmalbaf's film was a reaction to such changes which were beginning in that period.

Political sensitivities about the film led to a controversy, starting at the 1989 Fajr International Film Festival (FIFF). The film's release at the FIFF caused a sensation because of its unprecedented criticism. Some who had been linked with Makhmalbaf began to dissociate themselves from him. In an interview published in

*Figure 3.1* Advertisement for Mohsen Makhmalbaf's *Marriage of the Blessed* on the cover of *Mahnameh-ye sinema'i-ye film*. The picture shows Mehri visiting the hospital.

the FIFF's daily newspaper, fellow filmmaker Hatamikia described the film as dangerous. Many wondered if the film would ever receive public release. It did, but not before the intervention of Musavi who was the prime minister at the time (see my interview with Makhmalbaf).

The film came under attack from some conservatives. For example, in a newspaper article Hosseini and Khani (1989: 8) claimed that in this film, 'the values of sacred defence [the war against Iraq] have been sacrificed'. They further asserted that unlike Haji, the restlessly questioning protagonist of the film, a real *Basiji*[1] would have put his trust in the orders of Ayatollah Khomeini and other religious leaders and calmed down. In other articles, however, referring to the film, some writers posed similar questions as Makhmalbaf about where the Iranian society was heading as a whole (Ferasati 1989: 42–44; Taraqijah 1989: 37–39).

Before I proceed to my discussion of the film, I will introduce the filmmaker. In the next section, I summarize the plot of the film. I will then discuss a range of reactions to the film before discussing my interview with Makhmalbaf.

## Mohsen Makhmalbaf

Makhmalbaf is arguably the most prolific post-revolutionary Iranian filmmaker who has famously taken a metaphoric personal journey from being a religious guerrilla to becoming a rather secular world-renowned film director.[2] Before the revolution, he spent over four years in jail, where he befriended many other religious revolutionaries such as Mohammad 'Ali Raja'i and Behzad Nabavi. These friendships were to prove crucial when his former cellmates become high-ranking officials in the new Islamic regime.

In the early 1980s, after Makhmalbaf received some minimal film training, he began making a number of films with strong religious themes, beginning with *Nasuh's Repentance* (1983) and *Two Sightless Eyes* (1984).[3] Later, in his novel *Crystal Garden* (1986) and the film *The Peddler* (1986) Makhmalbaf demonstrated a shift in focus from religion to the issue of social justice.[4] Having changed direction, Makhmalbaf began to clash with the director of the Art Centre of the Islamic Propaganda Organization (henceforth the Art Centre), Hojjatolislam Zamm. Makhmalbaf and some others working at the Art Centre signed a petition for artistic freedom from Zamm, who expected them to produce what he wished (Hojjati 2003: 7). Disgruntled, Makhmalbaf and many others left the Art Centre.

Makhmalbaf's next film, *Marriage of the Blessed* (1989), proved to be an important moment of diversion from his earlier unconditional support of the regime. Although his next two films, *Time of Love* (1991) and *Nights of Zayandehrud* (1991), were banned after their screening at the FIFF, the script of the former, which was published as a book, became a best-seller and was reprinted several times. From then on, many of his films became box office hits and were also critically acclaimed (see Table 5.2 in Chapter 5). Makhmalbaf's activities were not limited to filmmaking. He wrote a number of articles and books, and gave interviews which established him as a controversial social critic. As Ridgeon puts it, 'he could almost be considered a dissident' (2000: abstract).

## The plot

The story is about Haji, a man in his thirties, who is a shell-shocked *Basiji* veteran of the Iran–Iraq war. Released from hospital into the care of his fiancée's family,

Haji is haunted by images of war, the revolution and hungry children in Africa. He often has seizures. His doctor believes that the upcoming wedding and his return to his old job as a photojournalist will help improve his health. His fiancée, Mehri, is the daughter of a wealthy vegetable wholesaler. Unimpressed by the prospect of their daughter marrying the half-mad man, Mehri's parents try unsuccessfully to turn her against the marriage.

Haji is hesitant about marriage in general, worrying that it might cause Mehri and himself to give up his ideals of social justice. He begins to work again, taking photos for a newspaper. On a shoot he is joined by Mehri, and together they take photos of the urban underclass, destitute petty thieves, drug addicts and the homeless. His newspaper does not publish the photos. Haji is shocked by the contrast between the prevalent poverty and the comfortable lives of the rich, some of whom, like his future father-in-law, now pretend to be religious. Dismayed, Haji believes that society is regressing to the period before the revolution.

When Mehri does not return home for three consecutive nights and stays at Haji's house instead, her father rushes the wedding plans in order to prevent his daughter bringing 'shame to the family'. The film climaxes with Haji's welcome speech at his wedding. Addressing the invitees Haji says, 'Those who have got mismatched socks are welcome; those with mismatched cars, also welcome. Those with mismatched wives are also welcome. Eat the sweets. They are *haram* [religiously forbidden]; *haram* things are delicious.' As he repeats the last sentence, he waves his fist in the air, as people do in demonstrations. He continues, 'We have sold the watermelons five toman more expensive per kilo to pay for the dowry of our daughter', at which point his father-in-law shouts to people to go and stop Haji. Haji has a fit again as he remembers scenes from the war-front. He is then taken back in the hospital. He escapes the hospital and phones Mehri to say goodbye, without saying where he is about to go.

### *Discussion*

The film is a polemical critique of the unfulfilled revolutionary promises of social justice. The tone is set in the first few sequences of the film, when Haji is being taken home in his future in-laws' expensive Mercedes. We watch through the windscreen of the car from the point of view of its passengers, as it is driven down backstreets. As it turns a corner slowly, revolutionary quotations are clearly visible on the wall in front of the car. A quote from Ayatollah Khomeini reads: 'I will take all the capitalists and feudal lords to court.' Another declares, 'We want the country to belong to shanty-town dwellers.' The contrast between the writing on the wall and the visible Mercedes logo on the bonnet of the rich man's car registered on the minds of many. Thus, ten years after the revolution, when this film was shown in Iran, Makhmalbaf's reminder showed the failure of the state to deliver. Elsewhere in the film, Haji's damning remarks at the wedding about his future father-in-law's immorally accumulated wealth complements the film's depiction of prevalent poverty in post-revolutionary Iran. This was not lost on audiences (see my interview about the film in this chapter).

*Table 3.1* Box office ranking for the top ten films in 1368/1989

| Film | Box office rankings in Tehran |
| --- | --- |
| Golnar | 1 |
| Horizon | 2 |
| Magnificent Day | 3 |
| Hey, Joe | 4 |
| The Cyclist | 5 |
| In the Course of the Cyclone | 6 |
| A Ship Called Angelica | 7 |
| **Marriage of the Blessed** | **8** |
| Canary Yellow | 9 |
| Lead | 10 |

Source: Produced by the author using box office figures in Javedani (2002: 204).

The criticism was all the more important because it was unprecedented in Iranian cinema. That it was articulated by Makhmalbaf, a *khodi* or 'insider' within the regime, was also significant. Makhmalbaf's *The Cyclist* (1989), which was released the same year, was also concerned with social justice. That film shows a destitute Afghan man's attempt to raise money for his sick wife's operation by cycling non-stop for a week for spectators.

*Reactions to the film*

As Table 3.1 demonstrates *Marriage of the Blessed*, was one of the top ten most popular films in Tehran in the year it was released. According to the MCIG figures, the film sold a total of 1,115,000 tickets in the whole of Iran.[5]

I watched the film in Iran at the time and remember the period clearly, when there was much dissatisfaction among many urban Iranians whom I knew. Although the war had ended a year earlier, there was no sign of the economic recovery which many hoped would begin with the end of the war. Because of the fear of the omnipotent regime, however, people only shared their views on such matters with those they trusted. Nevertheless, there were multiple expressions of resistance to the imposed social restrictions. Defiance of the strict dress code, by women as well as men, was one such expression. Others included prohibited activities such as dating, mixed-sex parties, making and consuming alcohol, listening to Western music and watching satellite TV (Sreberny-Mohammadi and Mohammadi 1994: 179–80). These expressions of resistance have been particularly significant for the secular middle class, who have mostly been excluded from the regime's definition of the Moslem nation. These counter-hegemonic practices continue to the present, although subject to the risk of punitive action, including arrest, detention, (public) flogging and/or paying hefty fines.

I remember hearing about *Marriage of the Blessed* from a friend who highly recommended it, particularly for its criticism of Ayatollah Khomeini in the sequences described earlier. I went to see the film with two friends – one a university student and the other a graduate working in Mashhad. The film was particularly important at the time when every day we were being bombarded with images on the conservative-controlled national television and also in the press that showed the country to be united behind the authorities.

In such an atmosphere, seeing the film in a packed cinema hall (around 1,000 people) had a special importance for me. I remember thinking that I was part of a collectivity which was critical of the status quo. This was a significant feeling that countered the isolation of not being able to share your thoughts in public. Now of course, after the 1997 elections when 22 million Iranians voted for the reformist Khatami, people opposed to the conservatives have a better sense of their numbers.

After the film we discussed it in the house of one of my friends. The following outlines some of what I remember from our discussions. What impressed us most was the opening sequence I have described, with Khomeini's quotes on the wall. Whether Makhmalbaf meant it or not, we took the scene to point to the failure of Khomeini to deliver on revolutionary promises. Khomeini was still alive when the film was being made and had just passed away when the film was released. To this day, there has not been any comparable critical reference to Ayatollah Khomeini in any other film.[6] Indeed, many years after his death, the Ayatollah is regarded as sacred. In January 2003, when the newspaper *Hayat-e No* published a cartoon which some conservatives claimed poked fun at Khomeini, the paper was banned.

Another sequence we found significant was during Haji's photography shoot with Mehri, taking pictures of the destitute on the streets of Tehran. When they try to take photos of two petty thieves stealing change from a public phone, a police car enters the frame. In what is perhaps the first instance of meta-fictional blurring of the boundary between fiction and documentary (which has since become the hallmark of Iranian art cinema), the police start to question the film crew about what they are doing. Makhmalbaf appears in front of the camera, showing the police officers his filmmaking permit. While the director urges the cameraman to continue shooting, a policeman asks him what his film is called and what it is about. He replies that he is making a documentary called *Marriage of the Blessed* in which he is 'showing things as they are'. The policeman says, 'There is nothing here [to film].' When the film goes back to its fictional mode,[7] the police take Haji and Mehri with them for questioning. As the police car drives off in the background, in the foreground the thieves are shown stealing from another phone booth. We found this sequence to be another amazing critical statement, showing the misguided scrutiny of the police who focused on the film crew rather than the 'real' criminals.

In spite of our secular divergence of opinion from the religious Makhmalbaf, what we shared with him was the idealization of social justice as a legacy of the revolution. Not so long ago, during the revolution, secular Iranians like my friends and I had happily marched side by side with religious persons like Makhmalbaf, shouting slogans for social justice and freedom. Now this was a timely reminder about those ideals, for both religious and secular individuals.

In 2003, when I was in Iran for my research, I discussed *Marriage of the Blessed* with a former *Basiji* and revolutionary guard called Rahim. Now a government employee in his forties, Rahim talked to me about his experience of watching the film in 1989. I interviewed him at his office one day after work.

I began by asking about his recollections of watching the film. (Henceforth in the interview transcripts, the initials SZ indicate that it is I commenting or asking questions.)

Rahim:      I saw the film during the FIFF, in Shahr-e Qesseh cinema I think. I went to buy a ticket at five in the morning, and the film's first showing was at nine that day. Tickets would run out for Makhmalbaf's films so I had to be there early.

SZ:         What were you doing in that period?

Rahim:      During the war, I was a student at high school and would go to the war-front frequently as a *Basiji*. After a while, I got into the public relations in *Basij* at the war-front, and part of my job was showing those earlier religious films by Makhmalbaf. Then in 1988–89 I was working in the Revolutionary Guards and that was when I saw the film. I was in the accounts department.

SZ:         Did you say you saw it with your friends?

Rahim:      I was part of a large group, but there were only three or four of us who were ready to wake up and go to the cinema that early in the morning. After the film we walked to Laleh Park. We went there to chat about the film, to analyse what Makhmalbaf wanted to say. Each one would say what they thought the film was about. On the whole we reached the conclusion that Makhmalbaf was going far ahead of us, and as an artist he was making the right moves. We were very pleased with him. His work was important because all the 'social films' that you see now started with him. He made the first ones.

SZ:         Had you seen his other films before this one?

Rahim:      I had not only seen those films, I had read all his articles, books and even knew about what he was doing. He was one of us. He was saying what we wanted to say and did not have the knowledge to say, or [talking about] things that he had seen and we had not. He had political experience, for example, and knew about political issues closely. He could see our present, and could see that our ideals were in contradiction with what was going on at that time. His criticism was from within and not from the outside. Like a father, a mother, or a son criticizing in a family. This is not offensive to the other family members [but] if an outsider says something, he is easily rejected.

            For us who were getting to know some of the problems in society in that period, [this film] was fascinating because someone had talked for our generation. There is a scene in which the father of the bride is aiming at the words of Imam [Ayatollah Khomeini] with his Mercedes [logo] as he is driving. This is a scene which everyone knows; that scene was so in-your-face. That was a quote about the poor and the rich. Well, this Mercedes was aiming at that. There is another scene in the film where Haji is asking his wife, 'Is 'Ali possible? Could you become Fatima?'[8] He meant to say, can we materialize the ideal of social justice that we had in mind. There was another scene in which Haji was saying, 'haram things are delicious'. This film was very interesting for people like myself who were starting to open up our minds in the political arena in that period.

At that time, people like me wanted things to go back to what it was like earlier in the revolution. Later I reached the point where I was hoping that the whole regime would change, I mean I wanted this regime to go and another to replace it. Now recently I say, no, let them stay because I think there is no need. We want to change the structure, not just the people at the top. Let the same mullahs stay, but our way of thinking should change. It is like Taliban have gone and perhaps others are now filling their pockets in Afghanistan. What difference did it make? We have to change our cultural perspective. This is something Makhmalbaf said many years ago and he was right. I told you he was always one step ahead of us. When I tell you one step only, I am boasting. Perhaps he was many steps ahead of us. I don't know how, perhaps that is his God-given gift. We could not go very far, we had set the red lines ourselves. We were saying, for example, if Imam [Ayatollah Khomeini] says die, we should die. These things were authoritative for us. Well, Makhmalbaf had a better understanding than we did.

Makhmalbaf continued his criticism in his next film. But he lost more fans after *Nights of Zayandehrud*. Because, for example, there is a scene in that film where the wife of a martyr kills herself. There is a university lecturer who had been a political prisoner during the Shah's time and he loses his job for political reasons. Once a student asks the lecturer in the class what would have happened if a certain political leader had not done what he did, and he answers, 'It would not have made a difference; things would not have changed much.' He hits the spot with such a comment, that this revolution did not change much. At points like this, he made a lot of enemies for himself. So those who used to support him became divided. They became two or three groups. Some became silent, [because] they did not know what to say. Some strongly opposed him. Some were still his fans. I knew people like that.

SZ:      What did you think about him after that film?

Rahim:  I did not disagree with him. Somehow his films have come from my heart as well.

My interpretations and Rahim's share the same assumptions. First of all, that Makhmalbaf's film was a critical commentary on the predicaments of Iran at the time and that some of what he meant to convey in his film would not be obvious and had to be 'decoded'. Everyone, even people who supported the regime, as Rahim did at the time, knew that not everything could be said openly. In addition, the Iranian poetic tradition of layered meaning played a part in our approach to the film. Hence, for us, the contrast between the Mercedes logo and the quote from Ayatollah Khomeini was laden with meaning. But the complexities involved in reading coded messages in cinema require a different approach from reading poetry. The interpretive strategy common among Iranians is to try to decode the film in a group. In such interpretive groups, which Rahim and I refer to above, meanings are debated and negotiated.

At the same time there were differences between secular Iranians' relationship to the film and that of supporters of the regime like Rahim. While for us, engaging with Makhmalbaf's film was a political act of resistance to the regime's ideological attempt to transform us ideologically into supporters of the Islamic establishment. For people like Rahim, who were included in the Moslem nation, Makhmalbaf's criticism had a different resonance.

The film and its maker had a role in raising consciousness at that particular moment in the Iranian history. The fact that the film was taken as social commentary shows that it was considered to point to systematic injustice rather than being just a fictional story or the depiction of an isolated 'real' case. The film's depiction of Haji's non-conformist attitude demonstrated that one did not necessarily have to follow the leaders unquestioningly. As mentioned above, Hosseini and Khani (1989: 8) criticized Makhmalbaf's film because they believed that Haji should have put his trust in the leadership of Ayatollah Khomeini and calmed down. Therefore, this film was a radical statement at that time, precisely because Makhmalbaf's restless anti-hero, Haji, did not blindly follow the leaders but posed important questions.

As for the communication of counter information in Makhmalbaf's films, Rahim's remarks demonstrate that Makhmalbaf's commentary was significant for people like him who were beginning to think critically about the post-revolution politics at the time. As Rahim states, he found Makhmalbaf always 'one step ahead' of himself. Makhmalbaf's timely reminders about the forgotten promises of social justice were part of the counter information in his films, as well as his other work.

Furthermore, the emotive way Makhmalbaf engaged with social and political issues in this film and in his writings was particularly significant in engaging his audience, which would not have been provoked in the same way had Makhmalbaf delivered them in a less effective manner. Aminzade and McAdam (2001: 17–18) emphasize the significance of such emotional investment by activists in raising consciousness. They do not consider emotion as operating in a binary opposition to rationality, but as capable of inciting more rational forms of response.

Because he was an 'insider', the criticism of people like Makhmalbaf was much more significant than that of disempowered outsiders. Apart from his religious credentials, he was a working-class hero who spoke for the *mostaz'afin* or the downtrodden. At the time he still lived in Serah Azari, a very poor suburb of Tehran. Following Downing (2001: 15), I suggest that, as the 'communicator/activist' who was organically integrated with the working class, Makhmalbaf was also an 'organic intellectual' who come from the ranks of the subaltern insiders.[9] Criticism by such intellectuals is particularly important because, as Gramsci states, ideologies cannot replace each other totally, rather it is through critique of what has already been accepted that new forms of thinking or consciousness can be advanced (1971: 195).

Makhmalbaf later called for collective action in support of the reformist candidate Khatami when he ran for president in 1997. Makhmalbaf's following among university students was considered important to the Khatami campaign. The campaign strategists released the letter of support from Makhmalbaf as the 'last ammunition in the canon of campaign' (Dad 1998: 55).

## Interview with Makhmalbaf

To discuss the film and find out about its passage through regulatory processes, I arranged to interview the director, whom I much admired. Arguably the most controversial figure in Iranian cinema, he was the first of the revolutionary generation to publicize his increasingly liberal views in his films, articles and books. The fact that these changes led to incrimination by many, who used to be close to him, was to my generation a sign of his courage. I also admire Makhmalbaf for his masterly filmmaking, particularly his experimentations. I looked forward to this interview very much.

Nervous about the meeting, I arrived at his office earlier than our agreed time. As I went through the door, he rushed to greet me with a smile and kissed me on both cheeks. I immediately felt relieved, and my nerves settled (see Figure 3.2). Before we started, Makhmalbaf asked me whether I had read his books, in which, he believed, he had said everything that needed to be said. I assured him that I had and that I wanted to talk to him about what he had not said up to then. I added that in Iran,

*Figure 3.2* Photograph of the author with Mohsen Makhmalbaf, June 2003.

generally when a film became controversial, at the time, in order not to let the crisis escalate, many things remained unsaid. Since much time had passed since *Marriage of the Blessed*, and I was not writing for the Iranian press, I suggested that he could talk with me with more ease. He nodded and we started. I began by asking him about the conditions under which the film was made. Showing his well-known passion for social/political issues, he discussed his film:[10]

*Makhmalbaf:*    The film is about a *Basiji* who has had many ideals and sees that people are paying for those ideals that have not materialized. The idea of the film was conceived at the height of the Iran–Iraq war, when the people were constantly suffering. The official version of the situation in the press and on TV was that everyone was ready to go to the war or give their blood [i.e. be injured or die for the revolution]. For me as a person living in my society, looking from within, I could see a different unofficial version of events. At that time, you could hear the whispers about this in people's houses, but nobody dared to disclose them [publicly]. Iranians live like people in Los Angeles at home and like Saudi Arabians on the streets. You cannot get to know this society from the streets. If you go to people's houses you see the real people.

Secondly, in 1998–99 ten years had passed since the revolution and this was enough time for a revolution to show whether it is still faithful to its ideals or not. In fact *Marriage* was the first film to censure the war and incidentally its completion coincided with the acceptance of the 598 UN resolution [that marked the end of the war]. The film is from the perspective of a person who used to be an idealist and has taken part in the revolution and the war, but now from within he sees a different picture.

As Makhmalbaf points out, his film is a commentary on the liminal predicaments of the country and this was not lost on Iranian audiences as I discussed earlier. However, while Makhmalbaf rightly draws attention to the public/private divide and acknowledges the double lives many secular Iranians live, his film does not focus on this divergence from the official line. Rather, Makhmalbaf has highlighted the disillusionment that he felt at the time with the failure of the revolutionary leaders to deliver on the promises given during and after the revolution.

*SZ:*    You said your film criticizes the war, but I think, rather than the war itself, the film criticizes society as whole, from the perspective of someone who has fought in the war.

*Makhmalbalf:*    That is right, but the film also shows the madness which was prevalent in the war. For example, in the first scene at the hospital you see a group of crazy shell-shocked war veterans who are playing a war game like children, using pots and drip stands, in their hands. In fact, in this scene, the war is being shown as a mad act. Part of the film goes back to my having been close to the generation that has gone to war and criticizes society, and the other is my criticism of the war.

In spite of Makhmalbaf's insistence, I was not convinced. In fact what legitimizes Haji's critical voice in the film is his status as a war veteran, just as Makhmalbaf's criticism at the time was justified by his religious credentials. In the above comments, Makhmalbaf was projecting his present-day views back onto when he had made the film.

*SZ:* In that period you had to hand in the script to the censors before you made your film; were there any problems with your script?

*Makhmalbaf:* I can talk about these things now. For 20-odd years we have been tricking the censors in Iran and we still do that. One of our tricks was that I would give them one script and use another for making my film. The truth is that the history of Iranian cinema is full of the tricks the filmmakers play on the censors. There are times we have gone outside Iran to say something we could not say here. At the moment Samira's film [*At Five in the Afternoon*] is like that; because they would not let us make it here, we made it in Afghanistan. For *The Cyclist*, they gave me permission with the condition that I should say that [the story] had happened outside Iran, so we were forced to go and make part of it in Pakistan. But in any case we have said what we wanted. There are other tricks I am still using so I cannot talk about them now (he smiles).

*SZ:* What about the screening permit?

*Makhmalbaf:* There is also another thing that I can tell you now. To get that permit, when the film was finished, I would give them one copy [to get permission for screening with that], then I would then give another copy of the same length [with unapproved scenes] for distribution. One such example in that film was a scene in which the [father of the girl] gets out of his Mercedes and urinates in the direction of ordinary people who are in the background. When [the censors] noticed it after it was screened in the cinemas, they censored the individual copies of the films.

*SZ:* What happened after the screening of the film?

*Makhmalbaf:* For three months the intelligence agents were following me. I was questioned in the Interior Ministry, in that building [he points to a high-rise building through the window] by Mr Shari'atmadari, the present director of Keyhan newspaper, who is one of the main supporters of violence in this country, together with 11 other agents. They made a lot of accusations and threats. But someone [like me] who had been to prison and had received a death penalty [does not get scared so easily]. There was a lot of pressure on me, which had started after I had left the Art Centre.

There is something that even now I do not really wish to say. I remember that [in 1989] Hatamikia insisted that I edit his film

Sentry. At that time, I had to edit my own films [*Marriage of the Blessed* and *The Cyclist*] but somehow I made time for him. At the time he used to say that I was his teacher and he had much respect for me. But after the film was shown at the FIFF, he got scared of the fact that he had been associated with me and that I had edited his film. So he started saying that my film was dangerous and was against the ideals of the revolution, etc. He also said that he was sorry and ashamed that I had made such a film. You can see how intimidating the atmosphere was at that time.

SZ:    Was the film taken off the screen anywhere?

Makhmalbaf:    No, and that is because of Mir-Hossein Musavi, the Prime Minister at the time. This is one of those things that I can say now. Because of the persistence of Musavi, the film was shown to his cabinet. And against the atmosphere that wanted to condemn this, he stood like a man, and that is why I still respect him very much. At the time Musavi had allowed the Association of Moslem Writers and Artists to start working and this led to his eventual removal from office. He passed a message to me saying, 'Don't call me, because both you and I are being watched.'

Makhmalbaf's comments demonstrate that, although the filmmakers resisted censorship through indirect devices, it was the behind the scene negotiations involving the prime minister at the time which played a much bigger role in his film being released. However, as Iranian filmmakers often do, Makhmalbaf emphasizes his own role in 'tricking' the censors rather than on his powerful political backing. Had it not been for the influence of Musavi, Makhmalbaf would not have been able to make and/or distribute his film. However, even within the same political camp[11] there were differences of opinion about how to deal with Makhmalbaf's daring stance. Beheshti, former head of Farabi Cinema Foundation, told me that at the time he was against strong political statements in cinema. He added, 'but we did not stop Makhmalbaf. [pause] I wish we could have stopped him from making these films. His films harmed Iranian cinema as a whole.' Beheshti is suggesting that because Makhmalbaf drew attention to cinema with his social/political commentary, the conservatives began to question the MCIG's handling of cinema and to create obstacles.

In the interview, Makhmalbaf also drew attention to the fact that intelligence ministry officials were fiercely involved in stifling intellectual and artistic activities which Musavi favoured. That Makhmalbaf stood firm in such an atmosphere was the reason for much public admiration for him and in turn for the appeal of his cinema. His reputation as a brave critic provided a sub-text to his cinema.[12]

As Makhmalbaf pointed out to me, in 1989, when *Marriage of the Blessed* was released, the press and the public broadcasters were portraying Iran as a monolithic mass supporting the regime.[13] Thus, the film's unprecedented commentary became a phenomenon in Iranian media. For the secular middle class such as myself, the film was important in two senses. First, the realization that some of our concerns were shared by regime insiders offered us a degree of symbolic inclusion. Second, the film offered us something basic: hope for a change in the stifling atmosphere to allow alternative views a space for expression. For the supporters of the regime, Makhmalbaf's critical stance played a significant part in raising consciousness, which would prove significant when such consciousness was allowed to make an impact at the ballot box in 1997.

## Glass Agency (Hatamikia 1997)

Like Makhmalbaf's film, *Glass Agency* is about a disgruntled *Basiji*. Written before 1997, *Glass Agency* was only allowed to be made when the reformists were in government (see Figure 3.3). The election of Khatami, who had shown his liberal

*Figure 3.3* Advertisement for Ebrahim Hatamikia's *Glass Agency* on the cover of *Mahnameh-ye sinema'i-ye film*. The picture shows Kazem in the travel agency.

attitude towards filmmakers at the MCIG in the early 1990s, brought much hope to filmmakers. As mentioned in Chapter 2, the new Cinema Deputy of the MCIG, Seyfollah Dad, acting on promises of freedom of expression, provided permits for the exhibition of previously banned films and the making of others such as *Glass Agency*. Made by the prolific Ebrahim Hatamikia, the film became a seminal work in the post-1997 cinema.

The controversy about *Glass Agency* began at the FIFF, when the Tehran Police filed a lawsuit against the film for its alleged showing of an 'unsuitable image of the police' (Saffarian 1998: 27). Dad met with the police chiefs to negotiate a settlement. The police were initially reluctant to compromise but Dad managed to convince them to do so after assurances that none of the people who had seen the film with Dad had thought that the police were portrayed 'negatively'. They then withdrew their lawsuit although some uncertainty hung over the film until its premiere at the FIFF.[14]

### Ebrahim Hatamikia

Like Makhmalbaf, Hatamikia has a religious background. After some training in filmmaking, Hatamikia joined the Revolutionary Guards. He went to the war-front, where he worked in the audio-visual section, shooting documentary footage. He later made two short films followed by his first feature named *Identity* (1986) which received an award at the FIFF.

Most of Hatamikia's films belong to the Sacred Defence genre, about the Iran–Iraq war. Beginning with *Matrimony of the Good* (1992) (which is widely believed to be intended as his 'answer' to Makhmalbaf's *Marriage of the Blessed*), he started making films about war veterans. His next film, *From Karkheh to Rhine* (1993), caused a controversy because in a sub-plot it showed a *Basiji* veteran applying for asylum in Germany, where he had been sent for treatment. Unlike in other Iranian films, the deserter was not demonized. According to Hatamikia, thousands of *Basijis* wrote a petition to the Supreme Leader asking for the film to be taken off the screens.[15] In spite of such objections, the film became the third best-selling film of the year. *Glass Agency* was his next most successful film at the box office.

### The plot

Kazem, a *Basiji* veteran in his forties, runs into Abbas, a fellow *Basiji* veteran, many years after the war. He finds out that Abbas is in Tehran for a health problem; a shrapnel piece left in his body from the war has moved slightly, is threatening his life, and must be removed immediately. Since the operation cannot be performed in Iran, Kazem accompanies his friend to a war veteran's organization to get financial support for the trip abroad. They are told that the organization is closing for the Nowruz holidays and they should come back afterwards. Kazem decides to finance the trip himself by selling his car and borrowing money. With the help of a friend, he manages to get the visas to the UK. On the day before the Nowruz holidays, the two go to a travel agency and manage to make a booking for the next day. Kazem fails to collect enough cash to pay for the tickets that morning, but promises the manager of the agency that he will bring the rest that afternoon. However, the agency will close for the holidays from that afternoon. Although Kazem promises to deliver the rest of the money to the manager wherever he wishes, he refuses Kazem's request and gives the tickets to another customer.

Kazem angrily argues with the manager who then gets an armed security guard to escort Kazem out. As Kazem is being led out, he grabs the security guard's gun, and takes hostage all those inside the agency. Kazem tells the authorities that unless they provide a plane for him and his friend to go to London the next morning, he will start shooting his hostages one by one.

While Abbas, whose condition is fast deteriorating, protests at what his friend has done, Kazem insists that the country owes Abbas this. The hostages either plead for their freedom or argue with Kazem, and as a result he lets some of them out. Salahshur, an agent from the Ministry of Intelligence, tries to negotiate the release of the hostages. Kazem and Abbas are joined by a fellow *Basiji* called Asghar. Salahshur attempts to disarm Kazem but fails. When Kazem's deadline is not met, he pretends to have shot a hostage. Later they are informed that top officials have ordered that Kazem and Abbas be allowed to leave Iran on a plane. However, during the flight but before their plane leaves Iranian airspace, Abbas dies, with his head on Kazem's shoulder.

### Discussion

Despite the similarity between the discontented *Basijis* in *Marriage of the Blessed* and Haji, there are major differences. Kazem does not criticize the direction that society is heading, as Makhmalbaf's anti-hero, Haji, does. Rather, Kazem rebels for what he considers to be the rights of a fellow *Basiji* that have been forgotten by society. In addition, his rebellion's objective remains within the bounds of accepted state ideology. Kazem seeks recognition for the national debt to war veterans, who are insiders within the Islamic state.

Hatamikia's *Glass Agency* is an adaptation of the Hollywood film *Dog Day Afternoon* (Lumet 1975),[16] in which two men's attempt to rob a bank goes wrong and they take the customers and the staff hostage. In the Iranian version, the motivation is not material gain; rather, Kazem's actions are based on his *javanmardi* – an ideal Iranian character type embodying selfless courage and generosity (Adelkhah 1999: 4, 6–7). Nevertheless, like the Hollywood original, *Glass Agency* is a gripping drama. *Dog Day Afternoon* ends with the killing of the hostage takers by the police. *Glass Agency* has a different bittersweet ending with the success of the hostage taker but the 'martyrdom' of Abbas.

Many elements in the film appear to encourage a reading of it as a commentary on Iranian society as a whole. The hostages comprise of people of different social classes, backgrounds and ethnicities, which make up a mini-Iranian society. While Kazem is addressing the people in the agency, he argues for Abbas's right to better treatment for having served his country in the war. The hostages and the intelligence agent often go beyond what is necessary in their arguments with Kazem. For example, the agency manager refers to the war against Iraq, saying, 'Did you ask for my permission for those eight years of killing?' Another hostage, a woman, refers to the state-supported benefits that the *Basiji*s enjoyed during and after the war: 'Who does not know that you [*Basiji*s] have taken enough pillage during the war: fridges, air conditioners, TVs, cheap airplane tickets, the right to study at the university and thousands of other things we do not know about. I don't know what else you want now.'

Different characters in the film represent a range of political viewpoints. Salahshur, the intelligence agent, for example, reminds Kazem that he should consider the stability and security of society as a whole. Salahshur also tells Kazem that Kazem's decade, i.e. the 1980s when war dominated domestic politics, is over. According to him, the decade in which the film is set (i.e. the 1990s) is one of security and 'reconstruction', which was the modern right's catchword at the time. Asghar, the *Basiji* who joins Kazem, seems to be a member of the far right vigilante group, Ansar Hezbollah. Such a collection of diverse perspectives in a film was unprecedented in Iranian cinema. *Glass Agency* appears to be heteroglot text, consisting of many voices which correspond to diverse political viewpoints outside the film's fictional frame.

### Reactions to the film

The film was featured at the FIFF in February 1998, where it received most of the major prizes, including Audience Choice Award. According to the MCIG, the film sold 1,280,000 tickets and, as Table 3.2 shows, it became one of the best-selling films of the year.

Commentators have not been unanimously supportive of the film. For example some criticized it for the treatment of the 'ordinary' people in the film. Mo'tamedi, a journalist from *Mahnameh*, told me, 'Hatamikia should not have shown the people in the agency, who represented the population of Iran as a whole, as powerless captives. This was unfair when just recently Iranian people took an active role in electing Khatami.'

*Table 3.2* Box office ranking for the top ten films in 1377/1998

| Film | Box office rankings in Tehran |
| --- | --- |
| Mard-e Avazi | 1 |
| **Glass Agency** | **2** |
| Psycho | 3 |
| Sunny Man | 4 |
| Help Me | 5 |
| Wild Jasmines | 6 |
| The Meeting | 7 |
| Mercedes | 8 |
| Life | 9 |
| Lady | 10 |

Source: Produced by the author using box office figures in Javedani (2002: 295).

Saffarian, a film critic, suggested that the violent act of hostage taking in the film was undermining the rule of law, which was an integral part of the reformists' agenda (Saffarian 1998: 25).

Behnoud, a dissident journalist who has since left Iran and lives in exile in the UK, described the film as 'deeply moving' (1998: 14). The reformists in the MCIG showed their support for the film at the FIFF by awarding it the major prizes, such as Best Film and Best Director.

Among my informants, many remembered sections of dialogue in the film. The quote mentioned above about bloodshed in the war and the other about *Basijis*' privileges were among the most commonly remembered as catchphrases.[17]

Arash, a 23 year-old student, told me that he was most impressed when the woman confronted the captor and likened the backdoor entry of *Basijis* into universities to war pillage. For a bright student like Arash, having to sit in class next to students who had not earned their place was particularly frustrating. He said he was surprised at the time that such dialogue could be included in the film at all. Like many others, Arash told me that he had not heard such dialogue in any other film before *Glass Agency*.

Arash was nevertheless unhappy with the ending of the film, which according to him was 'as the regime would have wanted it'. Rahim, the ex-*Basiji* whom I had interviewed about *Marriage of the Blessed*, shared Arash's criticism. According to him, this ending appeared to suggest that 'the Supreme Leader had directly intervened to allow the hostage takers to get away'. He added, 'I would have liked there to be a gun fight and the two to get killed. That would have been realistic. The way the film ended gave a positive representation of the regime.' 'Ali, a 30 year-old engineer, told me, 'This film should not have ended like that. Even in American films things do not end this way. Whenever they take hostages somewhere, the captors never succeed. In this film, they succeeded and the fact that Abbas died was nobody's fault.' Mehdi, 'Ali's friend, agreed, saying, 'In other words, you could say that it ended in favour of the authorities who had allowed the film to be screened. If the film had not ended this way, it would not have been made. It could only end this way.' The aversion to the ending was in spite of the fact they all said they liked the film on the whole.

Others were impressed with how Hatamikia had allowed multiple political perspectives to emerge within the same film. Saeed, a 25 year-old civil servant, told me, 'Hatamikia was telling the facts as they were, and you could decide for yourself what is right and what is wrong.' He added that one of the so far unacknowledged voices within the society was that of those who questioned the reasons for the eight-year war with Iraq. He repeated a catchphrase from the film,[18] and said, 'This is a perspective that was never shown in any film until *Glass Agency*.' According to Saeed and many others, in cinemas many people would cheer as these lines were being spoken in the film. Mehrdad, a master's student in his late twenties, added:

Hatamikia was trying to say that the different perspectives [of people] in the agency were all somehow right even if they were different from each other. I think this film was the peak of maturity for Hatamikia. [With this film] he showed he had now reached relativism, and was not the absolutist he used to be in the past.

Saeed agreed with Mehrdad and emphasized the importance of the relativist position in the film, saying:

When we talk about pluralism, in fact we are talking against the conservatives in this society, who think they are the embodiment of truth and truthfulness and everyone else is in the wrong. This is both in politics and religion. But here Hatamikia wants to say that they are all right to a degree. Hatamikia has not created a good/bad dichotomy.

Hatamikia's other films were seen as evidence of his pluralist perspective as well. Saeed added:

Hatamikia's pluralist perspective is not limited to Iranians. In *Dead Wave* [2001] he shows the Americans in a positive light. [In a scene in that film] the American forces who were in the Persian Gulf with their aircraft carriers saved the life of the wife of the [anti-American] hero. [Hatamikia] showed the Americans in a very positive light. This was very interesting for me because ideologically Iran has problems with the USA. But Hatamikia showed them as positive. This was new in 'social films'.

My informants interpreted the filmmaker's perspective as supporting not only a pluralist vision of the nation but also the reformists' more conciliatory attitude in international relations. Furthermore, the above comments indicate that the cinema-goers take a very critical and politically aware view of the films. While they generally disapprove of the ideological ending of the film, they like the oppositional catchphrases and the plurality of voices in the film as something new in cinema. The interpretive assumptions and strategies applied appear to be similar to the case of *Marriage of the Blessed.* Such films are an important element in the public sphere discussions that are challenging the conservatives' monopoly of political and religious power.[19]

### Interview with Hatamikia

When I asked Hatamikia for an interview, he agreed and arranged for us to meet at his house Shahrak-e-Gharb, a middle-class suburb in Tehran. At the interview, he seemed relaxed and happy to talk about his 1997 film, but it was not long before he was talking with much passion about his films and his convictions. I started by asking whether the censors had forced him to change his script and/or the film. He answered that the film was exactly what he wanted to make from the script which had been rejected before 1997, adding the following.

Hatamikia:   In the period before 1997, when I wrote the script, [the censorship was so strict that] they did allow me to make such a film. I was thinking I should put cinema aside because I could not make the type of films that I wanted. For five months I worked in my father's shop and I was also working as a taxi driver to prepare myself for a job other than cinema. At times like this, many filmmakers just give up on what they want to say, and compromise. I was not so desperate as that.

In 1997, when I got the permission, I still did not have it easy. When I started making the film, the police were not cooperative. I needed police cars and guns for this film, but they would not give them to me. So we only had one real gun in the film, which we borrowed from a government agency. The rest were wooden. [The police] were worried that perhaps the film would show them in a bad light. There were rumours that the film was questioning the position of the police. We were making the film under a lot of uncertainty, thinking that at any moment [the authorities] could stop the film, and this was the atmosphere during the filming and also when it was being edited.[20] So when the film was shown at the festival, the police wanted to block it. This went on until the film finally got the screening permit.

When it was screened at the Fajr Festival, it finally had an undeniable existence. When we were making it there was a feeling [among the film crew] that we were risking it all, and this affected everything. It actually made us bold. The film is the result of such an atmosphere.

SZ:          Some intellectuals criticized you for the violent act of hostage taking in your film, because at that time, under the reformists, there was a lot of talk about the establishment of the rule of law.

Hatamikia:   Cinema visualizes a fantasy which does not exist. This is the job of cinema, to create a dream. If there is violence, it is just a film. We are showing this so that it will not happen in reality. At the time there was a question whether this film could instigate some to revolt like the hero of my film. Actually, last year I was speaking somewhere about this and I reminded people that four years had passed since then and there had been no copycat hostage taking.

But a question I ask here is whether a democratic society will ever happen here without a cost. I believe there will be a cost. There is going to be violence, there are going to be problems [he emphasizes]. If anybody believes otherwise, they are too romantic. I think anywhere in the world this transition will not be easy and there will be obstacles in the way. In cinema, to show the contrast in a multi-vocal society, you need to show these people as well.

SZ:          At that time, you kept silent while a lot was being said about your film. Why was that?

Hatamikia:   At that time, different political factions claimed that my film confirmed their views. They were all saying that the film is *harf-e del-e mast* [literally 'it's the word of our hearts']. I was very happy that the film had not been claimed by one side only, so it was beyond political divisions. I thought at that time that I should not say anything, because whatever I said would be used by one political faction or the other to their own advantage. When I make a movie I am in charge, but when I am being interviewed a smart journalist can take you one way or the other and thus make certain interpretations out of what I say. That is why there are no interviews with me at the time. Those were feverish times, but through it all I was a loyal supporter of Khatami and I think he is like me in allowing everyone a voice.

Hatamikia is as passionate as Makhmalbaf about his political views, and this is reflected in the conviction with which his characters express themselves, as well as the enthusiasm with which he spoke to me. But unlike Makhmalbaf, who has long since distanced himself from revolutionary and wartime perspectives, Hatamikia still remains close to the revolutionary generations in the regime, some of whom also took part in the war. Like many of those war veterans, his views have become moderate, lending themselves to support for a pluralist point of view.

That Hatamikia's film appears to have been positively valued by people with differing perspectives, apart from Hatamikia's pluralist approach, may have to do with Kazem's act of *javanmardi*[21] which among Iranians is universally revered.

Hatamikia states that the ending of the film was not forced on him by the censors. Hence he agrees with my informants' reaction to the ending to whom it indicates that Hatamikia's film is not radical. Nevertheless, *Glass Agency* is significant for being the first film to acknowledge the multiplicity of political views in Iran. This was one step ahead of Makhmalbaf's *Marriage of the Blessed*, in which only Haji's critical perspective was highlighted. *Glass Agency* was released in the period after Khatami's 1997 election victory, when the reformist movement, with its pluralist slogans like 'Iran for all Iranians', had much momentum. The importance of reflecting a cacophony of voices in the film's social commentary was not lost on the increasingly politically aware cinema-goers.

One lasting legacy of *Glass Agency* has been the inclusion of oppositional catchphrases, which one could hear in everyday life in public (counter-)discourse but were never featured in films. For the first time, people could hear their criticism being spoken by larger-than-life characters on cinema screens. Hatamikia's inclusion of these oppositional lines in *Glass Agency* was unprecedented in Iranian cinema. Catchphrases play a major role in the word-of-mouth advertising for films. Nowadays, such catchphrases and one-liners feature in a number of films such as *House on the Water*, which was screened during my fieldwork trip to Iran.

## *House on the Water* (Farmanara 2001)

The release of *House on the Water* coincided with my second field trip to Iran in 2003. One of the questions I was pursuing in my research, was about the level of public enthusiasm for the reformist movement and how that affected their response to 'social films'. Until then, filmmakers had been enthusiastic supporters of reform and the reformists had in turn generally backed artistic freedoms. In all recent elections before my trip, the reformists had won landslide victories. Nevertheless, the conservatives had orchestrated a heavy backlash against the reformists. As mentioned in Chapter 2, many newspapers had been banned, a number of prominent reformists had been imprisoned, a few intellectuals had been brutally murdered. The setbacks the reformists had suffered and their inability to deliver on their promises had cast doubt in my mind about the continuation of public support for them. Nevertheless, hoping against hope, I thought that perhaps some degree of fervour remained.

I was soon disappointed. Almost everyone I talked to told me that they had lost faith in reformist politicians. Although many still believed in the integrity of Khatami, some thought that he was no different from the other politicians. An important reason for the disillusionment with the reformists was their failure to deliver a significant improvement on the economic front.

One of the telling signs of disaffection for the politics of reform was the low voter turnout in the municipal elections held in Tehran in February 2003. In spite of the campaign posters all over Tehran, I did not detect any eagerness about the elections. Although I meant to vote myself, I only remembered about it late on the polling night! Apathy had infected me, but I was not alone. The results showed that only around 10 per cent of people in Tehran had voted, with conservatives winning all seats in the capital. This was an incredible change from the huge support that the reformists enjoyed until less than two years ago. In the 1997 and 2001 presidential elections as well as the 1999 municipal and 2000 parliamentary elections, there was an overwhelming voter turnout resulting in the reformists winning in all elections. Popular support for the reform movement appeared to be a thing of the past.

A month later, the controversial *House on the Water*, which had previously been banned, was finally screened. Drawing a parallel between the film and the objectives of the reform movement, the pamphlet advertising the film and the ad for the film published in the reformist newspaper *Hambastegi* read, 'Your support for *House on the Water* is support for freedom of expression' (see Figure 3.4).[22] Owing to the decline in public support for the reformists, I wondered whether interest in 'social films' such as *House on the Water* was also in decline. In this regard, Downing (2001: 23) suggests that 'when [social] movements are at a low ebb, the flood of alternative media also subsides'. My examination of this film and *The Lizard* (2004), which was released at this low point for the reforms, could provide an answer to the question.

### Bahman Farmanara

Bahman Farmanara studied cinema at the University of Southern California. Upon completion of his studies he went back to Iran and began making short films. Later he tried his hand at directing with *Qamar Khanom's House* (1972). It was, however, his 1974 film *Prince Ehtejab* which established him as a New Wave director, winning the prize for Best Film at the Tehran International Film Festival that year. That was the first of his collaborations with the well-known anti-Shah writer

*Figure 3.4* Advertisement pamphlet for *House on the Water*.

Hushang Golshiri. Farmanara was also active in producing films, both festival films, such as Kiarostami's *The Report* (1977), and others, such as Sayyad's *The Night Never Ends* (1977).

His second collaboration with Golshiri, *Tall Shadows of Wind* (1978), was a highly metaphorical political commentary on power relations in Iranian society. The film was made when the revolution had already begun across Iran. It was banned not only by the Pahlavi regime, but also later by the Islamic Republic, for the same metaphoric images which were now interpreted as antagonistic to the new regime. As mentioned in Chapter 2, rather than being fooled by indirect narrative devices, the censors were highly suspicious of filmmakers' intentions, particularly those of a secular 'outsider' like Farmanara.

Soon after the revolution, Farmanara migrated to Canada, where he was active in film distribution and the organization of festivals. It was a difficult time for film-makers who had started before the revolution, many of whom were regarded with suspicion. This was particularly the case for Farmanara, because some conserva-tives claimed that he was a descendant of the Qajars who ruled Iran before the Pahlavis (Dorostkar and 'Aqili 2002: 103, 108–9, 207).

Farmanara returned to Iran ten years later to take over the affairs of his father's textile factory, where he has been working since. After his return, he attempted to make films, but his scripts were rejected. While some New Wave filmmakers such as Beyza'i had managed to make films in the 1980s, although with difficulty, Farmanara's efforts were unsuccessful until 1997. Under Mohajerani and Dad, the MCIG tried to close the gap between the *khodi* or insiders or those with a pro-regime background and the *gheyre-khodi* or outsiders, and secular filmmakers like Farmanara were able to work again. In addition, the outsider filmmakers now had a chance to enter negotiations over censorship of their films as well.

In 1999, Farmanara completed the self-referential *Smell of Camphor, Scent of Jasmine*, his first film since the revolution. The film told the story of a filmmaker, called Bahman Farjami, played by Farmanara himself, who had not been allowed to make films for years. It referred to the serial murders of intellectuals, which hap-pened around the time it was being made. It also included extensive documentary footage of a speech by Khatami about political freedom. Significantly, the film won many awards at the FIFF, including Best Film and Best Director. In 2001, Farmanara directed his next film, *House on the Water*, which also swept up the major prizes at the 2002 FIFF.

### The plot[23]

The central character is Dr Sefidbakht (literally 'white-fate', meaning fortunate), a gynaecologist in his fifties. It begins in a rather surrealist fashion: on a misty night, driving under the influence of alcohol and in the company of a prostitute, Sefidbakht hits something with his car. When he gets out of the car, he realizes that he has knocked a cherub[24] unconscious. As his touches the cherub, she grabs his hand for a moment, giving him an excruciating pain and leaving a sore. Sefidbakht drives away quickly.

In his ward at the hospital where he works, there is a seven or eight year-old-boy in a coma, who is a reciter of the Qoran. Talking to the boy's father, Sefidbakht suggests that the coma is the result of the pressure the family had put on the child.

Later, we come to know that Sefidbakht's attractive secretary Jaleh had been carrying his child before she had an abortion administered by Sefidbakht. As a result of the operation she suffered an infection which rendered her infertile.

Sefidbakht's son, Mani, comes back to Iran from the USA, where he has grown up with Sefidbakht's ex-wife and her American husband. Mani is a heroin addict. Upon meeting his grandson, Sefidbakht's father, who is in a home for the elderly, tries to get Mani to persuade Sefidbakht to take the old man back home. Mani fails. Sefidbakht puts Mani in a rehabilitation clinic from which he later escapes. In search of Mani, he goes to the poorest areas of town, where many streets are lined with drug users at night, but he fails to find his son.

When Sefidbakht notices that he is being followed everywhere by a car (see Figure 3.5), he decides to install an alarm system in his house. His secretary Jaleh, who still holds a grudge against Sefidbakht, is keeping those who follow him informed of his movements. They also approach the security shop where Sefidbakht bought his alarm system. Threatening the manager of the shop about the renewal of the shop licence, they demand the code to Sefidbakht's alarm.

One night, when Sefidbakht is in the hospital, the child in a coma suddenly regains consciousness. He asks Sefidbakht to take him away. On the way to his house, the child hears from Sefidbakht about the infection on his hand, which was caused by the cherub's touch earlier in the film. The child then tells Sefidbakht to

*Figure 3.5* Still from Bahman Farmanara's *House on the Water* showing Sefidbakht at a newspaper stand; he notices that he is being followed.

take off the bandage because he has been cured, which, to Sefidbakht's amazement, turns out to be true.

At his house, the child tells Sefidbakht why he went into a coma: when he realized his parents were exploiting his ability to recite the Qoran, he went into a coma 'for fear of God'. Later that night, Sefidbakht wakes up to the sound of the burglar alarm. He goes to investigate, but a group of men dressed in black surround him and stab him (as he stands on what appears like a spider's web on the floor – see Figure 3.6). When Sefidbakht yells out 'God!', a light shines upon the child from above and he goes looking for Sefidbakht. When he finds Sefidbakht taking his final breaths, he comforts him, caressing his head on his lap. Hearing the noise, the assassins return to finish the job. The child signals them with his hand to stop, as he recites verses from the Qoran. The assassins back off.

The film ends with a shot of a garden where Sefidbakht and the child are lying under a tree with their eyes shut, both dressed in white.

### Discussion

Farmanara has used the various subplots in his film to bring up a number of social ills such as drug addiction, prostitution and AIDS. The filmmaker has *woven* the sub-plots together to reinforce the film as a commentary on the country as a whole. 'Weaving' has an explicit as well as metaphoric presence in the film. Throughout the film, in shots that do not advance the plot, an old woman appears to be knitting, using colourful wool balls. The old woman also has a minor plot-related presence

*Figure 3.6* Still from Bahman Farmanara's *House on the Water*; Sefidbakht is murdered in his house.

in the film as Mrs Zamani ('of time or fate') in the same home for the elderly where Sefidbakht's father resides. At the end of the film, just as the alarm goes off in Sefidbakht's house, we see the wool balls rolling in different directions and eventually forming a spider's web pattern on the floor. Sefidbakht is stabbed as he stands at the centre of the web. Mrs Zamani makes a final appearance in the last sequence of the film, in which she is knitting under the tree where Sefidbakht and the child are lying. The religious connotations are easily read by Iranians (see group discussion about this film).

### Interview with Farmanara

I met the filmmaker at his textile company office in downtown Tehran, a week after the end of the film's cinema run. I started by asking him about the fascination with death evident in three of his films (*Prince Ehtejab* 1974, *Smell of Camphor* 1999 and *House on the Water*). He explained that to him death was a motivation for people to reassess their lives and see what more they could do: something he was now doing himself. He added, 'This is not about the afterlife and heaven or hell, because I do not believe in them, even though I do believe in God. Life ends here, although the idea of reincarnation is an attractive one.'

The obvious contradiction between his liberal spirituality and the orthodox religiosity in his film prompted me to raise with him the following:

SZ:   You said that you don't believe in heaven or hell, but something that stands out in *House on the Water* is its religiosity. For example, your protagonist Sefidbakht becomes repentant (by calling on God at the end) and the child character is a reciter of the Qoran. Religion in your film has a very traditional form that exists in Iran today. How do your personal beliefs relate to this film?

He responded that religion to him mattered at the level of morality, and added the following:

*Farmanara:*   [As for] what I say in the film, I don't mean that there is a heaven and hell and you will atone for your sins. I mean to say that hell for Sefidbakht is the one he has created for himself with his miseries. I wanted to give him comfort when he dies, otherwise hell is his own life.

This is not what Farmanara told 'Alipur, an interviewer from the reformist newspaper *Yas-e No*, when his film was screened in Tehran ('Alipur 2003: 5). Talking about his protagonist Sefidbakht, Farmanara started with a rhetorical question:

Why does this person become *rastegar* (forgiven, a person destined for heaven)? I think, as they say, if a person repents just before death, God forgives them. The God I believe in is much kinder than not to forgive [. . .] when [the protagonist] calls out to God, HE forgives him.

When he talked to me, however, he explained that the last scene of the film, rather than depicting salvation for Sefidbakht, is a political statement.

*Farmanara:* In the last scene of the film, we see him in heaven, lying under the tree next to the child [Qoran reciter]. I have actually used that scene to say that *they* would kill the boy who recites the Qoran if *they* thought it was necessary.

He is suggesting that extremist conservatives would kill an innocent child if it suited their agenda. By contrast, when talking to the reformist daily Farmanara played down the politics of that scene, which the interviewer clearly wished he had not. The interviewer asked:

The 'threatening' forces have already been seen in relation to Amir (an intellectual who disappears temporarily and is feared dead) in *Smell of Camphor, Scent of Jasmine.* [In *House on the Water*] there are the same forces who cause the death of Sefidbakht. Why are [your protagonists] in conflict with these forces?

Farmanara responded:

An interpretation I have heard, which is very interesting for me, is that they say that Sefidbakht is killed by his own demons. If I refer to the same level of insecurity in both films, this is along the same lines as other things I refer to in this film. [These are] things which have been seen or heard in our society. Although I think they should not be forgotten they are not my main focus.

Obviously Farmanara felt he had to be more cautious when he talked to the media in Iran compared to when he was talking to a diasporic researcher such as myself. Thus he stressed the politics of his film to me and its religiosity to the Iranian reporter. Unlike Makhmalbaf and Hatamikia who have more powerful connections to different factions in Iran he obviously lacks their confidence.

Unlike Hatamikia's and Makhmalbaf's more passionate discussions of their social convictions, which they dealt with in their films, Farmanara was much more subdued in conversation about his films. In addition, although his previous film, which was made at the peak of the reformist movement, had a strong reformist slant, in conversation with me he appeared to have lost faith in the movement. Considering the less than enthusiastic reactions to the film in contrast to the others discussed in this chapter, it appears that the political commitment of filmmakers has an impact on how the viewers consider the films.

## Reactions to the film

At the 2002 FIFF, the MCIG gave the film a special award for Best Religious Film. According to the director, this made the conservatives react against him, because 'they think religion is their exclusive area of expertise'. When he submitted his film for a screening permit, the censorship section asked him to make a number of changes to which he agreed.[25] When the film was about to be released, Mohammad Sadeq Tabataba'i, father of a well-known real-life reciter of the Qoran, wrote to the MCIG complaining about the film's portrayal of the father of the Qoran reciter, which he claimed was a distorted depiction of himself (Ghaffuri-Azar 2003: 59). This led to the banning of the film just before its release in December 2002. Furthermore, a religious organization claimed that the film had insulted Ayatollah Khomeini and had encouraged immoral behaviour (Anon. 2002: 12).

Frustrated by the situation, Farmanara wrote an open letter to the MCIG, criticizing it for not releasing a film for which it had already issued a permit. The next day the MCIG published an answer with an apologetic tone, explaining their problems with the judiciary about the film (Farmanara 2002: 12). *House on the Water* had received a production permit during Dad's period as Cinema Deputy and a screening permit under his successor Pezeshk, but was not released under him, and the Deputy had changed yet again in 2003. Such rapid changes create a sense of insecurity for filmmakers. Nevertheless, for the first time a filmmaker had managed to use the press to pressure the MCIG to follow through and enforce their own permit.

The film was eventually released in March 2003, but not before a final set of problems.

## Censorship of the film

Mohammadi of the censorship section told me that after a few showings of the film on its first day of release, 20 March 2003, the judiciary demanded further cuts. Caving in to them, between 6pm and 8am the next morning the MCIG cut more out of the 30 copies of the film, and made them available for screening on 21 March. The haphazard nature of the workings of censorship in Iran is well exemplified by the case of *House on the Water*. Faced with a complaint from the father of a real-life Qoran reciter, the censorship section decided to conduct a survey among the employees of the cinema section of the MCIG to determine whether the depiction of the matter in the film reminded viewers of the well-known Qoran reciter. Mohammadi told me that their effort did not produce any clear result, and the censorship section abandoned the idea.

Later a Tehran court ordered the banning of the film. To negotiate its release, Farmanara attended a session with a clerical judge. The judge asked him to make a few changes. Some of the original dialogue in the film, and the changes that Farmanara made through either dubbing or cutting of a scene, are detailed in Table 3.3.

The reasons given by the judge in charge of censorship demonstrate the sensitivity about 'subversive messages' being conveyed in the film. For example, in the case of (A) the clergyman told Farmanara that by 'the top', the speaker is referring to the Supreme Leader. Item (B), the judge suggested, was meant to refer to Ayatollah Khomeini's famous phrase that half the population of the country at the time of the Iran–Iraq war should become part of the *Basij* paramilitary force.

*Table 3.3* Censorship of *House on the Water*

| Original | Altered phrase after censorship |
|---|---|
| (A) 'In this country jealousy and envy are everybody's second job, *from the top to the bottom.*' | 'In this country jealousy and envy are everybody's second job, *from friend to enemy.*' |
| (B) Sefidbakht addressing a man who has 11 children and whose wife is expecting another: *'Was the order for the 20-million army addressed to you alone?'* | *'Are you the person responsible for population control in this country?'* |
| (C) Sefidbakht addressing Jaleh: 'A child needs a future that does not exist *in this country.*' | 'A child needs a future that does not exist.' |
| (D) A young girl who is HIV positive addressing Sefidbakht: *'When you were our age, you had a future. We have neither a future nor hope. As if we have built our house on the water.* (pause) *We have just learnt to swim well.'* | Removed. |
| (E) Verses from the Qoran uttered by the boy near the end of the film and the following sequence showing Sefidbakht and the boy lying under the tree at the end. | Removed. |

Sections of another sequence pointing to the corruption of customs officers was also censored. The scene showed Mani, Sefidbakht's son, being arrested at the international airport in Tehran for carrying drugs into the country. Sefidbakht is then called to the customs office. At first, Sefidbakht agitates the customs officers by suggesting that his son had made a mistake by bringing drugs into a country where there is already an abundance. Later, when Sefidbakht adopts a softer tone towards the officers, a telling smile exchanged between the bearded officers suggests that perhaps a bribe is forthcoming. Immediately after that there is a cut to the next scene showing Sefidbakht and Mani driving home. The comment about the abundance of drugs in Iran and the telling smile between the officers were both cut. Later on, in an interview with a reformist paper, Farmanara explained what some of the censored sections of his film were ('Alipur 2003: 5).

*Group discussion*

In spite of the protracted controversy, Farmanara's film managed to sell 224,300 tickets or only a third as many as *Glass Agency* had sold in Tehran.[26] Perhaps the cutting of those catchphrases in the film deprived it of more powerful word-of-mouth advertising. Nevertheless, as Table 3.4 shows, the film was the sixth most popular film in Tehran in 2003.

I had seen the film once before at the London Film Festival, but I saw it again in Mashhad with group of university students in their mid-twenties. The group, all old friends, consisted of six people: three men (Ramin, Hossein and Mohsen), and three women (Simin, Mina and Soraya). When the film was released in Mashhad,

*Table 3.4* Box office rankings for the top ten films in 1382/2003

| Film | Box office rankings in Tehran |
| --- | --- |
| Tokyo Non-Stop | 1 |
| The Bride who Brought Luck | 2 |
| Dona | 3 |
| Iranian Girl | 4 |
| Fifth Reaction | 5 |
| **House on the Water** | 6 |
| Pink | 7 |
| A Madman Flew Away | 8 |
| Black Eyes | 9 |
| This Woman Doesn't Talk | 10 |

Source: Produced by the author using box office figures published in *Mahnameh* (Anon. 2005: 297–379).

Hossein and Simin, who had been following the controversy in the press, said they were keen to see it and told the others about it.

We went to see the film in *Cinema Africa* which was long past its heyday in the 1970s, with its refurbishment overdue for decades. Once in the hall, we were ushered to the family section where men without female company are not allowed.[27] It was a 10am weekend show; there were about 100 people in the 1,000-seat cinema. During the show, I noticed that, as is customary in Iranian cinemas, people in our group were talking to each other. One reason for this is the low-quality sound, which sometimes makes it difficult to hear the actors clearly. But the reasons do not end there; engaging with films in general is a group activity.

After the film, we went to a restaurant for lunch. The group seemed to be quite keen to talk about the film. The following are excerpts from the discussion.

Simin:      While we were watching the film, Mohsen was asking me, why this or that happened. I said, 'Mohsen! Please keep quiet!' (Simin and Mohsen laugh.)

Mohsen:    Because the film was going well and then this little boy came out of the coma and started saying things like, 'I could suddenly see God everywhere' [with a sarcastic tone he refers to the scene in which the boy says to Sefidbakht that after trying to learn the Qoran he fell in love with it, etc.] and the film became a joke from then on.

Hossein:   He sounded so fake . . .

Mohsen:    Yes; and the sore on Sefidbakht's hand. The boy said, 'It is not there any more' (sarcastic tone). When Moses wanted to perform a miracle, he would at least wave his walking stick in the air. (Everyone laughs.) And all this for (Sefidbakht) who was not into this sort of thing. He was a womanizer and saw prostitutes and now suddenly a spiritual light (sarcastic tone) shone on him (everyone laughs) and then he changed. In the end what did [the filmmaker] want to say?

Mina:      Well the story could have got somewhere but the little boy spoiled it.

Simin:      The boy is a cliché part in religious films. You either have an old man who is the reciter of the Qoran, or a little boy.

Ramin:      At the beginning when Sefidbakht said they had put too much pressure on the boy [to learn the Qoran by heart] and that is how he went into a coma, I liked that bit. (Others agree.) I thought that it was good that somebody finally says that every child who is put under pressure could perhaps eventually memorize the Qoran. And if you put that much pressure on the child, this could be dangerous for the child's health.

Mohsen:     What was the spider's web at the end?

Hossein:    Well it looks like he wanted to make a religious film. For example, the title of the film, and the spider's web – that is all from the Qoran. The verses say that those who do not believe in God, it is like they have built themselves a house like a spider, which is very unstable. It is exactly what Farmanara is referring to, because of the way [Sefidbakht] dies on the web. It was as if this guy wanted to interpret that verse of the Qoran, saying that if you do as Sefidbakht did in the film, you will end up like him, and if you do as the child who had learnt the Qoran by heart you will end up differently. Well, this is not right. Part of it is correct, that if you do not believe in anything [and do as Sefidbakht does in the film] your life won't have a good end but when [Farmanara] says that if you learn the Qoran by heart you will end up better, this is problematic.

Mina:       Also when the boy said himself that [when he learned the Qoran by heart] his father was taking him around to show off, that is exactly what they do to the children we see on the TV. They always take them around to recite the Qoran. Once on TV they had an eight year-old child teaching five year olds the Qoran. (Others add their voices in support.)

The reactions of the group show that after over two decades under the Islamic Republic, ideological themes in what they refer to as 'religious films' are not easily accepted. The group also expect that cinema should not be going the same way as the conservative-controlled TV. However, there is a certain degree of tolerance of filmmakers pandering to the regime:

Ramin:      Don't you think that the bit about the child was added to the plot in order to get permission to screen it? Because I don't think that Farmanara is a religious person.

Hossein:    Perhaps. Because most of the film is fine until the reciter boy enters towards the end.

The film is understood in relation to its maker, Farmanara, who is known to be a secular filmmaker. In addition, there is obviously an expectation, based on his previous work, that the filmmaker should resist the dictates of regime ideology:

SZ:         There is a part when they go to get the code from the alarm shop.

Simin:      Yes, because they threaten the shop owner with not renewing his licence. It looks like they are agents of the regime. I think Farmanara is

|          |                                                                                                   |
|----------|---------------------------------------------------------------------------------------------------|
|          | referring to the serial killings [of intellectuals], because in his previous film *Smell of Camphor*, . . . he showed that as well. |
| Ramin:   | Well the part when he says that a child needs a future and the future does not exist is along the same lines as Sadeq Hedayat's nihilism. |
| SZ:      | Actually [in the uncensored version] he says 'in this country there is no future'. They cut that bit, and in the censored version, he just says, 'there is no future'. |
| Mohsen:  | (Facing me) Since you have seen the uncensored version, I have a question: when Sefidbakht's son is held at the airport does he pay a bribe to get his son released? |
| SZ:      | Yes, it definitely appeared so. [I then tell them about the censorship of that scene.] |
| Mohsen:  | They don't need to show all of it, even with the censorship we can work it out (he smiles with obvious pleasure). I thought, how could he get his son out so easily – especially when one of the customs officers was saying: 'There is no way I would allow it.' In this society, exactly those who say 'there is no way we are going to allow this or that' are the ones who accept bribes. |

Censorship can create loose ends that audiences take into account in their interpretive strategies. They seem to be very alert to any possible instance of censorship. In this case, as in others which I have observed, catching an instance of censorship and 'discovery' of oppositional meaning appears to be very pleasurable. In this case it is particularly so, because the customs officers in the scene are both bearded and appear to be religious. Corruption among the Islamic officials is often discussed in private but is a sensitive area for the public sphere; hence, the (ineffective) cutting of the scene.

|           |                                                                                                  |
|-----------|--------------------------------------------------------------------------------------------------|
| Hossein:  | [Farmanara] could have done things much better. For example, at the beginning I thought he had done so well to bring up so many social problems. I thought, good for him! |

To criticize in Iran still takes courage, and people of course acknowledge this.

|           |                                                                                                  |
|-----------|--------------------------------------------------------------------------------------------------|
| Hossein:  | I liked the film and I prefer to see a 'social film' like this to other films. Well, everyone who goes to the cinema gets something from this film. I can say that the child was not necessary. So, I say, OK, I would put the child aside myself. Other than that, you see in this film that everyone has got their own problems. I prefer seeing this film to seeing a cute story about falling in love. [Although] I agree that this film had problems. |
| Ramin:    | I liked it too, like a book that you read even though you do not approve of everything in it. |

In an instance of what Brecht refers to as 'cofabulation', the group members try to create their own narrative out of what is on the screen. As I mentioned in Chapter 1, according to Brecht, 'cofabulation' is the audience's active involvement in creation of their own story out of the material available to them in the play or in my case film. As the above discussion demonstrates, the efforts of conservatives within the Islamic Republic to inculcate religiosity, which is a feature of many TV pro- grammes, have resulted in widespread rejection of such ideological 'messages'. However, through 'cofabulation' these cinema-goers 'edit out' those parts on the one hand, and, ironically, include some parts which the censors have tried to elim- inate from the film, albeit unsuccessfully. Thus, they resist and subvert the regime's control of the political content of films.

As Turner suggests about how people engage with cultural performances in lim- inal circumstances, my informants discuss *House on the Water* as a meta-commen- tary about present day Iran. Nevertheless, it appears that these audiences do not suspend their critical judgement even when it comes to these social commentaries. This is unlike Turner's assumption about uncritical social acceptance of the cul- tural performances.

Films such as *House on the Water* attract attention to themselves by scenes and con- versations which can lead to censorship, but are approved overall and released with only minor changes. Some filmmakers do try this to gain some publicity for their films, while they are sure of their films' eventual release. A film editor who did not want to be named told me that since they can guess which parts of their films are liable to be censored, some filmmaker have the solution ready to fix those parts. For exam- ple, alternatives to potentially censorable dialogues are recorded and kept handy. This is a safe bet, because if the censors do not in the end pick them out, the film will include some daring dialogue. These memorable catchphrases are useful for word-of-mouth advertising, and work as the most effective way of promoting a film.[28]

Along the same lines, sometimes filmmakers try to grab headlines by publiciz- ing a vigilante attack on a cinema showing their film. Doubts have been cast on the veracity of at least one event reported by a filmmaker. Mo'tamedi, a cinema reporter, told me that when Mehrju'i, the director of *The Mix* (2000), realized his film was doing badly at the box office, he claimed in the press that vigilantes had been throwing stones at the glass front of a cinema showing his film in Tehran. When Mo'tamedi investigated and found no evidence to support Mehrju'i's claim, he wrote a piece in *Mahnameh* titled, 'The stones which were not thrown' (2000: 16). The film did not attract large audiences. Interestingly, while earlier on such reported attacks appear to have worked in boosting ticket sales, nowadays box office success is not necessarily guaranteed by them.

Finally, my earlier question about the direct co-relation between the weakening of social movements and the decline of alternative media is perhaps yet unanswered. It appears that the lower interest in Farmanara's film is perhaps more to do with his film's religious overtone which met with negative reaction on the part of some who are unimpressed by it. Whether the less-than-enthusiastic reaction to *House on the Water* also meant that people were no more interested in 'social films' was not clear. But the case of *The Lizard*, released almost a year later, suggests an answer to this question.

## The Lizard (Tabrizi 2004)

The much-awaited public opening of *The Lizard* was due on 19 March 2004. When the day came and there was no screening, rumours began to appear in the newspapers and websites regarding the banning of the film. The main reason was that Tabrizi had gone where no other filmmaker had gone before: a comedy about the clergy. The ascendancy of the clergy after the revolution has meant that in general the state treats them with reverence denied to ordinary citizens. For example, a Special Clergy Court deals exclusively with cases against them.[29] Hence making a comedy about the clergy was bound to be controversial. The release of the film in Iran coincided with my final field trip to Iran.

### Kamal Tabrizi

Kamal Tabrizi is from the same generation of religious revolutionaries as Hatamikia and Makhmalbaf. His first major involvement with filmmaking was at the Iran–Iraq war-front, with a documentary called *Martyrdom Seekers* in 1980. His ensuing feature films, *Passage* (1988) and *In the Slaughterhouse of Love* (1988), were about the war. The latter focused on an Iranian defeat in battle, and was banned temporarily.

His third film, *Leili is with Me* (1996), is significant because it is the first comedy ever about the sacred topic of the Iran–Iraq war. Because of the significance of its topic and its relevance to *The Lizard* I will now summarize its plot.

*Leili is with Me* is about Sadeq, who is a film crew member working for the Iranian national TV in the early 1980s at the time of the Iran–Iraq war. Sadeq needs a bank loan to build a house. Since he realizes that if he pretends to be interested in going to the war-front as a film crew member, he is more likely to get a loan, he begins to fake an interest. In the meantime, his boss, Kamali, who has to go to the war zone, picks him as his companion. The closer Kamali and Sadeq get to the front in their van, the more Sadeq is afraid (see Figure 3.7). Kamali misinterprets Sadeq's behaviour as impatience to get to the front as soon as possible. When they reach the front, however, it becomes clear that Kamali is also very scared of being there. Eventually, Sadeq finds himself in a bunker at the front, from which he destroys an Iraqi tank with a missile. The film ends with a shot of Sadeq lying in a hospital bed with his family around him.

With the popularity of *Leili is with Me*, Tabrizi's profile as a filmmaker grew in Iran. After some other critically acclaimed films, in 2004 he made the controversial film *The Lizard*. It won the 22nd FIFF's Audience Choice Award. Since it was rumoured to have run into trouble with the censors and to be banned before its public release, there were long queues in front of cinemas everywhere to see it at the festival. The events of the next couple of months showed that those rumours were justified.

### The plot

Reza Mesqali, known as the Lizard apparently for his ability to climb walls, is a professional burglar in his forties. He is taken to jail where he is to spend a life

*Figure 3.7* Still from Kamal Tabrizi's *Leili is with Me* showing Sadeq feeling sorry for himself on the way to the war-front.

sentence for armed robbery. Reza tells the prison chief, Mojaver, that he was not armed at the time, but Mojaver is not convinced. He sends Reza to solitary confinement a number of times for minor misconduct. Mojaver declares that his policy is 'to force the prisoners into heaven' using strict controls in order to make them atone for their 'immoral' behaviour.

Reza gets injured in a jail fight and is sent to a civilian hospital outside the prison where his room is watched by a prison guard. In the bed next to his there happens to be a friendly mullah. When Reza discusses his desperate situation, the mullah tells him that he should not despair because 'there are many ways to reach God'. Once, when the mullah goes to the bathroom, Reza puts on his robes and escapes from the hospital. Reza first visits a friend who suggests to Reza to acquire a fake passport in order to escape the country through the border with Turkey (see Figure 3.8).

Still wearing the robes, Reza sets off for the Iran–Turkey border to leave the country. When he gets off the train in a town near the border where he hopes to find a contact who will supply a fake passport, he is greeted by some villagers; they mistake him for their new mullah, whom they have come to meet at the station; and they take him to their village. Gradually, because of his lenient attitude on the one hand and his *javanmardi*[30] on the other, his popularity grows in the area, reviving interest in the mosque and attracting large crowds of worshippers.

Hearing about the new mullah's popularity, a local official, who wants to run for a new post in the upcoming elections, seeks to be associated with Reza. He imposes

*Figure 3.8* Still from Kamal Tabrizi's *The Lizard* showing Reza in his friend's house before he embarks on the trip to the Iran–Turkey border.

on Reza to give a sermon at the local jail. Meanwhile Mojaver, the jail chief from Tehran, who has followed Reza's trail to the area, is also in town and attends his sermon at the jail (see Figure 3.9). Although he does not recognize Reza immediately, he becomes suspicious. Later Reza goes to the border, but the checkpoint is temporarily closed, and the guards tell him it will open in two to three hours. Reza goes to the mosque to take part in a religious celebration. There, he is finally arrested.

### Discussion

The film has a number of elements that reinforce its religious themes, while it does not exude ideological features shared among many that are commonly referred to as 'religious films'. In addition, the film's subtleties and ambiguities have not only worked for the filmmaker in his argument with the MCIG censors, they have opened it to readings that are opposed to the conservatives' restrictive tendencies.

Among the religious motifs in the film, the mullah's robe is of particular importance. Having helped Reza's escape, it appears to prevent him from immoral behaviour. For example, when he wants to flirt with a girl from the village, the robe often gets in his way. On one occasion his robe gets caught in the window of the train compartment, preventing Reza from approaching the girl. At the end of the film, when he is being arrested, Reza treats the robe with reverence. As he hands the robe

*Figure 3.9* Still from Kamal Tabrizi's *The Lizard* showing Reza preaching.

to a child from the village, he says, 'These clothes should tame a man, right?' However, in Reza's case the robe may not have been successful in 'taming' him: just before handing the robe to the boy, Reza had attempted to escape across the border.

In spite of the narrative's religious connotations, while one could read a subtle change of heart into Reza's character at the end, there are other elements in the film which make it unlikely. One of these relates to a woman who makes a fake passport for Reza. Just as she is about to complete her work in his presence, she has a sudden religious awakening, triggered by a certain coincidence, and begins shouting 'Repentance!' She throws the faked documents, including Reza's passport, into the fire, much to Reza's annoyance. Reza raises his hand to hit her in the face but does not do so. Next, as the woman is being arrested, she says to the bystanders, 'Repent and God will forgive you as well.' In a dialogue a police officer tells another that the woman has gone mad. Reza's gradual and ambiguous change of heart stands in sharp contrast to this woman's sudden turn to religion.

An important and yet subtle point in the film is that, although at one level the film may reinforce a positive image of the clergy, the persona Reza takes on as the popular village preacher is one with an open-minded, non-restrictive view of religion. Nowhere is this better exemplified than his repetition of the phrase 'there are many ways to reach God', a phrase which he learned at the hospital from the real mullah. Often, when wondering what to say in his sermons to his congregation, he repeats this sentence to them and tries to interpret it. He also advises village parents not to compel their children into pious behaviour. For example, he tells the father of one of members of his congregation not to pressure his son to learn the Qoran by heart, which Reza believes should be a matter of choice for the son. He says, 'Don't try so hard to push him into heaven because he may fall off the edge from the other side into hell.' He also tells his congregation not to restrain their children from mixing with the opposite sex.

In essence, Reza's message stands against that of the prison chief, Mojaver, who tells Reza at the beginning of the film, 'I will force you into heaven.' This is a commentary on the paternalist attitude of the conservatives who want to force Iranians into 'Islamic' behaviour – for example, Ayatollah Khaz'ali, a powerful conservative member of the Guardian Council, who suggested that the Council had a duty to make sure the youth did not go to hell (Ansari 2006: 186).

An important element in the film is its ambiguous narrative closure which makes the film open to interpretation. It is unclear why at the end of the film Reza goes back to the village mosque when he hears that the border is closed for a couple of hours. If he has become repentant, why does he go to the border at all? Does he go back to the mosque because he does not want to cause suspicion by his absence? Could he not have waited at the border for that short period? Does he not want to let go of the respect he is receiving from the villagers?

The ambiguity proved useful for Tabrizi's argument with the MCIG and the conservatives for the film's release. Tahmasebi told me that in the negotiations for the release of his film Tabrizi argued that *The Lizard* was a story of transformation, because the thief who starts by imitating clergymen, goes from chanting *sho'ar* (slogan) to *sho'ur* (knowledge). When at the beginning he tells the villagers about the many ways of reaching God he is just repeating a statement by the mullah he met in the hospital without understanding it. But by the end of the film he begins to understand its implications. Tabrizi's argument was effective, at least with some of those the filmmaker negotiated about his film.

### Group discussion

Kaveh, a friend of mine, invited me to see *The Lizard* with him and some friends I had already met. After a few unsuccessful attempts to buy tickets to sold-out shows, Hamid managed to get some for a 10pm showing in *Sepideh* Cinema in central Tehran. As I was waiting for the others in front of the cinema, I heard a passing driver shout out to another who had obstructed the road, 'You, lizard!'

My friend Kaveh, his girlfriend Shiva, her cousin Shirin, and Kaveh's friend Farhad, all in their mid- to late twenties, arrived just minutes before the show. We were all excited to see the film at last. Farhad told everyone about the instances of censorship in the film he had heard about and the others were keen to listen to him.

The cinema was packed to its capacity of 750. There was a noisy, cheerful atmosphere, with a lot of people still talking at the start of the film, but it became quieter gradually before the bursts of laughter started early on in the show. During the film the audience laughed a lot and in one case, which I will now recount, some clapped. When Reza first meets him at the hospital, the mullah is not wearing his robe, so Reza does not know who he is. As Reza is complaining about his own predicaments, the mullah tells him that thinking about God will perhaps make him calm. Reza replies that these things are said by the mullahs to fool everyone. The clergyman says, 'There are good as well as bad mullahs', to which Reza answers that then the good ones must be waiting for the right season. Using an analogy with the ripening of fruits which are only available in season, he implies that this is not the right season, because there are no good mullahs around. Apart from this instance, many people also clapped at the end of the film as well.

Shirin, who was sitting next to me, made some comments about the film during the show. Once she pointed to an instance of censorship. When the film ended, I asked her about that. She said there was a sudden slight jump in the picture in a scene when Reza was talking to a young couple in the village who seemed to be dating. She told me Reza must have said something to them that was cut. Comparing that to what Mohammadi told me about the censorship of the film, I realized that she was right.

Farhad told me that in the middle of the film Kaveh had said to him that he was dreading that in the end Reza would become religious and decide to stay in the village. He said that he and Kaveh were both relieved when this did not happen. I agreed.

As we stepped outside the cinema,[31] Shirin said she thought that at the end of the day the film wanted to say that the mullahs were essentially good. Farhad disagreed, saying that the good mullah in the hospital was an exception, and even he said that there are good and bad clergy like in every profession. On the other hand, Reza in the film was unlike any real mullah. For example, allowing someone to sing in the mosque and telling the young men that they should be allowed to have relationships with the opposite sex.

To Farhad, the film was about 'the various ways of reaching God'; everyone could find their own way. This was the main contrast between the reformists and the conservative mullahs who believe in a narrow definition of religion. According to him, this was precisely the problem many have with the conservatives. He said that everyone, including the young people, should find their own way in religion and in life in general; they should be allowed to live their lives free of forced dogma. He laughed as he recalled the line that if you force people into heaven they may end up in hell. Farhad later said that by showing Reza's success as the open-minded mullah in attracting people to the mosque, Tabrizi (the director) is trying to say that if mullahs did so, many who have been alienated from religion in Iran would be attracted back.

Kaveh interpreted the film more radically, saying that he thought the film subtly wanted to say the clergy are actually thieves themselves which he thought was witnessed by what they have been doing to the country since the revolution. He said he was surprised the film had not been banned altogether, because it did not favour the clergy at all.

The film certainly added to the vocabulary of resistance. A couple of days after I saw the film, a friend of mine told me he had heard a group of young men calling a clergyman a lizard.

*Interview with Tabrizi*

I arrived in Iran in early April 2004, shortly before the film's eventual release. I rang Tabrizi the filmmaker to arrange an interview. Unfortunately he could only see me before the film was screened, but I accepted this, since I knew enough about it and had seen his earlier and rather similar comedy *Leili is with Me*. Because I was interviewing him at the very time he was experiencing problems to do with his film, I was worried that he might not be candid about the controversy. To my delight he was very open about it.

We met at his office in central Tehran. I began by talking about the fact that his wartime/revolutionary credentials gave him a licence to make films about controversial topics, as in *Leili is with Me* and *The Lizard*.

*Tabrizi:*   I think this is not strange or negative. Well of course we are closer to the [post-revolution] regime. We can mix more with the Minister of Culture or his Cinema Deputy. For example, I know Heydarian [the Cinema Deputy at the time] very well. We grew up together. Obviously, when I made *Leili is with Me* and *The Lizard*, it is because there is a kind of trust in me. There is a friendship which creates this kind of trust between us.

  [However] we do not make banal films. We make films that mainly consist of social criticism. Like Hatamikia, I always go against the flow. Although we might be taken as connected to the regime, with respect to the conservatives, our perspectives are almost the exact opposite. We have created a share for ourselves and we use that to say what we want. In fact we are very concerned about the future of our country and this regime, and that is why we want to criticize it.

*SZ:*   What did you want to say in *The Lizard*?

*Tabrizi:*   I wanted to say that you cannot change people with threats and pressure. You cannot influence people like that. People need this to happen to them in a slow process. This is exactly what cinema does with its audiences. That means that only things which are completely subtle can work. Films that are exaggerated and full of slogans do not have any effect, because the audience will not listen. The whole point of *The Lizard* is this. Because it says that in Iranian society, there are still those who believe that you can guide people to the right path by using a stick. One of the main ideas in *The Lizard* is that you cannot force people into heaven. People have to want it themselves.

*SZ:*   What was it like to make a comedy like *Leili is with Me* about the war?

*Tabrizi:*   Well, here there are some of us who think that an artist's job is to talk about social ills. The conservatives believe that we should not go towards matters of social criticism, etc. For example I remember that there was a young clergyman who was involved in the censorship of *Leili is with Me* and he was totally against it. He said that the film was joking with sacred matters and I must not do that. Because this guy did not know me beforehand, he had certain perceptions about me. He thought that I wanted to uproot the *Basiji* and the war-front culture. Well, there were other people there who knew me well and who told him that although I was criticizing, it was with sympathetic intentions. This is exactly the problem: I don't have to convince the people who know me well. It is the others who look at us suspiciously.

SZ: How did you convince those people?

Tabrizi: The clergyman was telling me, 'Kamali [in *Leili is with Me*] has such a beard and wears a *kaffieh* [the Palestinian scarf worn around the neck which became a identity marker for *Basijis* during the war]; how can you say that he is also afraid [of 'martyrdom']?' What I told him was that the issue of religious belief is a personal and internal matter. If you make it an external and public one you will suffer the consequences. If you believe superficial things like a beard and a *kaffieh* are markers of a *Basiji*, this is a disaster, because in our society, the opportunity exists for people to pretend and deceive. I gave the example of the person who put the bomb in the Islamic Republic Party headquarters and killed scores of people [in 1981]. He had made friends with those he killed. Well, that was an extreme example that I brought up, but in everyday life some try to deceive others.

SZ: Have they censored *The Lizard*?

Tabrizi: They insist a lot that I should go and see Heydarian today. They really want to take some dialogues out of this film.

SZ: I thought that these things were all resolved and that you were going to show the film on the 2nd of Ordibehesht [21 April]?

Tabrizi: Yes, it will definitely be shown, but they insist that I should cut some scenes. And I do not agree to that.

SZ: How did you end up going after this topic?

Tabrizi: Manuchehr Mohammadi had written and produced a film called *Under the Moonlight*, which was an earlier film made about the clergy. Then he decided to make a comedy about the clergy. He talked to me about it and showed me a one-page plot for it. I thought that it was a brilliant idea and that in the framework of comedy, in a delicate manner, we could enter an arena in which we can take a critical look at the place of the clergy in society; but a critique which they would like themselves, and not one that they would reject. As for the script, we talked to a clergyman. However, this clergyman had himself written a story for which he went to jail for a while (he laughs). His name is Hojjatolislam Za'eri and he is very open-minded.

SZ: Did you go and see any of the authorities before making the film?

Tabrizi: It is possible that [Manuchehr Mohammadi] may have had some talks with the Minister. Well, I did the job carefully so that I could defend this film [if I came under question]. Although this was still risky, I thought I had taken the necessary measures. When I gave the completed film to the MCIG, immediately they gave it a screening permit. But in spite of the permit, they stopped it. Here in this country, if you have a permit you should not think that it will be respected by all. Perhaps somebody influential protests against your film and then your whole project comes under question.

SZ: Who has stopped it now?

Tabrizi: Heydarian, the Cinema Deputy. He got scared. Heydarian's point is that he does not want a repeat of what happened to *House on the Water*. It would be bad for the MCIG if they give a film a screening permit and then somebody files a law suit against it and the judge gives a verdict to ban it [as was the case with *House on the Water*]. For the last two months, we have seen the film with many authorities [he laughs], such as the Minister of Intelligence and judges from the judiciary.

SZ: Didn't anyone oppose the film?

Tabrizi: Yes, there were many who said, we think you should change this or that. For example, when I saw the film with four judges from the judiciary, three of the judges told me that there is nothing wrong with this film and while we were watching they were laughing all along. But the fourth one's hands and legs were shaking with anger (he laughs). He said, 'You have destroyed the clergy totally. You have put us under your feet and squashed us like cockroaches!' See how different the perceptions of people can be. It all depends on one's outlook on life. The other three said, 'Why are you reacting like this? This is fine, there is nothing wrong with it.'

SZ: Did you convince him there?

Tabrizi: We argued for a long time. He asked many questions which I answered. I began to explain so many things, such as characterization in cinema and novels, but he was not convinced. But I thought that because the other three supported me, this guy should give in. Unfortunately in our country it does not work like that. Even one person can go and start a fuss.

Like his contemporaries Makhmalbaf and Hatamikia, I found Tabrizi to be serious about his political/social convictions. Nevertheless, like his films he does have a sense of humour which sets him and his films apart from Makhmalbaf and Hatamikia.[32]

As Tabrizi points out, he sees his role as primarily a social critic who, like many reformist politicians, believes that the only way for the Islamic Republic to survive is to evolve. Filmmakers like Tabrizi have to take part in complex negotiations with conservative authorities, who may later object to the film. Obviously this requires much patience and commitment to such projects which could stir the conservatives. As he mentioned above, friendships and connections are important in such times. However, this is not only because friends will be more favourable to someone they know. It is to do with the trust that they place in the filmmaker, whose commitment to the regime they do not question. As Tabrizi pointed out, he had to prove himself to those who did not know him beforehand. The system is based on traditional face-to-face negotiations, where success largely depends on trust between people who know each other.

Part of the complex negotiations, as Tabrizi points out, is to educate those who are objecting to a film about cinema. As is clear from what Tabrizi says, their lack of knowledge does not make them easy to trick. Unfortunately, as was pointed out to me, as soon as the authorities learn about cinema, they move on to other jobs and often the filmmakers find themselves explaining the same things to the new authorities.

### Curtains close on The Lizard

After its release, *The Lizard* inevitably ran into a storm of protest. Leading the charge was *Jomhuri-ye Islami*, a major newspaper. Not surprisingly, some claimed there was a conspiracy at work and demanded that the film be banned. This was followed by protests from seminary clerics in Qom and Tehran. Finally Ayatollah Makarrem-Shirazi, a senior Ayatollah from Qom, condemned the film saying it was 'offensive to the robe of the clergy' and backed the call for a ban. Screenings of the film ran into multiple problems in a number of towns around Iran. In major cities like Mashhad the film was not allowed to be screened by the local MCIG branches. A copy of the film shown at a cinema in Rasht was stolen. On 17 May, when the film was still showing at sell-out cinema halls in Tehran 27 days after its release, it was suddenly taken off the screens by the MCIG to end the controversy.[33] Already about a million people in Tehran had seen the film in cinemas. This is while a low quality bootleg copy of it was circulating in Iran at the same time. Since then, high quality bootleg copies of the film have become available very readily in and outside Iran.

On the last day of the film's run, a question-and-answer session was held with the director at the University of Tehran. A range of issues were brought up by those attending the session in the packed auditorium. A seminary student said:

> The philosophy behind this film clarifies some truths in society, that in any case some thieves are in the clothes of the clergy today in our society and this is an undeniable fact. Anyway, *The Lizard* helped a new perception of the clergy take shape in people's minds so that they understand that they should not imagine the clergy are all the same.

Referring to the famous sentence repeated by the protagonist, 'there are many ways to reach God', a student suggested that it relates to the concept of pluralism which in Iran is widely attributed to Soroush, a renowned philosopher.

Engagement with the film as a political allegory appears to be ubiquitous, demonstrating that there is much at stake when a film features a thief in the clothes of a cleric.

While interest in the politics of the reform movement has all but died out in Iran, *The Lizard* brings up some of the basic ideas of the movement, such as rejection of authoritarian tendencies, respect for social freedoms, and pluralism. Such ideas remain in circulation as popular catchphrases from the film in the everyday discourse of resistance to strict controls favoured by the conservatives. Such smouldering resistance may very well later galvanize into a fresh movement which will draw on the experiences of the reformists.

The massive interest that *The Lizard* generated at a low moment of the reformist movement also shows that perhaps unlike what Downing suggests, there may not necessarily be a direct relationship between the fate of the radical/alternative media and that of social movements. While interest in the reformist movement is low, the enthusiastic reaction to *The Lizard* shows that interest in radical media may not always necessarily ebb with the low moments of the social movement.

## A note on the economics of Iranian cinema

So far, I have focused on political aspects of the relationship between Iranian 'social films' and state ideological control. However, the economic dimension of such relationship must also be addressed (Melucci 1995; Cox 1997). As mentioned earlier in the chapter, Atton (2002), based on Melucci and Cox, suggests that radical media must be free from determination by the state and commercial interests.

The main producers of film in Iran are state-affiliated organizations (Naficy 2002: 40–41). Most cinema halls are also directly or indirectly state controlled. The question is whether owing to the control of the state over production and distribution of these films, they are politically compromised. In relation to Iran, one has to consider the make up of the state. As I mentioned in Chapter 2, far from monolithic, the Iranian state has been subject to fierce confrontation between the two political factions particularly after 1997. Filmmakers with a critical outlook have been at times helped by reformist authorities but restricted by their conservative opponents. Because of the split character of the Iranian state, funding from the state cannot necessarily be considered as complicity with an authoritarian regime. As mentioned earlier reformist politicians have fought hard in order to reform the system and bring in a measure of democracy to the country. Therefore, the stark binaries set up by Atton about complicity with 'the state' should be reconsidered.

In addition, in terms of the economics of Iranian cinema, an important question is whether or not large commercial gain is possible, given the predicaments of the industry. As Ghazian (2002) has shown, Iranian cinema is in a permanent state of financial crisis and therefore substantial gains are not achievable. My own findings accord with Ghazian's position. According to many people I spoke to who are involved in Iranian cinema, in order to cover its costs a film has to make two times as much money as originally invested. Only a handful of films manage to earn beyond that amount. The films discussed in this chapter made modest profits, apart from *House on the Water*, which broke even. Furthermore, as the director Sadr-'Ameli told me, it takes a long time to retrieve the box office returns from ticket sales outside the capital, adding to the industry's financial problems. There are also very few sources of private funding available. As a result, filmmakers need other sources of income: some, like Farmanara and Milani (see the next chapter), have a second job from which they make their living; others, like Makhmalbaf, engage in many other aspects of filmmaking, such as production, editing, scriptwriting; a few, like Makhmalbaf and Kiarostami, are able to seek international funding (see

Chapter 5); others, like Mirbaqeri, also work in the national TV. Given the small scope of the film industry in Iran, there are only limited possibilities to make money. Therefore, the minor commercial gain in itself should not be taken as a reason to consider it as compromising.

Most importantly, the wide circulation of banned films on illegal video CDs (or VCDs) and more recently DVDs defies state control and hence renders Iranian cinema closer to radical media for remaining outside the channels of distribution controlled by the state or commercial interests. In Iran, besides the official economy of the box office, there now exists an unofficial black market in VCDs and to a lesser degree DVDs[34] which is not regulated by the state and of course does not benefit the filmmakers either (see Figures 3.10 and 3.11). These illegal VCDs, which are easily available in Iran for less than the price of a cinema ticket, vary in quality from shaky images shot on handheld digital cameras to perfect copies. There is considerable tolerance of the low picture or sound quality of the bootleg copies. Since VCDs can be played on basic PCs, which are quite common in urban houses in Iran, this unregulated economy plays an important part in the circulation of films, particularly those which are banned or censored. Often uncensored and subtitled versions of these films are available in video stores (see Chapter 5 about censorship of 'art films'). The circulation of the VCDs plays an important part in the culture of resistance to state control in Iran.

*Figure 3.10* VCD stand, Central Tehran, September 2008; photograph by Hamed Ghofrani.

*Figure 3.11*  VCD stand, Central Tehran, September 2008; photograph by Hamed Ghofrani.

## Conclusion

In this chapter, I examined four 'social films' as nodes of media activity which are influenced to a large degree by the post-revolutionary context. My investigation of these 'social films' demonstrates that they are produced and perceived as commentaries on present day Iran. The role that this cinema plays conforms to Turner's theory of cultural performances. However, contrary to Turner's assumption about societies' trust in the performances, cinema-goers in Iran appear to be more sceptical.

With regard to radical media, it is important to examine the relationship between media practices and social movements or the raising of political consciousness. In terms of raising consciousness, 'social films' have pointed to significant social problems which audiences recognize as systematic and blame on the shortcomings of state authorities. As for encouraging collective action, many filmmakers have been involved in supporting the reformists at crucial moments. Makhmalbaf's statement in support of Khatami's candidacy in 1997 was followed by a campaign video made by two established directors, namely Dad and Afkhami.

Some films' metaphorical endorsement of pluralist solutions to the present predicaments of Iran are in synergy with the reformist movement. This is particularly important because, as Solanas and Getino point out, films attract people 'many of [whom] might not respond favourably to the announcement of a political speech' (1976: 129). The stimulation of counter public spheres is significant to social movements.

My examination of *Glass Agency* and *House on the Water*, however, highlights that the oppositional politics of 'social films' cannot be taken for granted in all respects. While the films and their makers are progressive in some ways, in others this has not been the case. Since audiences do not suspend critical judgement even when they engage with 'social films', in their cofabulation of meaning they detect and reject instances of conformity with state ideology.

Cinema-goers' sensitivity to political meaning in films is heightened by the controversies around them. In their engagement with the films, cinema-goers resist the state controls by recovery of anti-hegemonic meanings. The pleasure that this activity gives the viewers is twofold; one in the 'discovery of oppositional messages' in the films or guessing what a censored message may have been. The other is the social pleasure of sharing what one has noticed with others. The 'discovery' is pleasurable, regardless of whether such a 'message' is or is not intended.

Although public support for the reformist movement has diminished, 'social films' have remained an important vehicle of social/political criticism. The reactions to *The Lizard* demonstrate that interest in the core ideas of the reform movement remains and is stimulated by such films. As Downing points out, radical media's stimulation of resistance is a significant part of their role (2001: 31). Attention to the alternative dialogue stimulated by these films is important, because such dialogue can contribute to the fomentation of another movement when the myth of the conservatives' omnipotence is undermined.

'Social films' which focus in particular on women's issues are the subject of the next chapter.

# 4  'Women's films'

## Introduction

'Social films' which deal with women's issues to do with patriarchal domination such as divorce or polygamy are referred to by some as *filmha-ye zananeh* or 'women's films'. These films are political for the challenge they pose to patriarchal values and institutions in society, and consequently such films are subject to conflicting negotiations of gender identities and relations.

In this chapter I examine the negotiation of gender around controversial 'women's films' by focusing on two films: *Fifth Reaction* (2003) and *10* (2002). *Fifth Reaction* is directed by Tahmineh Milani, who is one of the best known female filmmakers in Iran. *10* is made by the renowned Iranian auteur Abbas Kiarostami.

The prominence of women's issues in some Iranian films, many of which are made by female directors, has led to much interest in the role of gender in Iranian cinema. Research so far has mainly concentrated on 'art films' or 'festival films', while generally either totally ignoring other films (Dabashi 2002) or only briefly mentioning them (Tapper 2002).[1] Furthermore, since so far no other study of the reception of films about women's issues has been published, the significance of these films in Iran has not been explored in depth.

I consider these films in relation to the pleasures they offer to women (Mulvey 1987); whether their strong characters are considered as role models (Inness 2004); or whether female viewers 'try on' their characters' identities in the sense that Ang (1990) suggests.[2] The 'performative' role of gender as enunciated by Butler (1990) will be examined in relation to Iranian cinema. She suggests women's agency is facilitated by repetition of counter-hegemonic performance of gender because such a repetitive performance is constitutive of gender identity. On the other hand, Skeggs (1997: 163) maintains that self-reflection in engagement with the media is part of 'the project of the self as a Western bourgeois project' and is irrelevant when considering other contexts.

Women's engagement with 'women's films' may not always happen in isolation from men. Since men both make 'women's films' and engage with them as viewers, it is important to address their involvement. Although the position of traditional patriarchy in relation to the feminist challenge through film is clear, that of the more modern men is not. In this regard, Sharabi's concept of neopatriarchy is relevant to my analysis. According to Sharabi, neopatriarchal order is marked by '*the absence equally of genuine traditionalism and of authentic modernity*' (1988: 23; emphasis in the original). Such contradictions manifest themselves among middle-class individuals. These men whose feet are not on the solid ground of patriarchal tradition, while wanting to be modern, cannot yet accept the reality of educated women in Iran today. Their engagement with 'women's films' is addressed in this chapter.

Having the above in mind, in this chapter I pursue the following lines of inquiry: Do women filmmakers face extra difficulties in order to make these films in contrast to 'social films' in general? If so, how? What reactions have these films caused in Iran? How do Iranian women engage with these films? Do they use them as a moment for self-reflection? If so, do these instances challenge or strengthen patriarchy? Do women appropriate the films in their negotiations of gender with men? How is the cinema space used by women after the revolution?

I also consider the films in relation to the women's movement in Iran and how they fit in the context of Sreberny and Zoonen's (2000) tripartite 'counter publics' model particularly with respect to consciousness raising. According to them the three consist of the women politicians who fight at the level of changing policies, the activists who promote awareness of the women's cause, and the weak public of the ordinary women and men supporters of the women's movement.

Feminist consciousness raising (referred to as CR) was pioneered by the feminists of the Women's Liberation movement in the USA in the late 1960s. They came to the conclusion that, rather than begin with political agendas, women should draw reflexively on their own life experiences and their emotional response to them in order to arrive at a collectively defined understanding of injustice in CR groups. Such awareness would enable the group members to relate their own personal lives to feminist perspectives, hence the personal becomes political (Hanisch 1978). Sarachild, one of the founding members, suggests that consciousness raising is more important than single issue political action which is often in danger of losing sight of the bigger picture. 'Naming the problem', as in consciousness raising, is 'radical action' also because it has the potential to involve many women who are not already politically minded (Sarachild 1978).

Consciousness raising is particularly relevant to the women's movement in Iran for a number of reasons. Owing to the scrutiny of the state, social organizations with aims which could be considered politically sensitive are difficult to form. In addition, many of the social changes which have led to women entering public life are rather new. Hence, at this stage, raising reflexive engagement with women's issues in order for women to understand injustice as systematic is significant. How cinema is engaged with this agenda is an important part of my inquiry.

Finally, I have attempted to comply with what Zoonen calls 'the feminist project of trying to rescue the experiences of women with the media from invisibility' (Zoonen 1994: 22). This is particularly important in the case of Moslem women. As Ansari (2002: 1) suggests, 'the dominant image of a "typical" Moslem woman combines powerlessness and passivity on an individual level with what seems like a fierce and active loyalty to her community and its shared values, especially religion and culture'.

Moslem women's wearing of the *hejab* also appears to have contributed to uncritical application of the stereotype. The present chapter will problematize such generalizations by highlighting their irrelevance to the situation in a Moslem society.

First, I provide an overview of the contemporary changes to women's social position in Iran. Then, I trace women's involvement with Iranian films from the early days of cinema in the country. Next, I proceed with the discussion of post-revolutionary changes in relation to 'women's films'. Finally, I discuss *Fifth Reaction* followed by *10*.

## Changes to women's social position in contemporary Iran: an overview

Women and issues related to them have steadily moved centre stage in Iran. Under the Pahlavi dynasty (1925–79), Westernization of the country also implicated women's lives. The forced unveiling of women in 1936 was an early move in the implementation of the state ideology. However, the Pahlavis took numerous progressive steps, which included the 1967 Family Protection Law that curtailed men's right to divorce and polygamy. During the same period, women's organizations, led by women who had close links to the ruling elite, drove forward on many fronts such as women's education. The opposition to the regime, however, rejected women's programmes under the Shah from different perspectives. The main discourse that found ascendancy after the revolution was that of Islamists who rejected Western-style modernization programmes for women in favour of an 'Islamic model' under which they believed women would be better off.

Under the Islamic Republic, initially the Islamization of the country resulted in a reversal of the advances made under the Pahlavis and a return to more traditional configurations of gender relations. The 1967 Family Protection Law, for example, was declared un-Islamic and was therefore abandoned. Some university courses such as mining and agriculture were prohibited to women. Wearing of *hejab* also became compulsory. Initially secular women resisted these changes, but their protests were swiftly brushed aside (Keddie 2004: 257).

Ironically, however, the Islamization of public spaces in Iran led to increased participation of women from the more traditional backgrounds (Gerami 1996; Higgins and Ghaffari 1994). Under the previous regime, these women would not engage in public life which was considered secular. Traditional women's public participation also received a boost because of the 1980–88 Iran–Iraq war, which took many of their men away to the war-front, necessitating women's involvement with life outside the home.

In the less restrictive atmosphere after the war, debates to do with women, which had been buried after the revolution, gradually began to appear, but this time in an Islamic framework (Mir-Hosseini 2000). The debates were initiated by a group of women, including 'Azam Taleqani, Faezeh Hashemi, Ma'sumeh Ebtekar, Monireh Gorji and Shahla Sherkat, who all had links with the Islamic regime's political elite. A number of secular women such as lawyers Mehrangiz Kar and Shirin Ebadi, and the writer and publisher Shahla Lahiji, were also active in lobbying for changes to discriminatory laws/regulations to do with women, and also lent their support to the former group. Mir-Hosseini refers to the former group as 'Islamic feminists', a label which is disputed by Moghissi and Moghadam who believe that feminism is only constrained by an Islamic context (Moghadam 2002; Moghissi 1997). However, the term coined outside the country in exile is often rejected by those to whom it is meant to refer, such as Shahla Sherkat (Khiabany and Sreberny 2004: 29). As I discuss later, such rejections have more to do with political pragmatism rather than genuine disagreement with feminist ideology.[3]

Although the above actions by women may not be organized and coherent, they do constitute a part of a women's movement which aims to address the private and public inequalities that women face. Women involved in the movement have taken part in several public acts demanding women's rights. These include the 'One Million Signatures Campaign' demanding an end to discriminatory laws against women, as well as several public gatherings in support of such changes to the law. Several prominent Iranian women including the Nobel Prize laureate Shirin Ebadi and the filmmaker Manijeh Hekmat have been active in the 'feminist' movement.[4] Following Mir-Hosseini, I use a minimalist definition of feminism as 'a broad concern with women's issues and an awareness that they suffer discrimination at work, in the home and in society because of their gender, as well as action aimed at improving their lives and changing the situation' (1999: 6).

The women's press, directed by the Islamic feminists, has been active in raising debates about women's position. Dailies and periodicals such as *Zan*, *Zanan* and *Farzaneh* published hard-hitting analyses and commentaries about issues such as women's rights and their participation in public life including employment (Khiabany and Sreberny 2004).

The public debates have been the precursor to changes to a number of laws and policies. Earlier restrictions on university courses women could study have been removed; divorce laws have been altered to limit men's right to divorce and to compensate women after it; family planning and contraception have become freely available, etc.

Although the women's journals seem to have much bearing on discourse at the level of state politics, while many of my female informants knew of these periodicals, they mostly did not read them. On the other hand, Iranian films that raise 'women's films' are particularly popular among women. Some women emphasized to me that films which show the victimization of women or their resistance to patriarchy are very important to them. While these educated women could easily access and read the women's periodicals, seemingly my informants found the dramatizations in films more engaging than the factual analysis in the press.

## Background to women and Iranian cinema

The involvement of women in Iranian cinema has been fraught with problems right from the beginning. This is because, prior to cinema, owing to religious prohibitions women were denied a presence in performing and visual arts and even in

Persian classic poetry (Chelkowski 1979; Najmabadi 1999). The first Iranian talkie, *The Lor Girl* (1933), which featured Sediqeh Saminejad, the first Iranian woman to appear on film, led to much trouble for her. During the shooting of the film, the actress was physically and verbally abused offstage, and for years afterwards
she was often subjected to insult and physical attacks (Baharlu 2002: 25–26). In the silent feature *Haj Aqa, the Cinema Actor*, made in the same year as *The Lor Girl*, the problem of women acting was a major theme in the film. *Haj Aqa, the Cinema Actor* is about a traditional man known as Haj Aqa who refuses to allow his daughter to act in films. A filmmaker then secretly films him as he goes about his daily business. When he later sees himself on the big screen and is cheered by the audience, he changes his mind about cinema and allows his daughter to act. In real life, the situation was very different from the film's happy ending. The acting school which Oganians, the director of *Haj Aqa, the Cinema Actor*, had established in Tehran failed to attract any female students (Baharlu 2002: 25).

Later on, with the popularity of *film-e farsi* from the 1960s, more actresses began to appear in films. However, as Lahiji states, owing to these films' exploitation of the female image, women's roles can be summed up as 'unchaste dolls' whose function was 'to display their bodies to satisfy the poor film-goers' (2002: 219).

While the representation of women for the male gaze was an important feature in the films at the time, what was even more significant was the denial of agency to female characters and the films' adherence to patriarchal values. In many films, typically the young female character would leave home because she was 'led astray and deceived' sexually by a man who would subsequently leave her. With nowhere to go, she would end up in the 'shameful' profession of singing and dancing in cafés for ruffian male customers (such as in *Ashamed*, Kushan 1950; *Shelterless*, Fahmi 1953; *Golnesa*, Azarian 1953). The male hero would usually rescue the young woman from the 'unchaste life'. The woman would then repent, put on a *chador*[5] and marry him, thus becoming chaste. Next, she would join the background figure of the hero's mother as an obedient housewife. Thus apart from satisfying the voyeuristic desires of the predominantly male cinema-goers in the first part of the film, the films attempted to please them by having the male hero take charge of women's lives and direct them to 'the right path'. Basically, in these myths of transformation from unchaste to chaste or vice versa, the women were denied any agency.

In the New Wave cinema of the 1960s and 1970s, women did not fare any better. The intellectual filmmakers, who were critical of modern lifestyles, also cast women in roles with little agency. Some reworked the unchaste-to-chaste transformation formula of *film-e farsi* (for example, *South of the City*, Gaffary 1958), or the restoration of family honour after the rape of a female family member (for example *Qeysar*, Kimia'i 1969). However, these films had more realistic story lines, superior filmmaking techniques and included little or no voyeuristic exploitation of the female image. In addition, apart from ignoring the woman's question, they were socially conscious.[6]

The representation of women as objects of desire in the cinema before the revolution was the main reason for the clerical establishment to declare cinema *haram* or religiously forbidden. Religious leaders including Ayatollah Khomeini compared cinema to prostitution. Representation of women as sexual objects was particularly alarming for the traditional clergy, for whom female sexuality was inherently dangerous to social order (Mir-Hosseini 2003). But in spite of religious sanctions, cinema attendance grew, particularly in the 1970s.

Cinema-goers before the revolution mainly consisted of young men (Sreberny Mohammadi and Mohammadi 1994: 35). In the 1970s, when some films did attract middle-class women to cinemas, they were accompanied by their male folk. This is something that I recall clearly myself. In the late 1970s, while my female relatives would take part in public life, they would not go to the cinema unaccompanied by men. When I went to the cinema in Mashhad with my family, the women would sit in the middle with the boys on either side to shield them.[7] The practice was not limited to Mashhad. In Tehran, our female relatives would not go to the cinema without male company either. The dark space of the cinema was not considered a safe place for female-only groups. This changed after the revolution.

### Women in cinema after the revolution

Since the establishment of the Islamic Republic in 1979, the Islamization of Iran has had far-reaching consequences for the representation of women in cinema. Women have to appear modest in appearance and behaviour, to comply with the rules of *hejab*. They can only appear with head cover and loose clothes that hide their bodies. For many years close-ups of women who were deemed young and attractive were not allowed. Women were dominantly portrayed as housebound and appeared in the background.

Gradually, however, some exceptions began to appear. In films such as *Bashu, the Little Stranger* (1985), which was released in 1989, strong female characters appeared, breaking the earlier stereotypical characterizations (see Rahimieh 2002 for an in-depth analysis of this seminal film).

A number of women also began to work both behind the camera and in front of it. In sharp contrast with the pre-revolution period, when there were hardly any female directors, in the 1980s filmmakers such as Tahmineh Milani, Rakhshan Bani-Etemad and Puran Derakhshandeh began making films and later were joined by others such as Samira Makhmalbaf, Marziyeh Meshkini and Manijeh Hekmat. After 1989, when a space for social critique opened in cinema, many films were made about women's issues as well as the taboo subject of women's romantic love. Makhmalbaf's *Time of Love* (1991) presented three versions of a married woman's love affair. Bani-Etemad's *Narges* (1992) was the first film about a love triangle involving two women and a man. The former was strongly condemned and banned for transgressively vindicating a woman in an adulterous relationship.

The reformists' rise to office and their relaxation of earlier restrictions on filmmaking meant that many films about women's issues appeared in Iranian cinema. In 1999 two films, namely Jeyrani's *Red* and Milani's *Two Women*, broke new ground in the representation of women. For example, *Red* is about a young woman whose psychotic and physically abusive husband torments her every day. In an unprecedented ending for an Iranian film, the woman kills the man. The two films ranked first and second respectively among the box office hits of that year (Javedani 2002: 310–11). In addition, thanks to the easing of restrictions since 1997, there have been many teenage love stories starring good-looking young female and male actors. These generally low-quality films, often referred to as *film-e dokhtar-pesari* (literally girl-boy films), are commonly characterized as *mobtazal* (sleazy). In contrast, following the popularity of *Red* and *Two Women* a number of films were made which focused on women's issues. Two such films, namely *Fifth Reaction* and *10,* are discussed in this chapter.[8]

## Fifth reaction *(Milani 2003)*

The controversial *Fifth Reaction* was written and directed by Tahmineh Milani, one of the most renowned female directors in Iran (see Figure 4.1). When it was shown for the first time at the FIFF, it met strong adverse reactions from both conservative and reformist reporters (see later section entitled 'Reactions to the film'). Later, while the film was on general release, one of the cinemas showing it came under an arson attack.[9] Like Milani's previous works, the film was condemned by the more secular critics for its 'one-sided' view of gender issues, for blaming men for women's misfortunes. Obviously the film had touched some raw nerves.

*Figure 4.1* Cinema Pars in central Tehran showing Fifth Reaction, May 2003; photograph by the author.

## Tahmineh Milani

Milani studied architecture at university. While the universities were closed in the early 1980s during the so-called cultural revolution, she took up work in film studios to support herself. Having worked in a variety of different capacities, in 1989 she directed her first feature, *Children of Divorce*. Her films are produced by her husband, Nikbin, who is also an architect and her partner in their architectural firm. Her comedy, *What's New?* (1992), became the best selling film of the year. It was, however, *Two Women* (1999) which established her as a filmmaker concerned with women's issues.

Since my informants' discussion of *Fifth Reaction* refers to *Two Women*, and Milani too mentions it in my interview with her, I will briefly recount its plot. Fereshteh (angel) and Roya (dream) are students together at the university in Tehran. When the universities close in 1981, Fereshteh goes back to her rather traditional hometown. One day a stalker who used to harass her in Tehran finds her and chases her car on his bike. During the chase, the stalker runs over a child and kills him, while Fereshteh injures another child. The stalker and Fereshteh both end up in jail. Ahmad, a family acquaintance, helps get Fereshteh released from jail. Her father strongly urges her to marry Ahmad, and she agrees reluctantly.

Fereshteh's friend Roya, however, has better fortune and marries a fellow student. Her marriage appears to be based on mutual love and respect. In contrast, Fereshteh's husband is jealous about her contact with other men, and locks her up in the house where she only has her two young children for company. Years later, after the stalker is freed from jail, one day he finds Fereshteh on the street near her house. She runs away, chased by the stalker, who is in turn followed by Fereshteh's husband. Trapped in a cul-de-sac, with the knife-wielding stalker standing over her, she sits on the ground and addresses him: 'All of you did not let me live the way I wanted, you, my husband, my father.' When the husband catches up with them, the stalker kills him. In the final sequence, Fereshteh gets together with her friend Roya and wonders what to do with her new found freedom.

*Two Women*'s controversial and unprecedentedly strong polemics divided the critics, some of whom praised it while others condemned it as *zedd-e mard* (anti-man). For example, Afshari criticized Milani for making an unrealistic film whose 'dictatorial' male characters do not represent contemporary Iranian men. He reprimanded her for her harsh portrayal of Fereshteh's husband, whose death creates a feeling of 'freedom and comfort' for Fereshteh and also the audience (quoted in Mazra'eh 2001: 263).

In her next film, *Hidden Half* (2000), Milani turned her attention to the brief period of political freedom immediately after the revolution, during which the universities were the hub of political activity in Iran. That period ended with the heavy-handed repression of all leftist parties and organizations. Shortly after the film's release, Milani gave an interview to a reformist paper in which she said that a lot of the young victims of repression at that period genuinely cared about Iran. She stated that what happened to those who were persecuted was a shame and she wanted to bring the issues up for the society to deal with them (Milani 2001: 230). Publication of the interview was followed by Milani's arrest and imprisonment. She was freed after six days. The issues surrounding Milani's films and her arrest led to her becoming better known as a controversial and outspoken social critic, particularly relating to women's issues. As the aforementioned arson attack on the cinema in 2003 shows, sensitivities to films such as Milani's still remain.

### The plot

*Fifth Reaction* starts where *Two Women* left off: the death of the husband of the protagonist, Fereshteh. As in the earlier film, Fereshteh is a 30-something mother of two young boys. She lives in the house of her traditional and overbearing father-in-law, Haji Safdar, who is the head of a large truck-driver's guild. Haji tells Fereshteh that he wants to take custody of his grandchildren, and to her dismay she finds out that she can do little to stop him legally. The only solution Haji suggests is for Fereshteh to marry Majid, Haji's other son. Only then can she stay in the house with her children. According to Haji, it would be morally inappropriate for her to live in his house while his unmarried son Majid also lives there. When she refuses, she is forced to leave the house without her children.

Haji allows Fereshteh to have the children only at weekends. After a couple of months, he decides to send the children to another city to live with his daughter. Desperate to stay close to her children, Fereshteh decides to escape from Iran with them. Her best friends, Parisa, Nasrin, Farideh and Taraneh, who teach at the same school as her, offer to help. Apart from Parisa who is single, her friends all have problems with their husbands. Farideh's husband has married a second time and hardly pays any attention to her. Nasrin's husband, a prisoner-of-war in Iraq for 12 years, has totally changed from how he was before captivity and Nasrin does not love him anymore. Taraneh's husband is abusive.

Farideh organizes Fereshteh's visa and a ticket to go to Dubai. Taraneh picks Fereshteh and her children up from school just before the weekend to take her to the airport. However, the plan fails because of Haji's vigilance. Fereshteh decides to go to the southern port city of Bushehr, where her brother lives, to use his help to escape by sea. Taraneh offers to drive her to Bushehr. As their first stop, they stay with Farideh's brother in a town near Tehran. On the way a truck driver recognizes them and reports to Haji, who goes after them. Realizing that Haji knows their whereabouts, Fereshteh and Taraneh decide to drive straight to Bushehr. Haji finds out about their plan through his network of truck drivers, and follows them south.

When Fereshteh reaches Bushehr, she stays in her brother's room in the house of Zeyrmadineh, a southern matriarch with much influence in the area. When Taraneh's husband demands it, Taraneh returns to Tehran. Haji arrives in Bushehr and finds Fereshteh before she can escape.

He reports her to the police who take her into custody. Warning Haji of her local influence, Zeyrmadineh tells him that she will not allow him to take away Fereshteh's children. In the final sequence, Haji stands over Fereshteh, who is crouching on the floor of her cell crying, and he tells her that she can keep her children but only 'under certain conditions'.

## Discussion

Milani herself does not dispute that *Fifth Reaction* was inspired by the Hollywood film *Thelma and Louise* (Scott 1991), which is also about two women who run away from home by car.[10] In Scott's film, the two women who are taken for granted by their male partners one day decide to run away from their unhappy routines. They set off on the interstate highways in Louise's car. Their journey, however, turns into flight after Louise kills a man who has tried to rape Thelma. They decide to go to Mexico, but soon they are hunted down by the police. Obviously, the dramatic turn to violence marks one major difference between the two films.

There are certain similarities between the two films which are relevant to consider. *Fifth Reaction* is also a fast-paced, engaging road movie featuring two women being chased as they drive across the country. A particular element in Scott's film that appears to have inspired Milani is the bonding between the main characters and their escape by car. Fereshteh is backed by her other friends and Zeyrmadineh, the southern matriarch, as well.[11]

As in the Hollywood film, in *Fifth Reaction* the women's attempt at escaping patriarchy is doomed to failure. At the end of *Thelma and Louise,* surrounded by the police, the women drive off a cliff into the Grand Canyon. The film ends with a freeze-frame that captures the moment when the wheels of the car are off the ground and before its inevitable descent. In *Fifth Reaction*, although Zeyrmadineh forces Haji to compromise, in the final shot – which also ends with a freeze frame – the figure of the patriarch stands tall over the crying Fereshteh. The woman's submission to male oppression did not go unnoticed by my female informants (see 'Group discussion' later in this chapter).

In spite of the endings, the two films' representations of women's challenge to patriarchy, and their sense of freedom from male domination during the escape, matched by the open road scenery of the escape route, defy being tidily wrapped up in the final sequences. This is a significant element in terms of women's reactions to the film.

*Fifth Reaction* includes references to the discriminatory laws which disadvantage women. In one scene, included in the version screened at FIFF but cut from the version on general release, Nasrin complains about the disregard for women in laws that legalize polygamy and are of course written by men. In another scene, which was not censored, Zeyrmadineh complains about the total disregard for women's point of view when laws such as those about custody were written.

### Reactions to the film

At the 21st FIFF in 2003, which I attended, *Fifth Reaction* was one of the much awaited events. Milani's film was the only one with a female director, while none of the other films dealt with women's issues.

I saw the film in the packed auditorium of *Esteqlal* (independence) cinema, which was hardly ever so full during the ten-day festival. The press conference following the screening of the film was attended by a very large number of reporters. The filmmaker met with a hostile reaction from conservative reporters/critics. The first question was from the reporter for the conservative paper *Qods*, who asked: 'Do you have any other ideas for film apart from the injustices done to women by men, or verbal attacks on the civil laws of this country which have their roots in religious teachings?' That was followed by another asking: 'If we men promise to commit suicide as a group, will you promise to stop making these repetitive films?' Defiantly, Milani answered, 'I do not make such a promise. I think if I have a story about women, who make up half the population of this country and are *really* suffering, I will still make that into a film.' The challenge that Milani's cinema poses to patriarchal views of gender is easy to see in the reactions of the conservatives.

Some of the more secular critics did not react to her films positively either. Qaderi, who regularly writes for *Mahnameh*, claimed that Milani had tried to create a controversy by a one-sided story in which 'all the men in the world want to treat [Fereshteh] cruelly' (Qaderi 2003: 7). He continued that 'Milani loves women to gain male characteristics', and that '[her] *zan-gara'i* (this could roughly be translated as feminism) is no different from men who are fanatical about their manhood'. Qaderi's attitude towards Milani is typical of many male critics who are simply against her feminist agenda. Since her work is considered 'low-brow', she is an easier target than other female filmmakers such as Bani-Etemad, whose films also have strong feminist themes but are considered 'high-brow'.[12]

Although, as Table 4.1 demonstrates, the film was one of the top ten in terms of ticket sales that year, the number of tickets sold for it in Tehran, which were 236,000, showed a sharp drop from *Two Women*'s over a million tickets. This was surprising because, by 2003, Milani was a better known director than she was in 1998. Furthermore, her new film was technically accomplished and had a famous cast. The lower than expected box office figures should be considered in relation to my qualitative investigation.

*Table 4.1* Box office rankings for the top ten films in 1382/2003

| Film | Box office rankings in Tehran |
| --- | --- |
| Tokyo Non-Stop | 1 |
| The Bride who Brings Luck | 2 |
| Donya | 3 |
| Iranian Girl | 4 |
| **Fifth Reaction** | **5** |
| House on the Water | 6 |
| Pink | 7 |
| A Madman Flew out of the Cage | 8 |
| Black Eyes | 9 |
| This Woman Doesn't Talk | 10 |

Source: Produced by the author using box office figures in *Mahmaneh* (Anon. 2005: 297–379).

*Cinema as women's space*

An acquaintance of mine, Manijeh, a 31 year-old mother of one, talked to me about the film. She and her husband Hossein are both educated professionals. Manijeh had just seen the film with her 29 year-old sister-in-law Zahra, who is also married with children. She talked to me shortly after having watched the film.

*SZ:*   Did you like the film?

*Manijeh:*   Yes. At the end, Zahra and I were saying we should have brought our husbands. Because the film was very anti-man and would fix them properly (she laughs). The women behind us were saying, 'Why doesn't Fereshteh agree to marry the good-looking brother-in-law?' (She laughs.)

*SZ:*   How did you decide to see this film?

*Manijeh:*   Because of Milani. She makes good films about women. In general I like 'women's films' about women and their rights. This is because [women's rights] are ignored here, or [they are supported] just in words, when it is *shown* on the screen it is great (she emphasizes the word). Women are happy to see a film which talks about 'the pains of their hearts' or [the films that] show that men want to make decisions for women.

   [In this film] now that the husband is dead the father-in-law wants to put his opinion first. That is why she cannot keep her own children. Some films which are made like this are protesting about discrimination against women. For example, custody laws. Here, I think the father-in-law thought he was being kind by taking the children, so that Fereshteh could get married again. Well, in his view a woman is a child-bearing factory who needs male support to have more children.

*SZ:*   Did you like Fereshteh in the film?

*Manijeh:*   (Pause) There are always women in films like Fereshteh who have a lot to say in their own hearts, but they are always suffering internal conflict. Or perhaps they are resolute in their own mind, but in real life they are not so.

*SZ:*   Do you know women who are similar to Fereshteh?

*Manijeh:*   I am like that at times. In theory, I say I would do this or that and be strong and resolute when a tough situation happens. But when it comes down to it, sometimes I let things take their own course and sit back. A few times it has been like that. That is why I am in internal turmoil sometimes. (Pause.) I'd like women to be braver. I'd like to see more films which show women taking rational decisions instead of trying to run away with their children. To find better ways to deal with things.

*SZ:*   Like what?

*Manijeh:*   Zahra and I were talking about this. She could have put on her *chador* and sat in front of the father-in-law's house and said, 'I'll just sit here to look after my own children.' What could the father-in-law do? Not much.[13] But [in films] this sort of thing is sinema'i [literally 'cinematic', connoting 'dramatized for cinema'], otherwise would someone who loves her children so much risk escaping across the Persian Gulf in a [small wooden] boat?

After the revolution, women's use of cinema space has changed. As mentioned earlier, before the revolution it was uncommon for women to go to the cinema unaccompanied by men. Since the revolution however, a section of cinema halls is set aside for couples, families, women with children, and groups of women.[14] In order to further Islamize the cinema space, and to make sure 'immoral' acts do not take place there, the house lights are not turned off but only dimmed.

As a result of these changes, the use of the cinema space by women-only groups, is now quite common, and I noticed it on most visits I made to cinemas in Iran. Manijeh and other women take pleasure not only in watching a film with feminist themes but in sharing the experience in all-female company, while interacting with other women in the cinema. In addition, the presence of noisy young children is tolerated in the cinema, facilitating the access of young mothers. As Manijeh mentioned above, Zahra and Manijeh took advantage of this opportunity to take pleasure not only in 'anti-man' dialogues in the film, but also in talking about an attractive actor in it.

Manijeh's reaction to Fereshteh demonstrates the complexity of her engagement with the film. Although she clearly did enjoy the film, her reaction is neither detached pleasure nor close identification with its main protagonist. She says she relates to Fereshteh in her moments of doubt. However, this goes beyond what Ang (1990) has described as a momentary fantasy.[15] Manijeh is reflexively critical of Fereshteh for not being resolute in standing up against the patriarchy with which Manijeh struggles herself.

Reflection is not limited to individual contemplation. The ability of women-only groups to go to the cinema provides them with the chance to collectively reflect on gender issues as well. According to Manijeh, she and Zahra discussed what the woman could have done differently to deal with her situation. Such collective reflection is important in terms of prompting women's consciousness in relation to discussion of injustices to themselves and seeing their personal circumstances politically.

As for the question of how the presence of men would affect the dynamics of watching and discussing films, I found out about that when I watched and discussed the film in mixed company. As mentioned in Chapter 1, as a man, my access to women-only groups was restricted. Therefore, I rarely managed to discuss the films with women without the company of other men, and as a result the groups below consist of members of both sexes. Although this may be a limitation in one sense, since negotiations of gender do occur between men and women, the discussions afforded me the chance to witness gender discourse in the process of making meaning about 'women's films'. In the discussions, my presence and their knowledge of my feminist perspective had a bearing perhaps in encouraging my female informants to also manifest such opinions.

*Group discussion*

I saw *Fifth Reaction* later with a group of university students aged between 20 and 25 – two women (Parvin and Mahnaz) and two men (Hamid and Sirus). The women, who had seen Milani's *Two Women* and *The Hidden Half* (2001), said they were keen to see her new film. We watched the film at a cinema in central Mashhad and discussed it afterwards in the basement flat where Hamid lives. When we got home to Hamid's place, the girls took off their manteaus and headscarves, as some women do in private. We had something to eat and talked about the film.

Sirus started by saying that almost all men in society, from the Haji to Taraneh's husband, did not respect women because 'apart from exceptional cases women have not yet gained the respect of men in society'. Two notable exceptions, to his mind, were the poet Forough Farrokhzad and the filmmaker Tahmineh Milani. At this point Parvin's response was rather angry:

*Parvin:* If women have not reached their due status in society, it is not because of women themselves but because of the norm here. Traditional beliefs in our society have always been so rigid and stupid that they have not allowed such a thing to happen. Then usually things start in small numbers with women like Forough, who break traditions, and things gradually change. Women now know where the problem is and they know they can fight it.

When Sirus retorted that he does not see much change in society, Parvin said, 'So how do you categorize this film? Is it not a fight to change things?'

*Sirus:* It shows the perspective of men towards women.
*Parvin:* It also shows the struggles of women against injustice and it shows women want to make a difference.

Next Mahnaz talked about the rise in the number of female students at universities as evidence for women's move for independence. When Sirus claimed that 'this independence has become the beginning of loose behaviour', Mahnaz responded with the following.

*Mahnaz:* I don't know what your position is, Sirus. On the one hand, you say that independent women become 'loose', on the other hand [you say] that women have not become independent. Forough Farrokhzad [whom you mentioned before] was known as 'loose' in her time, not the sacred virgin.
*Parvin:* Look, you are talking from the same position as the old traditional men.

Parvin's comment seemed to win over Sirus who did not seem to want to be associated with the way 'the old traditional men' talk. He simply answered, 'I dislike that sort of talk' and that was the end of that line of discussion. Later they moved on to the theme of the film and its treatment by Milani.

*Mahnaz:*    I liked that the film talked about women's rights, which I totally agree with. A mother must have the right to the custody of her children, and not the grandfather. I think this is common sense. But the film itself looked a bit artificial to me. The characters and the situations were sort of arranged in a certain way, for example the father-in-law had to be the head of a truck guild and the brother of Fereshteh had to be a student in Bushehr for the story to work.

*Parvin:*    [The film] was a bit hurried in the way that it wanted to put a lot of women's issues into a fast-paced film.

*Sirus:*    What about the ending of the film, when the Haji says 'under certain conditions'? I think he was forced to compromise at the end, but he had not changed much, because he still had his own conditions.

*Parvin:*    I think if this was a better film it would show that in the end, in spite of Fereshteh being an ordinary woman, she could still get her own rights and somehow could keep her children. I liked *Two Women* though. It ended much better.

*Hamid:*    I think another problem was that the filmmaker had made a za'ifeh (literally 'weak female person', a derogatory way of referring to a woman) out of the woman. In the end, the film finished with the man's finger on top of her head.

*Parvin:*    That was pathetic.

*Mahnaz:*    Ah, yes.

*Hamid:*    If I didn't know who the director was, when I saw it I would say it must be a woman. Because she is asking for our sympathy for the victimized woman.

*Mahnaz:*    No, there are other films by women which are not like this. Like *Women's Prison* or *Under the Skin of the City*.

The rather confrontational exchange is indicative of the fact that negotiations of gender evoke strong reactions from women and men. The interactions should be studied on two levels, as suggested by Potter and Wetherell (1987: 110). They argue that the question one needs to ask about audience discourse about films is 'how these images are used and to what end, and thus what they achieve for the speaker immediately and interpersonally, and then in terms of wider social implications'.

First of all, by challenging Sirus early on, Parvin asserts her own point of view. In the process, she denies the male members of the group a monopoly on negotiation of gender. Parvin's assertion demonstrates that, like Sirus, she has interpreted the film as a commentary on the Iranian society as a whole. She maintains that the film represents injustice to women. She also interprets the film to mean that 'women want to make a difference'. The collective action of the women on the screen could perhaps be one example, albeit unsuccessful.

The discussion easily extends to the world outside the film frame and to women as a whole. That women are successful in university education, and that women like Milani make films become significant points not just to score with Sirus but perhaps to remind themselves about women's active social participation.

Most importantly, Mahnaz manipulates a weakness in Sirus's neopatriarchal mindset to the women's advantage. When Sirus voices his concern about the moral repercussions of women's independence, Mahnaz accuses him of being 'traditional', an unwelcome association for these men who aspire to be 'modern'. Faced with this challenge, Sirus was disarmed and began to listen. This method is also used by Milani, who told me that it is effective in her dealings with the censors (see my interview with Milani later in this chapter).

Although the women seem to take it for granted that a mother has more right than her father-in-law to keep custody of her children, they contrast *Fifth Reaction* unfavourably with Milani's earlier *Two Women* because of its ending, which they obviously dislike for appearing to affirm the dominant ideology. Fereshteh fails to defy the patriarch, whose continued dominance is emphasized by the ending of the film. By contrast, in *Two Women* the ending challenges the patriarchal ideology: the woman's oppressors are defeated; the husband dies at the hands of the stalker, who will in turn be imprisoned for the murder. Fereshteh's final words in *Two Women* are 'I feel free like a bird'. Second, because much time has passed since *Two Women*, the novelty of the representation of woman as victim has worn off and some other films have already pushed women's issues further.[16]

*Interview with Milani*

Apart from her films, Milani expresses her anti-patriarchal views in public fora and interviews as well. I met her at a film seminar called 'Women in Cinema', on 6 January 2003 in Tehran's 'Artists' House'. She appeared on the stage for a question-and-answer session after a screening of *Two Women*. She was asked a number of questions, many of them by women sympathetic to her perspective. However, a middle-aged man asked her why Ahmad, Fereshteh's husband in *Two Women*, had such an 'exaggerated character'. Milani disagreed and asked the man in turn, 'Have you not heard any of your female relatives, your sister, your aunt, ever being beaten or humiliated by their husbands? If not, perhaps you do not live in Iran.' While a group of young women were cheering her, Milani continued, 'Ahmad in my film was not such a bad man. In fact, he did not beat his wife. He was not an "exaggerated character" but like many men he thought he had total control over his wife's life. So he acted as a prison warden for her.'

Milani's emotive and persuasive protest about injustice to women is significant not only for highlighting discriminatory laws. But also, as Aminzade and McAdam (2001: 17–18) emphasize, such emotive involvement by activists is important in raising consciousness. This is because they evoke similar emotionally charged as well as rational responses from others.

Although I had read her interviews in the past and was well aware of her position on women's issues, I could now appreciate her role in raising awareness about systematic injustice to women. At her speeches and Q and A sessions at universities and cultural centres in Tehran and elsewhere, large crowds gather, many of whom are supportive women. In such public sphere interactions, Milani adds an extra-textual layer of meaning to her films by articulating the inequities women face.

Later I arranged to interview her. On the day of the interview, I went to her flat in a posh northern suburb of Tehran. We sat in the living room and began to talk. I began by asking the following:

SZ:    I saw the film after the festival at a cinema, and there was a sentence which had been cut from the film. One of the women was complaining about why men are allowed to have more than one wife. Was there more censorship?

Milani:    Well, we censor ourselves.

SZ:    But I thought that you did say what you wanted in your films.

Milani:    Yes, we find a way. Nevertheless, we cannot be very candid and say all that we wish 'from the bottom of our hearts'. I will give you an example, we have a very complex society. You have seen *Two Women*, haven't you? Well in that film there are two girls, one of whom, Roya, is comfortable [with herself] and the other one, Fereshteh, is najib [modest, chaste]. The modesty is not just because of the censorship at the MCIG. I believe, if I show Fereshteh saying to her friend, 'Look at that guy, he is so good looking', that would be a very natural thing. But I cannot show this in the film because I work differently. I want to take the [male] viewer and say, this is the chaste girl that you always like. She does not talk about boys and she is not a 'bad girl', but look what you do to her. Although if I showed that she had a boyfriend, it would not make her a 'bad girl'. But automatically I censor myself.

There are other social problems I show in my films. This is Iran, and all women have got such problems. For example, some women know that their husband has married again, but they keep quiet about it to save face. She could abandon everything and leave the man, but for the sake of her children she stays. That is like Farideh in *Fifth Reaction*. Taraneh has a different problem with her husband, who thinks it is all right for him to go to a restaurant with his secretary, yet he is unhappy to see his wife going out of the house with her friends. Not that he is worried about other men going after his wife. He just wants to keep her under control.

SZ:    As you said once, we have a lot of male intellectuals for whom the problem of women is still unresolved.

Milani:    Yes, my films are quite painful for them. Among our intellectual filmmakers there are some who have two wives. Aren't they intellectuals? Could a real intellectual do this? Some of them have made films defending women's rights, but what they claim has not had any effect on their own intellect. They want to be intellectuals but they cannot, because when their inner self is involved they cannot be loyal to what they have proclaimed. There is one of them who is a close friend [a famous filmmaker whose name she asked me to omit] who came to see *Two Women* when it was being shown at a university in Tehran. At the end of the film, when Fereshteh's husband was killed by the thug, the audience started clapping. At that moment he leaned forward and punched me on my leg saying, 'Look, they are clapping!' The punch hurt. Then afterwards he asked me, 'What is wrong with the guy not letting his wife contact anyone?' This is exactly what he used to do to his own wife, and finally she left him. [Another famous director] has recently married a second wife and his first wife is very embarrassed about that. I am not saying they should not fall in love again, or should not have an affair, etc. This is not a moral judgement. Iranian men, including many intellectuals, have done their best to abuse the laws that give them an opportunity. Even the so-called intellectual filmmakers, such as those making films about women, hypocritically criticize abuses to women in their films themselves.[17]

Our intellectual male filmmakers are sexist. For example, recently Manijeh Hekmat [a female filmmaker] applied to the directors guild for a director's certificate. They told her that since she is not experienced enough to make a film, they have to see a short film she has made before they can give her a director's certificate. Instead, she registered the film, *Women's Prison*, under the name of her husband Jamshid Ahangarani (a director himself) and went ahead and made it. Then again she applied for the director's certificate and sent a [self-contained] part of the film to the director's guild as a short film.

I was the only woman on the directors' committee reviewing the film. The men on the committee were very biased against her, and gave her very low marks like 2 or 3 out of 60, so that she would not get the certificate. Only one other director and I gave her a mark over 40. I told them, 'She has finished the film and it is a good one; you are just going to make yourselves look bad.' One of the directors told me, 'Ms Milani is playing feminist again just because a woman has made the film.' I told them that I liked the film and that I have a right to give my own judgement. Nevertheless they did not give her a director's certificate. She then hassled the MCIG so much that she got the certificate through the administrative channel. Since then the film that all these male directors rejected has been shown at film festivals all around the world, including Venice.

SZ:    I heard you had problems with the trailer of your film. What were the changes the censors wanted you to do to the trailers?

Milani:    We made eight and only one of them was accepted. I went to talk to the member of the committee which reviews the trailer. He said, 'Where are traditional men like Haji Safdar in this country?' I said, 'You are one' (she laughs). I said, 'Haji Safdar is not different from you. He represents a type of thinking. The fact that you are sitting behind that desk and can impose your will on me, means that you are like Haji Safdar. I came home that night and I told my husband that the censor would now give me permission because he would not want to be considered like Haji Safdar (she laughs). And then he actually did give me permission for that trailer to be shown five times. This is one way to resist, by making them want to prove to you that they are open-minded.

SZ:     Some say that your female characters are weak and that you show women as victims.

Milani:  Let me talk about my film; in *Fifth Reaction* there are two women: Taraneh and Fereshteh. Taraneh is the more natural of the two, because of the way she treats her husband. She makes her husband buy her things, saying to her friends, 'These things do not matter to me, but I have punished him like this.' She also defends her personal dream. By comparison, Fereshteh is a very primitive person in this respect, she is just defending her rights as a mother. She never says, 'What about me?' or, 'What if I fall in love again and want to marry a second time?' She is just defending her natural rights as the person who has given birth to those children. This is not to symbolize the power of Taraneh or the weakness of Fereshteh. This is social realism which says they do not give a woman like Fereshteh her dues in this society because she is truly najib [modest, chaste]; I really hate this word because in fact it means a doormat. Even their motherhood rights are not taken seriously. This is a very important issue, much more than anything else. The more submissive she is, the more the problems created for this woman seem unjust. Therefore, this is the power of the film and the power of that character. I am saying, 'You with your dirty laws are going to eliminate such a woman.'

SZ:     Traditions are also to blame.

Milani:  Yes, we have unwritten laws. These laws are ruling this country. A simple example is the social position of women and men. If a boy has a girlfriend the family talk about it proudly, forgetting that his girlfriend is the daughter of another family, and they praise him for his achievement. But they could never allow their daughter to have a boyfriend. They are unable to accept such a natural thing. These are the unwritten laws of the country.

[As for the laws relating to women] in the film, you see that about the custody laws. The mother can keep the child but the father-in-law can say that she is morally corrupt, as Haji hints by saying Fereshteh goes out with her friends. The law gives the children to the mother, but he can easily take them back. You see, the law in this country backs such behaviour.

SZ:     In Iran they know you as a feminist, and you yourself accept that. What do you think about that?

Milani:  This is a strange society where words lose their meaning. For example, anywhere else, if you say somebody is a liberal, that is not a bad word. Here it is an insult. When the rightists want to condemn the leftists, they call them liberals. And the leftists now want to prove they are not liberals. The meaning of '-isms' changes when they get here, and the same goes for feminism. They call me, 'You feminist!', meaning to insult me. They don't know that I enjoy being called a feminist. They are so stupid to think that this is a label that should make me tremble. Our female filmmakers are always giving interviews saying they are not feminist. I think that is good, because all the honour can then be mine [she laughs]. In a recent interview, the actress in my film, Niki Karimi, said that she was not feminist, and has no relationship with my way of thinking.

The reason for the emergence of the feminist movement has been a need across the world. There were rights that have been denied to women and therefore the basis of the movement is very progressive. So feminism created a means of opposing discrimination based on sex. When it comes to Iran you have to know that you cannot talk about the basics of the arguments of feminism. For example, there may be a woman who gets married but does not want to have any children. If you tell [Western] feminists this, they will laugh and say, 'Of course, she does not have to.' But in our laws it is women's duty to have children, and if not, the husband can take the woman to court. Perhaps no man would do this, but what I want to say is that, suppose you are a feminist and you want to defend a woman who does not want to become pregnant. They can easily take you to court. Or if you support a woman who does not want to wear the hejab. These are basic rights by world standards, but can we talk about them here? Forget about abortion, lesbianism, etc., because if you [advocated those], they would kill you. If you want to be a feminist in the Western sense of the word in Iran, that is not possible.

Nevertheless, this place has its own laws, and you can zigzag through. I use a trick, in order to say what I want. For example, if I know that a woman whose children are taken from her is in the right, I will protest against it. But this is a delicate matter and you have to be careful how you protest. For example, if in *Fifth Reaction* I had questioned the custody laws, my film would have never got a permit. I question the law that says the child does not belong to the woman by asking the question whether that is possible under these conditions. So, I zigzag through. After seeing my film, the viewer is going to say, how *na-mard* [cowardly; the opposite of *javanmard*] they are to take her children from her. See what a trick I use to say what I want. For example, in *Two Women* Fereshteh wants to go to university. Is there anything more basic than what she wants? But here, for a woman to study, she needs the permission of her father or her husband. To approach this problem I get the girl to say to her father, 'I want to study in order to be able to help you and my siblings.' This gives legitimacy to the girl's desire to study; and then I pose the question, 'Why don't you let her study?' This is how I can enter their hearts. If I said, 'I am a feminist, the feminists' in the world would laugh at me. That type of feminism has no meaning here. But I can say that I do my best to stand against discrimination against women. That is all I can do here.

By the end of the interview, Milani told me she felt exhausted.[18] This was no surprise, since she was sitting on the edge of her chair passionately emphasizing every word she was saying. She left me in no doubt that she was committed to the cause of women's resistance, and that her filmmaking about these issues is because of her commitment.

Milani's answers are revealing on a number of levels, including that of the difficulties faced by female filmmakers. As she suggested, to be able to advocate women's rights, at times she has had to adapt her narratives so as to legitimize her female characters' wishes in the eyes of the censors. Nevertheless, she still has to take part in face-to-face negotiations with the censors, which requires an ingenious use of persuasion and manipulation. Like Parvin,[19] she manages to put the censors in a position where they agree with her in order to prove they are not 'traditional'. Such skills are an important asset in these face-to-face negotiations.

Female filmmakers not only have to deal with authorities, but also with sexist male filmmakers who create obstacles for them. However, as Milani points out, persistence and inventiveness in negotiations enable female filmmakers to get through the barriers. Women filmmakers at times draw on mutual support. Hekmat, director of *Women's Prison* (2002), told me in an interview that at a time when she was feeling low about her film project, Bani-Etemad came to visit her film set to offer her support. She said that emotionally that gesture was very important to her.

Milani is one of the few who openly admit to being feminist. Although many others engage in a critique of patriarchy, they deny being feminist, for fear of hostile reactions from the conservatives as well as marginalization and attacks by sexist critics and filmmakers. Some of the leaders of the Islamic Republic have spoken out against feminism. For example, Ayatollah Khamenei told a group of female MPs that they must avoid 'feminist inclinations' when raising women's issues (Anon. 2001b). Obviously feminist discourse is subversive both to the traditional patriarchy and to those with a neo-patriarchal mindset.

Milani expressed disapproval of the hypocrisy of some male filmmakers whom she considered sexist but still make films about women's rights. However, such insider knowledge about the private lives of directors is not in the public domain and hence has no impact in Iran. Owing to the lack of gossip columns in the press, only the filmmaker's films and the political/social views they express in the press can influence public opinion about them. As for their films, many of those made by male directors about women's issues have been popular, for example Beyza'i's *Bashu, the Little Stranger* (1985) and *Killing Rabids*. Another example is Kiarostami's *10*, which is the focus of the next section.

As Milani asserts, *Fifth Reaction*, as with all her previous work, relates to women's issues. In the film Milani not only conveys critical ideas about women's rights, but also portrays an informal women's 'action group' in support of one who is being victimized by male injustice. Milani's emotive and articulate public appearances and interviews also contribute to her social criticism and become sub-texts to her films.

Milani's stated feminist agenda concurs with that of my female informants who easily relate the film's narrative to systematic injustices to women in Iran, including the inequity inscribed in the patriarchal laws. The women's emotional and articulate engagement in the discussion about the film shows that it has set in motion new articulations of the issues that it raised in its fictional frame. My informant

Manijeh appears to engage reflexively with the film and thus examines her own circumstances in the light of the female characters' stories. Such reflection is now facilitated by the Islamization of the cinema space which allows women to see films even when they have their young children with them. Women appear to empathize with the film characters' circumstances, although this does not seem to prevent them from being critical of the choices the characters make or from criticism of the film when they do not find it realistic enough.

## 10 *(Kiarostami 2002)*

Abbas Kiarostami's *10* is the first film that the world-renowned director has made about women's issues. Incidentally, it is also his first film to be banned in Iran. The censors considered four of the ten sequences that make up the film, including one that features a prostitute, unsuitable for public viewing. The ban was followed by attacks in the conservative magazine *Sureh*. which accused *10* of encouraging prostitution and social corruption. Kiarostami, who had previously refrained from adverse comments on censorship, now condemned it for the first time.

### *Abbas Kiarostami*

Kiarostami started his career in film in the 1960s with TV commercials. He recalls that after his first 50 ads, a friend observed that there were no women in any of them. Surprised by what he calls 'an unintentional omission', he began to use female characters in later commercials (Baharlu 2000: 16). In the 1970s, Kiarostami's career developed with a number of short films about children made for the Centre for Intellectual Development of Children and Adolescents.

After the revolution, his 'Koker trilogy' (filmed in a village by that name) made up of *Where Is the Friend's House?* (1987), *Life and Nothing More* (1991) and *Through the Olive Trees* (1994), as well as the semi-documentary *Close Up* (1990) brought Kiarostami and hence Iranian cinema much international acclaim. Later, his *Taste of Cherry* won him the Palme d'Or at the 1997 Cannes Film Festival and sealed his global prominence. He made two other films, namely, *The Wind Will Carry Us* (1999) and *ABC Africa* (2001), before making *10* in 2002. Among the major criticisms of Kiarostami's post-revolutionary films, especially from expatriate Iranians, are that he avoids political issues and in particular that his films do not feature strong and articulate women.

Farahmand, for example, suggests that 'Kiarostami's films are conservatively in line with the religious belief that allocates a marginal position and a subordinate gender role to women' (2002: 100). Dabashi (2001: 254) condemns Kiarostami's representation of women even more harshly by accusing him of depicting the (symbolic) rape of a young girl in a sequence in *The Wind Will Carry Us*. I find both these comments unfair, and equally could point to several strong female characters in Kiarostami's films before *10*, but it is certainly the case that he had not previously featured outspoken urban women in important roles (Zeydabadi-Nejad forthcoming).

### In lieu of plot

*10* is an experimental film which does not have a typical beginning, middle and end. It opens with a dialogue between a 10–12 year-old boy, Amin, and his mother, Mania, in a car she is driving. This is the first in a series of ten sequences that make up the film. Apart from one shot that lasts less than 30 seconds, the film is made using two digital cameras mounted just behind the windscreen of the car – one focused on the driver, the other on the passenger, both seen in medium close-up. In all ten sequences, Mania has a passenger in her car, all female except for her son who appears in the first, sixth, eighth and tenth sequences. In the second, she drives her sister home. In the third, she happens to meet a pious old woman to whom she gives a lift to a shrine; in the fourth, a prostitute gets in her car by mistake. In the fifth and the ninth sequences she offers a lift to a young woman she met at the shrine, and in the seventh she goes to a restaurant with a friend newly separated from her partner.

Mania, a woman in her late twenties, has divorced her husband because he would not let her follow her career as a painter. She admits to Amin that in order to be able to initiate a divorce, she lied in court, saying that her husband was a drug addict. Talking to her sister, Mania worries about her relationship with Amin, who has recently started living with his father. Amin does not accept Mania's new husband, Morteza. Mania attempts to convince her surprisingly articulate son that her decision to separate from his father was correct and that she has rights as a woman. The following is an excerpt from a conversation between the two, which deteriorates into a shouting contest.

*Mania:*   I will say two more sentences and I will keep quiet.

*Amin:*   OK, tell me.

*Mania:*   Then I will shut up and will not talk anymore. [Now] I feel fresh, like a river I am flowing. Then [when I was married to your dad], I was a stinking swamp that was rotten. My brain was rotten.

*Amin:*   OK, that is finished. You said three sentences. You talked too much and what you said were lies because I will not accept what you said.

*Mania:*   Why?

*Amin:*   I will not accept what you said because you want to say, with all this rubbish you talk, you want to say, 'My divorce from your dad was the right decision.'

*Mania:*   Well you may think that it was wrong but for me it was the right decision. I am happy.

*Amin:*   Are you happy? That is because you only think about yourself.

Amin later complains that Mania works long hours and does not do housework. At one stage he complains that he has to eat leftovers for dinner some evenings.

In another sequence, Mania is in the car with a friend who cries uncontrollably as she tells Mania about her separation from her partner of seven years. Mania is unforgiving of her weakness and of women in general.

*Mania:*   We women are wretched, we are like this. We don't like ourselves, can't be for ourselves. What does all this mean? That is enough; you cannot sum up everything in one person. What a pain! In such a big universe why you should become dependent on one person. I cannot understand.

Later she adds these thoughts:

*Mania:*   I went to the gym and the dirty woman who is in charge says, 'A woman should have either a big ass or big breasts. You have to make your breasts big because men like asses [and] breasts.' Ugh, ugh, ugh! This is a weakness. You have to make yourself for a man.

Mania later offers a lift to a pious old woman who is on her way to a shrine. The old woman says that she recently sold all she had in order to go on pilgrimage to Syria. In the next sequence, a prostitute gets in Mania's car by mistake and talks to Mania about her job and about sexuality in a matter-of-fact way. She calls Mania 'a stupid woman' for believing in men's love confessions, adding that her male customers sometimes call their wives, saying such things to them while they are in bed with her. Later, Mania goes to the shrine to pray for her relationship with Amin and to ease the feeling of guilt she says she feels at times. There, she meets a young woman in love who has been praying that her beloved will fall in love with her in return. In the penultimate sequence, this young woman tells Mania she has found out that the man loves someone else and she is very upset about that. As she is talking to Mania, she lets her scarf slip back, revealing that she has recently shaved her head. As the tears roll down her face, she says that since she has done that she feels better. Mania sympathizes, saying, 'He has gone now and you have changed drastically.' In the final sequence, which is the shortest, Amin gets into the car and says he wants to go to his grandmother's house, and the film ends there.

### Discussion

*10*, Kiarostami's first 'women's film', bears the hallmarks of Kiarostami's cinema, including a brilliant performance from a child actor, scenes filmed inside a moving car and a meditative pace, as well as an open-ended narrative. Unlike *Fifth Reaction*, where there is a clear distinction between the oppressor and the victim, in *10*, as in other films by Kiarostami, things are less clear cut. Mulvey refers to this as Kiarostami's 'uncertainty principle' (1998). Throughout the film, Mania's arguments for her own rights as a woman and mother, and for women in general, are compelling. On the other hand, Amin is very articulate and talks back. At times Mania appears to be arguing with him as if he were an adult. While to a degree Amin raises sympathy as a child (see the group discussions later in this chapter), as Geoff Andrew points out, he also appears to be an

> archetypal chauvinist male in miniature . . . Amin, in fact, is not only a child but the embodiment of masculine arrogance and power in a film devoid of

speaking parts for adult men. As [Mania] Akbari has said, 'he represented quite enough masculinity for the whole film.'

(2005: 44)

Kiarostami foregrounds Amin's presence in the film by only showing him, with no single shot of Mania, in the first sequence which lasts 16 minutes, when the two are having an argument. As Andrew (2005: 42–43) states, this opening gives the impression that Amin is to be the central character in the film, 'an impression which, of course, turns out to be false'. Although women's voices (particularly Mania's feminist one) dominate the film, as the discussions with my informants show below, Kiarostami's emphasis on Amin's presence appears to have opened up the film to patriarchal readings as well.

## Reactions to the film

I watched the film for the first time in 2002 at its premiere in London's Institute of Contemporary Arts (ICA), in the presence of both Kiarostami and Mania Akbari, the film's protagonist. During the question-and-answer session following the screening, as he had done at premieres elsewhere, Kiarostami talked mainly about his fascination with the new possibilities available to filmmakers with the use of DV cameras.[20] It appears that in spite of the overall feminist tone of *10*, women's issues are not a major concern for Kiarostami. However, I was intrigued by his turn to women's issues as his subject matter. Previously, whenever he was asked about lack of central female characters in his films, he would answer that it was because of the filmmaking regulations in Iran that did not allow a realist representation of women on film.[21] During the Q and A session, I asked him about this. Kiarostami replied that it was a mistake for him not to have done so earlier, adding, 'Women are beautiful and complex which makes them good cinematic subjects.' He also said that the representation of women in Iranian cinema so far had not been realistic, because female characters in the films are limited to devoted mothers, scheming seductresses, or women who are unrealistically strong. He added that in Iranian cinema, making films about women is a trend from which he could not stay away.

On one field trip to Iran, I took with me a VHS copy of *10*, which many people were very keen to see.[22] They had read about it in the newspapers and women in particular were curious to see it. I watched the film with two different groups, each made up of two women and two men.

## Group discussion 1

In the first session, I showed the film to a group of four university students aged 23 or 24. The women in the group were Parisa and Nushin; the men were their boyfriends Mehran and Hamid. Mehran organized the viewing in his own house in a middle-class suburb in Mashhad.

Early on, the main discussion concerned what the film was about. The men, who were not particularly impressed with the quality of *10* as a film, insisted that the film was about pluralism and it suggested that everyone could live life according to their own standards, from the prostitute to the pious woman. But the women disagreed.

*Parisa:* Not exactly. Because if it was like that, Mania would talk about different things to different people; but she was talking with everyone about the problems of women in the society and the injustice to women.

*Nushin:* The film was more about women and many of women's problems were discussed here. It was about a woman who was going against the flow. I liked it very much. This is a contradiction which exists in Iranian society, where women who have [financial] independence want to have many other things as well, but society is not ready for that. This film shows this contradiction in Iran very well.

The men supported the boy's perspective.

*Mehran:* The boy was not getting what was his right as a child.

*Hamid:* I agree. The child was saying, 'I do not want to eat last night's dinner.' What do children want? They want food. So this shows that he was unhappy with the food he was getting.

Nushin, on the other hand, saw the boy not just as a child but as representing patriarchy.

*Nushin:* (Rather annoyed) He was a man. Very early on [in his life] he had learned to shout and shout louder [at women]. But perhaps she was teaching him this, because sometimes when he shouted louder she would give in. In a sense she had given in to her own son, but she wanted [other] women to be stronger. This was wrong because this boy was going to grow up to be a man who shouts and expects obedience. I think this was showing that mothers play a big part in the way their children grow up.

*Parisa:* I agree with Nushin.

*Hamid:* I think Nushin is taking Amin as a man, although he is only a boy. I think the child could have been a girl here. Wouldn't a girl want the same things? If you gave last night's dinner to a girl tonight, wouldn't she complain?

*Nushin:* Even if the child was a girl, the problem would be the same. That means if she expected only the mother to cook dinner and never the father, that would not be right.

Soon the discussion turned to speculation about the relationship between Mania and her ex-husband, and what in general couples could expect from each other in a relationship:

| | |
|---|---|
| *Mehran:* | This was an ordinary story, which you can see if you look around. This film did not say whether Mania's ex was good or bad. He had some needs and expectations, right or wrong, and the woman is an artist who had to go out a lot, so the two had separated. This is an ordinary situation and they actually could communicate, for example to arrange to pass Amin to each other. |
| *SZ:* | The ex-husband and Amin expected the woman to put her family ahead of herself. |
| *Mehran:* | The woman had some expectations. For example, to have a servant in the house. The man had to provide the money. Well, the woman cannot have it both ways. I don't know. Perhaps they should have reached an agreement. |
| *SZ:* | Well, the woman was working. She was not financially dependent on the man. |
| *Mehran:* | I do not understand. When two people marry each other, should they not expect things from each other? |
| *SZ:* | I don't think there is anything wrong with that. |
| *Mehran:* | Well, when I get married, I will say to my wife, 'These are the things that I can provide for you. For example, I could give you a car and we could go on holiday. But I have also expectations from you, [for example] that when I come home we should have food.' |
| *SZ:* | If the man is the only one working, then it is as you say. But when the woman is working as well, then it is a different story. |
| *Mehran:* | That's what I was saying; these two have not talked about their expectations from each other. For example, I will tell the woman I want to marry that I do not want my child to be raised by anyone else. She may say, 'I will be out all the time and we will put the child into childcare or with this or that person.' If the two do not want to compromise, they should not get married. |
| *Parisa:* | I think sometimes people make compromises and at the start they say, 'I love this person so much and it is worth making concessions.' But in practice things may not work so easily . . . |
| *Mehran:* | OK, so this is a mistake that [Mania and her ex] had made. |
| *Parisa:* | Well, you cannot say that was a mistake. Because it is perhaps not so easy. I think the problem here is that although the mothers and fathers both work nowadays, the children's expectations from them are still based on the traditional [gender] roles of the father as the breadwinner and the mother as the housekeeper. |
| *Nushin:* | I agree. I also think [Mania] had not been able to teach her own child that she could still keep her independence while she is a mother. I believe that in Iranian marriages men keep their independence more than women. So nobody expects men to work at home, but women, even when they work outside, have to do all the housework as well. Women have no free time for independence. |

As a point of comparison, Nushin talked about Western examples, saying that she thinks Western men help more at home and that is something she had seen from films and a book, about which she said the following:

Nushin:   I have been reading an American story book which is written from the perspective of a child who thinks his parents are not thinking about him. I like this book. The child says, 'We did not have food at home when I came home and I argued with my father or my mother or the two of them together.' Not just his mother.

And as for their future married life . . .

Nushin:   When I marry I think I will be like Mania, because I want to keep my independence.
Parisa:   Nushin is right. But I think this film left the judgement to us. I mean perhaps Nushin thinks that an ideal woman is one who is independent and who is friends with her husband. I think that a woman should still cook at home and treat her children in a certain way.

While Parisa was less inclined to sympathize with Mania, the main character in the film, the looks she exchanged with Hamid, her boyfriend at the time and now her husband, suggested to me that his presence had much bearing on her more restrained expression of her views. She often agreed with Nushin's more feminist position, but would not express herself as strongly. Nevertheless, I believe she was speaking reflexively when she pointed out that the compromises one may make at the time of marriage could be subject to re-negotiation later. Although Nushin had her boyfriend Mehran there as well, she did not hesitate to make her points.

Even with the men present, Parisa and Nushin took the opportunity to discuss the films reflexively. They also rejected the patriarchal definitions of wife and mother. Although Nushin declared that she wished to be independent like Mania, this did not stop her from criticizing Mania's choices, such as the way she had brought up her son Amin. This was unlike how Ang (1990) and Inness (2004) suggest women 'identify with' film characters. Nushin, and to a degree Parisa, used Mania's character as a point of reference to base how they would want to be as married women in the future.

Nushin was also very vocal in her support of the women's cause and in arguing against the men's views. This was rather surprising to me, because, although I was aware that Nushin was highly articulate, I did not think that she would argue in such a heated manner. That she did so on this occasion, I believe, had to do with her emotional engagement with the film.

As I mentioned earlier, perhaps the strong presence of Amin has laid the film open to patriarchal interpretations. Nevertheless, since Mehran and Hamid do not speak from the more solid basis of traditions which would take women's inferiority for granted[23] and are not yet ready to adopt modern alternatives easily, they appear to be ready to negotiate. However, Mehran appears to take his own advantage in the negotiation for granted as 'the only bread-winner'. Although these women are likely to work in the future, unfortunately because of lack of the necessary legislation to address discrimination based on sex, they are not likely to earn as much as men even for doing the same job. Nevertheless, as future working women they appear to be ready to demand that their future husbands take on some housework. As Parisa suggests negotiations between couples are ongoing processes which do not end easily with initial compromises as Mehran seems to hope. The heated discussion triggered by films like *10* could be part of these processes.

*Group discussion 2*

In Tehran, Mansur, a friend whose wife was very keen to watch the film, organized for us all to see it, together with his brother and his wife. Mansur is an engineer in his late thirties; he is married to Elaheh, a doctor, and they have two children. Mansur's younger brother, Nader, is a businessman; his wife, Mahsa, is a high school teacher. Mansur invited me to Nader's flat to watch the film over a take-away dinner.

When I arrived at Nader's flat I was greeted at the door by Nader and Mahsa. Unlike Elaheh, Mahsa was not wearing a scarf in my presence. Elaheh (whom I had met earlier) and Mahsa did not talk to me much before watching the film, but chatted together on the other side of the large living room. The men sat with me to chat. Nader is quite a forthright person and at times rather obnoxious. His older brother Mansur, on the other hand, is a soft-spoken intellectual.

After dinner, we started watching the film. Nader, Mansur and I sat on the floor while Elaheh and Mahsa were sitting on chairs. Nader, who was sitting next to me, pointed out irrelevant things such as the name of the streets down which the car was driving, or tried to speculate about the make of the car. At other times, when Mania was arguing with Amin, Nader commented, 'What a dirty woman!' or 'Poor child!' Mahsa and Elaheh were watching the film very intently, while Mansur dozed off towards the end.

Afterwards, as we talked about the film, Nader and Mansur, like the men in the first group, said that the film was not particularly good. Mansur suggested that Kiarostami could have written a story instead of making a film, because he did not do anything with the camera. He thought his previous films such as *Where is the Friend's House?* had beautiful scenery and a kind of gentleness which was missing here. Mahsa disagreed, saying that Kiarostami's *Taste of Cherry* was similar to *10* for doing little with the camera, and that film was about men while this one was Kiarostami's first 'women's film'. Elaheh continued the conversation.

*Elaheh:* I was saying [to Mahsa] that this film was more interesting for us because what Mania says are our words. This is how we women feel about things. Nader and Mansur are not in a position to understand.

Early on, the discussion about the film turned to morality.

*Mahsa:* Why did the girl shave her head at the end of the film?

| Nader: | She wanted to be like the prostitute. She wanted to get out of the house without restrictions, without a care. She just wanted to show her head. Like the prostitute [who] had cut herself loose from all the limitations of propriety. Then this one thought, 'I will go my way as well.' |
| Mahsa: | I do not think so. |
| Elaheh: | No. She had made a change to mark the end of what was and to make a new start. |
| Nader: | But the woman wanted to do what I said. |
| Mahsa: | I think the prostitute is surer of herself than Mania. Right or wrong, she seems to know what she is doing. |
| Elaheh: | She had accepted her circumstances as a fact of life. I do not think any woman would wish to be a prostitute. So she was thinking, 'Now that these are my circumstances, I should not have any feelings.' |

Later Nader asked what Kiarostami meant to say with this film.

| Mahsa: | He wants to say that the world of women is larger than the world of men. Men's world is limited to their stomachs.[24] |
| Elaheh: | Well, the film shows that this is what men pay most attention to. |

Surprisingly for me, the men did not react to what Mahsa just said, so I asked them what they thought about that.

| Nader: | (Smiling) Let's go to the other room and we will tell you. |
| Mansur: | (Also smiling) We would have to turn off the tape recorder as well. |
| Nader: | (With a serious tone) A man makes a woman complete. It is said in the Qoran. |
| Elaheh: | (Angrily) This sort of thing is the interpretations of the *ulama* [jurisprudents] who are all men. This is not what the Qoran says. |
| Nader: | Read it. |
| Elaheh: | I have. Twice. |
| Nader: | Arab literature says so. |
| Mahsa: | We are Iranians. |
| Nader: | Men's *diyeh* [blood-money] is twice women's, and that is in the Qoran. |
| Mahsa: | (Angrily) Well, that is because women need less; that is why. (She paused and then added) I think this discussion will not lead anywhere. Neither can a woman say she is stronger, nor can a man. When a person has reached *kamal* [perfection] then they can claim that they are stronger.[25] |
| Elaheh: | The role that Islam considers for the woman is much greater than that of a man. |
| SZ: | How do you mean? |
| Elaheh: | Humans are the most complete creatures on earth. If the responsibility for bringing up such a creature is entrusted to women, then our religion accepts her capabilities. I think this is the highest role that a person can have in the world. |

Elaheh directed the conversation to the issue of the mother–child relationship in the film.

*Elaheh:*    In the first sequence, I did not know who is right and who is wrong.

*Mahsa:*    I think Mania and her son have a relationship which is similar to one of my friends and her mum's, who fight a lot of the time but then a minute later they hug and make up. I think divorce is a very difficult situation for a child to accept. In the end, the children are going to say, 'Our parents did not consider us.'

*Elaheh:*    I think this is a very interesting film about women because the other films so far show clearly that they are pro-women. This film is not like that. It is showing a woman going from one phase of her life to another and I feel Mania had not completely accepted her own choices at the beginning. Through her interaction with other women she wanted to reach a certainty. Mania's view of her relationship with her child was not about sacrificing herself for him. This is against the norm here. I think at the beginning she still had not convinced herself that she was doing the right thing and that is why she had a feeling of guilt. She was trying to convince the child and herself that what she was doing was right. But it was only at the end that she perhaps got closer to resolving this issue within herself and she was ready to accept that her son thought differently. That is why at the end, when the child says he wants to go to his grandmother's house, Mania says, fine. She was not fighting anymore. Perhaps in the end she reached an equilibrium.

That Elaheh referred to what Mania said as 'our words' at the beginning, and her comments about how the film ended, show the women's reflexive engagement with Mania's filmic circumstances. Elaheh is a working mother with children and thus deals with similar issues to Mania's. Interestingly, she interpreted the open ending of the film to mean Mania's reaching an equilibrium. Thus, she gave an empowering interpretation to the film as a whole. Mahsa's interpretation of the 'message' of the film as, 'women's world is much larger than men's' was a polemic and emotional response to the film. As I had seen before, these women's emotional engagement with the films was important for winning the arguments, but the reasons did not end there. On other occasions I heard women say that films like *Killing Rabids* (Beyza'i 2001) and *Women's Prison* showed how 'dirty Iranian men were'.[26] On these occasion there was no argument going on, and the comment came as an emotional statement of facts. Two married men also confided to me that their wives made similar damning comments after watching *Two Women* and *Women's Prison*. Obviously the gender discourse that these films mobilize is subversive to male dominance. The repetition of these polemics in engagement with 'women's films', as Butler's (1990) concept of the 'performativity' of gender suggests, could perhaps be constitutive of identity for the women who frequently voice such polemics.

On the other hand, Nader's argument is informed by a traditional gender discourse based on the assumption of women's 'natural' inferiority to men. However, both Elaheh and Mahsa challenged him, using their own knowledge of religious texts as well as their power of persuasion. This further demonstrates the vulnerability of the position of men with neopatriarchal mindsets, whose position is no longer on the solid knowledge base of tradition. As Sharabi points out, the position of men in neopatriarchal society is informed by neither genuine traditionalism nor authentic modernity (Sharabi 1988: 23). Hence, they are also challenged by the modern interpretations.

As in the first group, the women in the second engage in negotiation between women's religiously sanctioned responsibility for raising children and their new roles as working women. Their position and the men's discussed above show the transitional nature of the Iranian society. The women's feminist consciousness as demonstrated here could have a strong bearing on the direction and pace of change.

Another significant instance of redefinition of gender was the discussion of morality with regard to the prostitute and the woman who unveiled her head in the penultimate sequence.[27] The traditional gender discourse attributes greater sexual desire to women than men. According to the discourse, women's sexuality, 'if left uncontrolled by men, runs havoc, and is a real threat to social order' (Mir-Hosseini 2003: 10). This assumption in turn justifies men's control of women. Drawing on the same discourse, Nader worries about the same effect in 10, claiming a cause-effect relationship between the prostitute's words in one sequence and the woman's unveiling in another. This was rejected outright by the women. They did not consider the prostitute or the girl who had shaved her head in moral terms. Nader's moralist unfavourable reaction to the woman unveiling in the film was in contrast to his own wife, who appeared in front of me without head cover. Obviously, Mahsa denied Nader's control over how she dressed.

As for *hejab*, its practice in film is taken for granted in Iran. The appearance of women in *hejab*, even when at home, with their filmic family or alone, has been accepted as a convention because viewers understand how the filmmaking restrictions work. Therefore, in general the veil hardly gets a mention in conversations about films. When it once did in my presence, it was to do with fashion. Elaheh commented that 10 must have been made about a year and a half earlier. When I asked how she managed to date it, she told me that Mania's manteau was trendy at that period in Iran. As Mir-Hosseini notes, women's use of hijab as a fashion statement can subvert the official gender ideology (1999: 278).

*Conversation with Mania Akbari*

During my field research, I tried to arrange an interview with Kiarostami. Unfortunately, his busy schedule prevented me from meeting with him. However, I did manage to have a conversation with Mania, the lead actress in 10. In real life, Mania is no different from her persona in 10. She is divorced from Amin's father and like in the film she is a painter. She has since directed her own first feature 20 Fingers (2004), an award-winning film about women's issues.

I began by asking about her representation in the film.

*Mania:*   What you see on the screen is what was in my subconscious, and it flowed out of me. I cannot see the Mania on the screen as separate from myself. In fact, the film is 80 per cent true to my life.

I think Mania is fighting against stereotypes. Her struggle with Amin was a struggle against the taken-for-granted norms of life in Iran [and] the mentality of most of the men here. These are stereotypes like a 'good woman' or a 'good mother'.

Later she talked about 'modern Iranian men'.

*Mania:*   [They] are no different from our traditional men when it comes to dealing with women. This I think is to do with their mentality. I know many men who are avid readers, are very well aware of what is going on in the world, but when it comes to women they are extremely narrow-minded. Iranian men are influenced by the culture of this society. There are words that have been handed down to them and they have accepted without question, such as *gheyrat* and *namus* [roughly, jealousy and sexual honour]. I have heard these words more often from intellectual men than from traditional ones. I think these words are very superficial, that they are a means to maintain the status quo.

Having met Mania Akbari, I was assured that in real life she was just as strong-minded, career-focused and passionate about women's issues as the Mania 'character' who talked about these issues in the film. Mania's friends and family also 'acted' in the film, which took shape in front of the camera.

As Andrew (2005: 7) contends, Mania had much bearing on the way *10* was made. The film is as much Abbas Kiarostami's art as it is Mania Akbari's life and one could argue for a sort of joint authorship of the work for her. *10* is not the first instance of an actress's involvement in feminist representation in Iranian films. Beyza'i has attested that Taslimi, the lead actress in *Bashu, the Little Stranger,* had much input into that film's narrative as well. Such contributions are important in bringing women's agenda to the fore in films and hence in the discussions that they generate.

*20 Fingers* is about a young couple in a turbulent relationship, and, like Kiarostami's *10*, blurs the boundary between fiction and documentary. As with other women directors, Mania has made an obvious choice to deal with women's issues about which she feels passionate.

## Conclusion

In this chapter, I have focused on two 'women's films' – *Fifth Reaction* and *10* – whose narratives were both significantly shaped by women. I concentrated on the processes of negotiation of gender around these films as nodes of media activity. As Milani revealed to me, women filmmakers face more barriers than men do. Part of these difficulties relates to discrimination by some of their male colleagues, who are deeply sexist. On the other hand, the censors at times take issue with feminist perspectives in films and seek to block them. Nevertheless, as Milani indicated, by adapting her scripts, she and perhaps other female filmmakers manage to reduce the chances of their films being censored. Rather than self-censorship, this is an instance of adaptation and resistance.

In contrast to the black-and-white certainty of Milani's narrative and embodying Kiarostami's principle of uncertainty, *10* remains open to both feminist and neopatriarchal readings. My female informants showed more enthusiasm for the complex and open-ended indeterminacy of *10* than for the rather closed narrative of *Fifth Reaction*. But overall, they welcomed both films with their different but equally prominent feminist polemics which raise similar issues.

Women viewers appear to engage with the female characters' circumstances more closely than Ang (1990) and Inness (2004) have suggested. They use the opportunity to reflect on their own circumstances. Therefore, unlike Skeggs suggests, women's self-reflection in engagement with the media is not the preserve of Western women only (1997: 163).

The two films' polemics engaged women emotionally as well as intellectually. In all the discussion groups, the women participants indicated that the films focused on injustice to women. Hence in their reflections on their own circumstances, women viewers saw their own personal experiences as part of a larger political reality of patriarchy. Now that women can use the Islamized cinema space in women-only groups, they are able to reflect on issues collectively in relation to film. These groups may also foster building solidarity through sharing of experience. The discussions of 'women's films' are a significant moment of raising consciousness which is not dissimilar to 1960s CR groups in the USA.

While discussing these films, my female informants generally took an assertive position in their arguments and interpreted the films as reasons for their condemnation of patriarchy. The repetition of these polemics, as Butler's (1990) concept of the 'performativity' of gender suggests, could be constitutive of identity for the women who engage actively and frequently with the numerous 'women's films' in Iran today.

As the reactions of my male informants demonstrate, they take these instances of discussion about gender in relation to film very seriously. These men, with their neopatriarchal attitudes, no longer stand on the secure footing of tradition, therefore these negotiations of gender identities are particularly significant. This is because in the course of such discussions they have to engage with the women's arguments and inevitably assimilate some of their points. The situation is similar for male filmmakers, such as Kiarostami, who wittingly or unwittingly contribute to the women's movement by joining the trend of making films about women's issues.

Some of the 'women's films' have been part of the post-revolution 'art films' or 'festival films' that have entered the international film circuitry. In the next chapter, I will explore Iranians' reactions to the phenomenal acclaim of these films.

# 5 Transnational circulation and national perceptions

## Art films in the Iranian context[1]

## Introduction

Global media flows are generally considered as a straight line and not one that loops back to the place of origin. These loops do exist. Often films are viewed at an international festival before they are seen in the home country. These travels have consequences for the films' reception and perception in the place of origin. Marks (2000: xii) suggests that on their travels films build up impressions 'like a palimpsest' which they then pass onto other audiences.

Iranian cinema has been phenomenally prominent at international film festivals since the late 1980s. For example, in the Iranian calendar year 1382 (21/3/2003–20/3/2004) Iranian films had 1769 'appearances'[2] internationally and won 103 prizes (Atebba'i 2005: 66). On international film circuits, the films are often collectively referred to as the New Iranian Cinema.

The implications of these contacts on the politics of Iranian cinema deserve attention. Farahmand (2002) claims that filmmakers have had to compromise with the Iranian authorities to facilitate their films' participation at international festivals. Hence, she argues, their films have become apolitical. In order to test the validity of such arguments, in this chapter I examine the consequences of the international prominence of Iranian cinema.

In Iran, there has been a range of reactions to this international standing. These reactions are implicated in the discourses of identity. As I discuss below, some middle-class Iranians reject the films for their focus on the urban poor or villagers rather than modern middle-class lives with which they can identify. At times the films are viewed from the eyes of a presumed orientalizing Western 'other' who would find the lives of the characters in the films, and hence Iranians in general, 'backward'. Thus, some films which are supposedly telling demeaning stories about 'us' are rejected. In this chapter I will engage with these perspectives.

Perceptions of what constitute appropriate representations of Iran in film are complicated by the Iranian practice of keeping a clear demarcation between 'private' and 'public', a concept which extends to the boundary between 'inside' and 'outside' the country. Accordingly, what is at the core or inside should be protected or hidden from the outsiders, and this particularly applies to the discussion of 'problems at home'. Hence, defensive strategies such as disguise, allusion and ritual courtesy are employed in social interaction. Iranian cinema's traversing of national borders is an important instance of enunciation of Iranian identity when the 'inside'/'outside' or 'us'/'them' boundary is bridged and inevitably causes sensitivity and apprehension among Iranians.

The Iranian diaspora have also reacted with much emotion to the films. For many expatriate Iranians, such as myself, films have played a part in our identity construction. According to Sreberny (2000), the media play an important role in the exilic/diasporic group members' construction of identity by facilitating their 'looking back' at their country of origin, 'looking inward' to their (new) national host context and to 'looking around' transnationally.

The films have not only been a way of 'looking back' where we come from. Watching the films is also an occasion to get together with compatriots at festivals. Or at times, when we have seen the films with non-Iranian friends, they have been an occasion to talk about our culture/society/identity, sometimes defensively, after watching a film that seems to confirm Western prejudices, and generally proudly, after films that go against the stereotypical Western media representation of Iranians as 'religious fanatics'.

Some diasporic Iranians have been very active in organizing and promoting Iranian film events in the West, hence perpetuating the phenomenon of Iranian cinema. Some exiled opposition, on the other hand, have rejected post-revolution cinema, owing to their antagonism to any sort of dealing with the Islamic Republic. Both groups have written about the phenomenon. Celebrating the international appeal of Iranian art cinema, Naficy (2002: 54) asserts that this cinema is independent of Iranian tastes. Sayyad (1996: 3), an exiled Iranian director, believes that filmmakers who work under the restrictions in Iran have compromised their integrity.

The questions which I pose in this chapter are: How has the political engagement of Iranian cinema been affected by the international acclaim? What are the claims made about art films (festival films), by whom and to what ends? How and why do the reactions to the international prominence of Iranian films before and after the revolution differ from each other? Are the films that represent Iran internationally 'independent of Iranian tastes' as Naficy claims? How are boundaries of Iranian identity negotiated in the discourse about the films?

This chapter consists of four sections. In the first, I discuss the 1960s–70s Iranian New Wave cinema which was the precursor to the post-revolution films. Next, I examine the post-revolution 'art cinema' and give a quantitative perspective on the phenomenon. I also analyse the relationship between art cinema and the Iranian authorities. In the third section, I examine the role played by award-winning Iranian filmmakers. Finally, I consider audience reactions to the phenomenon.

This chapter addresses the under-researched implications of global media flows for discourses of identity.

## Reactions to the New Wave films (1969–79)

With the international acclaim for *The Cow* (Mehrju'i 1969) at a number of European and American festivals, critics in Iran and abroad declared that a New

Wave had begun in Iranian cinema. In Iran these films were celebrated as *sinema-ye motefavet* or Alternative Cinema. *The Cow* tells the story of Hassan, a middle-aged villager, who owns the only cow in the village and is obsessed with her. When the cow, which is pregnant, dies, Hassan is unable to cope with the loss, goes insane and gradually takes on the identity of the cow. The film met with much critical praise in Iran and did well at the box office before it came to the attention of international festivals two years later. *The Cow* was famously only released when the censors inserted a note at the beginning of the film saying that events depicted in the film took place before the Pahlavi period. The 1959 censorship code prohibited presentation of 'backwardness' which would 'damage the state's national prestige' (Golmakani 1992: 20). Obviously the film's acknowledgement of the existence of such poverty-stricken villages in Iran was embarrassing for the Pahlavi regime, which claimed to have created a modern state.

Unlike the authorities, none of the commentators writing about *The Cow* at the time demonstrated any sign of self-consciousness about the film's depiction of the poverty-stricken village to the outside world. The commentaries which were published in popular periodicals of the time were mainly written by a number of intellectuals, some of whom such as Farrokh Gaffary were filmmakers themselves (Omid 1998: 538–49 for a number of reviews written at the time). The same applies to *A Simple Event* (Shahid-Sales 1973), which was also filmed in a village and once again was not criticized by Iranian intellectuals for its focus on the deprived life of villagers (Omid 1998: 659–62).[3]

Considering the fact that after the revolution many have disapproved of award-winning films centring on the urban or rural poor, it is surprising that no similar criticism was voiced before the revolution. Several factors could have contributed to this. First of all, at the time Iranian intellectuals were preoccupied with *gharbzadegi* (West-struckness), i.e. Western influences in relation to their identity. The self-consciousness of Iranian middle-class intellectuals was due to the difficulty of reconciling their traditional (often rural) backgrounds with the modernity of their current social stratum (Fischer 1984: 172). In the midst of the social changes of the 1960s and 70s, many Iranian intellectuals indicated the need to find an essential Iranian identity to which they could return (Al-e Ahmad 1982; Shari'ati 1979). Village life, and hence how it was represented in *The Cow*, seemed to possess a certain authenticity which life in the newly modernized cities lacked. Along the same lines, many of the populist films of the period were about the pains of urbanization and longing to return to villages (Rohani 2000: 286–90). In addition, a focus on life in a village was an implicit criticism of the urbanization and modernization of society under the Pahlavis. Lastly, at that time urbanization was quite a new phenomenon and many people maintained a close link with their rural places of origin.

As mentioned in Chapter 2, although the New Wave filmmakers generally continued working until 1978, the output of this cinema was in decline by the mid-1970s and had slowed to a trickle at the dawn of the revolution. The rising cost of filmmaking and the discontinuation of adequate funding from the state institutes made it difficult for filmmakers to continue their work. The inundation of the local

*Table 5.1* The international appearance of Iranian cinema in figures

| Year Iranian (Gregorian) | Number of presences | Number of awards | Number of Iranian jury members at festivals |
|---|---|---|---|
| 1358 (~1979) | 38 | 3 | – |
| 1359 (~1980) | 43 | 2 | – |
| 1360 (~1981) | 65 | 9 | – |
| 1361 (~1982) | 36 | 1 | 1 |
| 1362 (~1983) | 43 | 3 | – |
| 1363 (~1984) | 30 | 3 | 1 |
| 1364 (~1985) | 51 | 4 | – |
| 1365 (~1986) | 52 | – | – |
| 1366 (~1987) | 47 | 2 | – |
| 1367 (~1988) | 94 | 5 | – |
| 1368 (~1989) | 174 | 19 | – |
| 1369 (~1990) | 540 | 22 | 2 |
| 1370 (~1991) | 390 | 27 | – |
| 1371 (~1992) | 313 | 23 | 1 |
| 1372 (~1993) | 519 | 40 | 5 |
| 1373 (~1994) | 514 | 21 | 4 |
| 1374 (~1995) | 753 | 43 | 12 |
| 1375 (~1996) | 687 | 27 | 7 |
| 1376 (~1997) | 766 | 49 | 9 |
| 1377 (~1998) | 749 | 70 | 13 |
| 1378 (~1999) | 770 | 74 | 15 |
| 1379 (~2000) | 1155 | 114 | 30 |
| 1380 (~2001) | 1184 | 123 | 24 |
| 1381 (~2002) | 1462 | 110 | 31 |
| 1382 (~2003) | 1769 | 103 | 35 |

Source: Produced by the author using box office figures from Atebba'i (2004a: 337) and Atebba'i (2005: 67–68).

market with Hollywood also played its part in the decline of screening opportunities for the New Wave.

The examination of Table 5.1 indicates that the number of international appearances of Iranian films has been steadily increasing since the late 1980s. This is while the number of awards and jury members were steadily increasing until the year 2000 and have since been stable. The 1990s appear to have been the heyday, when New Iranian Cinema was still novel. Now (2000 onwards) this cinema is established on the world scene, and hence there is more of a plateau.

While in Table 5.1 festivals and their awards are considered indiscriminately, it is important to note that festivals are of course not considered equally important as one another. On a few occasions (see later), the Ministry of Culture and Islamic Guidance (MCIG) authorities have lauded the achievements of Iranian filmmakers at Cannes Film Festival while other festivals' awards have not received equal attention. Nevertheless, the fact that tables such as the above are published in *Mahnameh*,which is a major film periodical as well as a book published by the MCIG (Atebba'i 2004a), indicates the significance of the numerical data in Iran.[4]

Some characteristics are common to a large number of Iranian films which have won awards at festivals. They are mainly made with non-professional actors, are filmed on location rather than in studios, contain a number of long takes, blur the boundary between documentary and fiction, and many of their narratives are open ended. A main feature of many such films is that they appear to be 'a slice of life', with seemingly little dramatization or fictionalization. The stories are often about the urban or rural poor.

Outside Iran, these films have often been characterized as 'humanist', while the terms 'poetic realism', which has been used in relation to French cinema in the 1930s, and 'neorealism', which is a film movement in Italian cinema in the 1940s and the 1950s, have been employed in relation to Iranian cinema as well. The MCIG labels such films as *mokhatab-e khas* (literally for 'special audiences' in contrast to *mokhatab-e 'amm* or for 'common audiences'). While generally 'art film' and *mokhatab-e khas* coincide, at times the designation of the title appears arbitrary. I discuss this issue using the example of *Women's Prison* (2001) later in this chapter.

## State authorities and international success

Gradually, along with the political leaders' rhetoric of exporting the revolution, the authorities began to promote Iranian cinema abroad. 'Ali-Reza Shoja'nuri, Farabi's head of International Affairs at the time, was initially met with little enthusiasm from international festivals, with only 1 per cent of his letters being answered (Atebba'i 2003: 79). Sacred Defence films, such as *Realm of Lovers* (Karbakhsh 1984), which were sent to festivals were rejected (Babagoli 2003: 13). In 1985, however, Naderi's *The Runner* was accepted by some major festivals and subsequently won a number of awards. Far from ideological dogma, and set in the period before the revolution, *The Runner* was about the daily struggles of a determined orphan child. The success was followed by Kiarostami's *Where Is the Friend's House?* (1987) another film about a resolute child. These were followed by the critical acclaim for *Bashu, the Little Stranger* (Beyza'i 1985, released in 1989). Since then Iranian cinema has never looked back.[5]

To a degree these films coincided with the values of the Islamic regime for being about the lives of *mostaz'afin* (the downtrodden) whom the ruling elite claimed to represent. At that time the new cinema authorities insisted that filmmakers should avoid making films about affluent Iranians (see Golmakani's comments in Chapter 2).

Although one would expect the triumph of this cinema to have been a cause of celebration for the Iranian authorities, their reactions were more complicated than that. Beheshti, former head of Farabi Cinema Foundation, who is closely associated with the reformists, told me in an interview,

> from 1989, we saw in practice that if we announced the international success of Iranian cinema in the country, this would work against cinema as a whole. That is why we blocked [the news getting out]. [But] when it was reported in the international media, it was publicized inside the country by Iranian

journalists. The reason why we refrained from reporting it ourselves was that we knew it would become a politically sensitive issue.

By referring to the possible detrimental consequences for cinema as a whole, Beheshti is pointing to his fear of conservatives becoming suspicious of the motives behind foreign awards. They would then create obstacles for the way cinema was run under him and that would perhaps threaten the continuation of his role as the head of Farabi. Beheshti told me that some conservatives, who he did not name, did harbour such suspicions. Beheshti was asked questions such as 'how could an Iranian film win at a festival where France, Germany, Italy, and other Western countries have films?' Along the same lines, the (then conservative-minded) filmmaker Hatamikia wrote at the time, '[At the festivals] there is a political perspective at work. There is no way anything would happen without the existence of such perspectives' (Hatamikia 1991: 170).

Such suspicion was fuelled by the fact that the FIFF, with which they were most familiar, was (and still is) influenced by political considerations (see also Chapter 2). Furthermore, such suspicions were reinforced by the expert opinion of some prominent film critics, who use Hollywood cinema as their yardstick. For example, Khosrow Dehqan, a famous critic, claimed, '[T]he main problem with Kiarostami's work is that it is a stranger to the main elements of cinema, namely mise-en-scene, camera and editing. The whole of cinema is made up of these elements' (quoted in Mohammad-Kashi 2000: 64).

The misgivings of the conservative authorities were further nourished by the fact that some of these films were overtly political and came close to the 'red lines'. This was particularly true of the works of Mohsen Makhmalbaf. For example, in 1991 two of his films, *Time of Love* and *Nights of Zayandehrud,* caused much controversy. *Time of Love* told three versions of the love affair of a married woman. Reacting to these films, some conservatives went so far as calling them 'satanic art'. Ayatollah Jannati, a powerful conservative figure, said in a Friday sermon,

> Sometimes [cinema authorities] say proudly that our film[s] are praised abroad and they conclude that art is revived in Iran. What an achievement! Shall we be happy when those who are responsible for the spread of [moral] corruption in the world praise us . . .?
>
> (Anon. 1991: 88)

Apart from the conservatives' general lack of appreciation for art cinema, their political concerns play a major part in shaping their reactions. In general they do not miss any opportunity to attack their reformist rivals and often cinema has provided them with the excuse for an offensive. When it suits their political agenda, they often claim that conspiracies must be at work. At that particular period, Makhmalbaf's films were used by the conservatives to attack Mohammad Khatami, then Minister of Culture and Islamic Guidance. On the other hand, as the self-appointed guardians of public morality, some of the conservatives do believe that the West wants to exert a 'morally corrupting' influence in Iran. For example, during the same period, Ayatollah Khamenei, the supreme leader, warned against the Western 'cultural aggression' which the media, including the satellite TV, were allegedly launching against Iran (Siavoshi 1997: 514). As mentioned earlier, shortly afterwards the embattled Khatami resigned from the ministry.

The early 1990s saw the gradual replacement of the reformists in charge of cinema by conservatives who generally had little understanding of it. However, as some of the new authorities learned more about cinema, their views of it changed. This is perhaps best illustrated with an example: Atebba'i, a former Farabi official, told me in an interview that when Talebzadeh replaced Shoja'nuri as the head of International Affairs at Farabi in 1996, things seemed to be about to change.

At his first meeting with those working under him, Talebzadeh told them that, from then on, they had to promote films which contained revolutionary values, such as the Sacred Defence films. He also said he would stop sending secular films to festivals. Atebba'i and his colleagues tried to dissuade him by warning him about the negative publicity which stopping the films would create for the Islamic Republic. In an effort to change Talebzadeh's mind, Atebba'i and others got the Ministry of Foreign Affairs involved. Atebba'i recalls a ministry official saying that in the bulletins of international news agencies Kiarostami's name was mentioned twice as many times as the Iranian foreign minister's. Finally, the intervention of middle-ranking officials in the Ministry of Foreign Affairs resulted in Talebzadeh changing his mind. After about a year at the job in 1997, Talebzadeh revealed his reversed position by saying he had recently told some Sacred Defence filmmakers to try to make 'beautiful films like Kiarostami's' because 'film festivals were concerned with the quality of our films'.

Since 1997, conditions have been rather easier for Iranian art films' international exposure. The government has relinquished its monopoly on the promotion and distribution of films abroad, although they require filmmakers to get their permission prior to screening their films internationally.[6] The reformists have been more eager to claim some credit for the international acclaim by celebrating non-controversial films and honouring some award-winning filmmakers by special ceremonies on their return to Iran. For example, referring to humanist values of the films Khatami claimed, 'Iranian cinema is the most honourable cinema in the world.'[7] Nevertheless, the reformists have generally tried to avoid controversy by not drawing attention to films which raise contentious issues. For example, in 2000 Mohajerani (then Minister of Culture and Islamic Guidance) honoured Samira Makhmalbaf, Bahman Ghobadi and Hasan Yektapanah for their films which had recently won awards at Cannes Film Festival, but totally ignored Jafar Panahi, whose controversial film *The Circle* (2000) had won the top prize at the prestigious Venice Film Festival (see later in this chapter for further discussion of the film).[8]

Farahmand (2002) shows a similar attitude to the Iranian reformists in her selective focus on apolitical films (see 'Reactions among cinema goers' later in this chapter). She suggests that a connection exists between the diplomatic concerns of Western countries and the festivals they host. She claims:

The growing attention given to Iranian cinema in the West must also be linked to attempts in recent years to develop diplomatic ties and cultural exchanges between Iran and the West.

(Farahmand 2002: 94)

Yet, contrary to Farahmand's reasoning, the prominence of Iranian cinema in the West has continued regardless of ups and downs in diplomatic relations. This is evidenced by a large number of Iranian films in festivals in the USA after George Bush's denouncement of Iran as a member of the 'axis of evil'.[9] Moreover, both before and after 9/11, the US immigration authorities on several occasions treated Iranian filmmakers with disrespect. Panahi was detained in chains for several hours while in transit at the New York airport and Kiarostami was once refused a visa. If there had been a genuine and concerted attempt at 'ping-pong diplomacy' using Iranian cinema as Farahmand (2002: 95) claims, such incidents would have been highly unlikely.

Farahmand, explicitly, and Sadr (2002a: 227), implicitly, suggest that Iranian authorities used films about children in order to promote a humanist vision of Iran abroad. Farahmand claims that the proliferation of children's stories in Iranian cinema 'should be linked to the emerging post-war concern to renegotiate an image of Iranian society and to counter the militant revolutionary stereotypes of Iranians through representations of children' (2002: 105).

I argue that rather than a conscious decision on the part of filmmakers or the MCIG to portray such an image, the use of children was necessitated by factors such as funding and stylistic considerations. Since the beginning of the New Wave in the 1960s, the Centre for Intellectual Development of Children and Adolescents (or the CIDCA) was one of the major funders of art cinema. Even before the revolution, they funded many award-winning Iranian films, such as Kiarostami's *The Traveller* (1974), and Naderi's *Harmonica* (1974). In the first decade after the 1979 revolution, the CIDCA was perhaps the only source of funding that was not strictly controlled by government. Their financial support was important for secular filmmakers who did not have access to other governmental sources.

Apart from the funding issue, a close consideration of the stylistic necessities of Iranian cinema made working with children a logical choice for the filmmakers. Many Iranian directors of art films use non-professional actors, often children or villagers, and shoot on location. This is partly because, as Kiarostami has shown, children are easier to manipulate in order to get them to 'act' realistically. For example, early in the filming of *Where Is the Friend's House*, Kiarostami took a Polaroid photo of a child, who carried the photo everywhere with him. Just before a particular shot when the child was supposed to cry, Kiarostami ripped the photo and the child began to sob, creating the realism he desired. Kiarostami has also just as easily worked with adult villagers whom he has controlled as effectively. In addition, many of these filmmakers avoided risks of confrontation with the conservatives by staying away from political sensitivities and instead focused on children instead of adults (Sadr 2002a).

Once a few films about children had won awards in the late 1980s and the early 1990s, a trend began with numerous films with child protagonists emerging from Iran. Understandably, filmmakers tried to emulate the earlier films, knowing that such films would be easy to promote internationally.

### Promotions of Iranian cinema at the FIFF

The main occasion for the involvement of Iranian authorities, notably the Farabi Cinema Foundation, in the promotion of Iranian cinema is Fajr International Film Festival (FIFF). Every year since 1982 the FIFF, the biggest film event in Iran, has been held in February, coinciding with the anniversary of the revolution. Since 1997, it has been divided into two main sections: 'Iranian cinema competition' and 'International competition'. While in the former all Iranian films are included, in the latter only those Iranian films which are considered likely to do well at international festivals are shown. This arrangement makes it easier for international guests of the festivals to decide which films to see. Since the introduction of the 'International competition', the jury of this competition includes a number of international festival representatives.[10]

Every year, a number of festival representatives and critics from around the world are invited to attend the festival. Initially in 1991, Shoja'nuri, then head of International Affairs at Farabi, claimed that inviting foreign guests to the festival was for promoting 'revolutionary thought' elsewhere in the world. However, the conservatives such as a filmmaker and critic called Avini doubted Shoja'nuri's sincerity in wanting to export the 'culture of revolution'. He wrote at the time that if Shoja'nuri genuinely wanted to do so, he would have tried to promote the making of films for 'ordinary foreign citizens' rather than catering for the elite critics (Avini 2002: 177). In spite of such objections, the warm reception of foreign festival representatives and film critics became more elaborate over the years.

In 2003 when I attended the festival, international guests stayed at one of Tehran's top hotels where they watched films at exclusive screenings. In the evenings a 'Film Bazaar' was organized at the hotel where the guests mingled with filmmakers and representatives of production companies.

Although Farabi no longer has a monopoly in the promotion of Iranian films at festivals outside Iran, it still has a prominent position in this regard. Farabi not only promotes the films it produces internationally. In order to be associated with the success of films which could win awards, it gives minor financial incentives to the filmmakers to encourage them to have Farabi distribute their films abroad.[11] In spite of such promotions, apart from few exceptions discussed below, filmmakers generally gain only prestige and recognition, and not money, when their films are shown abroad. They rely on the exhibition of their films in Iran for financial returns.

### Exhibition of art films in Iran

Before 1997 screening schedules in Tehran were dictated by the MCIG. At the time a number of the better cinema halls in the capital were assigned to art films. Of particular importance among cinema halls was *Azadi*, one of the most popular in Tehran. *Azadi* was not only in a prime location, it also had up-to-date picture and sound equipment as well as comfortable seating. Most cinema auditoriums have not been refurbished in years and their picture and sound quality are poor. Since *Azadi* often showed art films, it had a major impact on those films in terms of box office takings. In 1997 *Azadi* burnt down in an accident, dealing a blow to art cinema economically.

Since 1997, the number of movie theatres allocated to art films has been reduced. Thus, being labelled *mokhatab-e khas* (for special audiences) by the MCIG is a liability. Furthermore, the theatres set aside for these films are not in prime locations, and this has been a further blow to art cinema. Makhmalbaf told me in an interview:

> Now that *Azadi* has burned down and *Asr-e Jadid* [another cinema that used to screen art films] shows banal films, there is no cinema in *Iran* for you to show your films.[12]

As for the fact that it is now the cinemas in downtown Tehran that show art films, instead of *Azadi* and *Asr-e Jadid*, which were located close to most universities, Makhmalbaf said:

> That is like taking a book which is to be sold in front of the university to downtown Tehran and afterwards say, 'Look, the book does not sell well.' You should sell a medical book in front of the school of medicine. We have lost the cinema halls for art cinema.

Makhmalbaf told me that the limitation on screening of art films amounts to a new type of censorship in Iran.

The labelling of films by the MCIG has not been consistent with how the films have been received internationally. For example, in spite of the international acclaim for *Women's Prison* (Hekmat 2002), it was *not* labelled as *mokhatab-e khas* and was therefore released in a large number of cinemas.[13] The wide exposure helped the film to become a box office hit.

### *Censorship of art films*

Some of the films the Iranian authorities have deemed unsuitable for exhibition in Iran are popular with International festivals. A compromise which has developed over the years has been to censor these films for screening in Iran while giving them a permit to be screened outside the country with little or no censorship. While some filmmakers have been willing to allow censorship of their films, others have resisted, resulting in standoffs with the authorities. For example, when Manijeh Hekmat, the director of *Women's Prison*, was faced with the banning of her film, she allowed it to be censored in Iran while the complete version was screened at festivals overseas.

Kasehsaz, former head of the censorship section of the MCIG, who made the decision about the censorship of *Women's Prison,* told me in an interview:

> After I censored the film, [the conservative politicians] saw it, and said things like, 'You should have cut more; if this film is shown in Iran or abroad it is against the interests of the regime', etc. But I refused. When the film went abroad, [Iranian exiles] were saying this film is portraying Iranian prisons to be much better than they actually are. I just did my job regardless of such claims.

Aware of how films are often interpreted by the Iranian exiled opposition, the censors' main concern is the reactions inside the country, where only the censored version of the film is supposed to be seen. Nevertheless, uncensored versions of many such films make it to the local video stores. For example, in 2003 when I was in Iran, while the censored version of *Women's Prison* was being shown in the cinemas, a subtitled version in its entirety was readily available on video.

In spite of the advantages of compromising with the censors, some filmmakers have resisted censorship altogether. Panahi sent his films *The Circle* and *Crimson Gold* (2003) to the Venice and Cannes festivals respectively, without a permit from the MCIG (see Figure 5.1). This was of course not without adverse consequences (see my discussion of *Crimson Gold* later in this chapter). At times filmmakers seeking international permits have had their films confiscated by the MCIG. For example, Jalili's *Abjad* (2003) was withheld from Toronto and other festivals where it had already been advertised.

*Figure 5.1*  Still from Jafar Panahi's *The Circle.*

The advent of digital filmmaking has contributed to a lessening of the control of the MCIG's censorship on filmmaking. The low cost of digital films has resulted in a higher number being made by young filmmakers, many of which take part in festivals abroad. According to Tahmasebi, a middle-ranking official from the MCIG, the sheer number of digital films produced in Iran poses a challenge for the censors in terms of monitoring what is sent abroad. 'The MCIG just cannot enforce censorship,' he said with a smile on his face.

## Art cinema filmmakers

In the 1990s, films by Kiarostami and Makhmalbaf came to exemplify Iranian cinema abroad. Kiarostami, and many others who followed his style, generally made films about children or villagers in stories with philosophical implications. Films by Mohsen Makhmalbaf, however, as discussed in Chapter 3, generally remained engaged with the grim social realities of urban Iran, such as the aftermath of the war, poverty and gender inequality.

The screening of the films abroad was often accompanied by commentaries from the filmmakers in interviews and Q and A sessions, which were translated and published in Iran. On those occasions, Makhmalbaf was outspoken in his criticism of the lack of freedom of expression in his native country. In contrast, Kiarostami tried to avoid contentious issues, as he had done in his films. For example, rather than criticizing censorship, he would often justify it, saying that even without such restrictions he would make the same films. In one interview, he explained, 'I will not be proud and pleased to make a film which gets banned. I have to use my knowledge of the government and the socio-political situation to pass under the censorship blade. I don't want the cut-up pieces of my film be taken out of a box years later' (Tabe'-Mohammadi 2000: 44).

An often-quoted instance of Kiarostami's avoidance of a clash with the censors is the circumspect ending of his film *Taste of Cherry* (1997). The film tells the story of Mr Badi'i who has dug a grave by a dirt road on the outskirts of Tehran and is looking for someone to bury him there when (and if) he commits suicide. He approaches a few strangers, none of whom agree to do so. In the end, Baqeri, a middle-aged taxidermist, agrees to his request, but tells Badi'i that he too had decided to commit suicide as a young man, but when he had gone up to hang himself from a tree, he had eaten a mulberry and the simple sweetness of the fruit made him change his mind. He reminds Badi'i of such simple pleasures such as the taste of cherry. Badi'i asks him to go the following morning to the grave, where Badi'i will be lying from the night before. He insists that Baqeri should make sure he is not simply asleep before burying him. That night Badi'i lies in the grave under a sky which is occasionally lit up by lightning. The final sequence of the film, shot on a handycam, shows behind-the-scenes footage, including long shots of Badi'i talking to Kiarostami.

Hamid Reza Sadr, a well-known film critic, has criticized the filmmaker for the inclusion of handycam footage at the end of the film. While the penultimate sequence is imbued with the grim prospect of the man killing himself, to Sadr the added footage of behind-the-scenes action appears to lighten the mood (i.e. what you just saw was a film after all) making the ending ambiguous. In spite of Kiarostami's insistence to the contrary, Sadr believes that the scene was a compromise. Because to suggest that the man commits suicide would have led to perhaps a permanent ban, given the authorities' religious view of suicide (Sadr 1999: 13).

Along the same lines, as mentioned earlier, Farahmand condemns 'political escapism' in Iranian cinema, claiming that in order to be allowed to go to foreign festivals, internationally successful filmmakers have refrained from politically contentious issues (Farahmand 2002). According to her, the Iranian authorities have in return facilitated the films' attendance at festivals. Farahmand's argument echoes that of the earlier mentioned claim by Sayyad (1996: 3), who asserts that working under the filmmaking restrictions in Iran compromises the filmmakers' integrity. While there is certain truth to Farahmand and Sayyad's claim that the films do not (and I in fact cannot possibly) challenge the basis of authority in the Islamic republic, as I have shown in this thesis, it is inaccurate to claim that the art films are all apolitical.

As I demonstrated in the preceding chapters, not only do the authorities treat many 'social films' politically, but also the reception of the films shows that they are interpreted in political terms as well. Farahmand ignores many films that have been politically engaged, such as those of Makhmalbaf, Bani-Etemad, Milani and Panahi. Furthermore, pointing out the difficulties that Kiarostami encountered before and after sending his *Taste of Cherry* to Cannes Film Festival, Devictor (2002: 74) demonstrates that the conservatives in Iran have not been particularly favourable to Kiarostami either.

Rather than becoming apolitical, over the years many filmmakers have become more engaged with the political situation. As I discussed in Chapter 4, Kiarostami's *10* (2002) deals with a number of contentious issues.

Recent moves by Kiarostami, such as the making of a controversial film, are taken as an indication of his *javanmardi*, an Iranian ideal type denoting *shoja'at* or bravery and *sekhavat* or generosity (Adelkhah 1999: 4, 6–7). In May 2000, Abbas Kiarostami was given the San Francisco Film Festival's Akira Kurosawa award for lifetime achievement in cinema. Kiarostami then called a veteran exiled Iranian actor, Behruz Vosuqi, to the stage and handed him the award to loud applause by the Iranian expatriates present at the ceremony. To help revive Vosuqi's career,[14] Kiarostami said, 'This is an award for all the years he's worked in the cinema in Iran, and all the years he's awaited work here in this country. And I look forward to his return to the cinema' (Avila 2001). Iraj Karimi, a director who is a friend of Kiarostami's, told me that upon his return to Iran after the festival, Kiarostami noticed a change in the way he was treated by his neighbours and some others who used to ignore him previously despite his international fame. Now they all treated him with respect, praising him for his gesture to an actor who had acted as a *javanmard* in many films before the revolution. Renowned critic Ahmad Talebinejad told me that another instance of Kiarostami's *sekhavat* or generosity was that wherever he was a festival judge he would make sure that Iranian films won awards.[15] In 2003, when Kiarostami's *10* was banned in Iran, for the first time he spoke out against censorship at a public event in Tehran and was applauded by the audience, who were taken by surprise by the filmmaker who previously justified censorship.[16] This showed his courage or *shoja'at*. Such acts are interpreted as Kiarostami's demonstration of *javanmardi*. Another courageous move by Kiarostami was writing the script for *Crimson Gold*, a banned film made by his controversial protégé Jafar Panahi.

Panahi too started his career making films about children, but has moved on to films about the harsh realities of life in urban Iran. His *The Circle* was about the plight of a number of underclass women on furlough from prison. The women seem to be released from a smaller jail into a bigger one in which they are continually victimized. In spite of their attempts to avoid going back to jail, the women are all rounded up at the end at a police station. The film was banned by the MCIG.[17] Panahi told me that because he was worried about *The Circle* being 'confiscated and mutilated', he made multiple copies of his film and hid them in different places in Iran. Later he sent a copy of the film abroad before seeking permission from the MCIG. Knowing that a copy of Panahi's film was already in Venice, the MCIG gave him a permit just days prior to its screening at the festival.

Sending films to festivals without permission from the MCIG is not without its risks. I interviewed Panahi in Tehran three days before the premiere of his *Crimson Gold* at Cannes. He was still hoping for an 'international permit' from the MCIG and he said he was in contact with the MCIG several times a day about that. The MCIG had asked him to cut some sequences out of the film, but he refused. Panahi told me that he was worried about the future of his career if he showed his film without their approval. Nevertheless, when the permit did not arrive, he did not withdraw his film from the festival.

The question to ask here is why Iranian filmmakers like Kiarostami and Panahi have become more radical. Panahi claims that his refusal to give in is setting an example for the younger filmmakers to follow, as well as making it possible for them to continue filming, as he explained to me:

> When people like me do these things, we know what position we are in. We are recognized around the world and so [the authorities] cannot pressure us too much. If something happens to us, it will be reported everywhere and even here [in Iran]. We have to risk pushing the limits for those kids who are just starting off. Those who are making their first films are forced to do whatever they are told; they allow the censors to mutilate their films. If we do not stand up to the censors the conditions will be worse for the young filmmakers. This would mean that this cinema would not continue; it would be suppressed and end with the few people who make films now. A cinema can survive if it has new filmmakers and makes new films. If we don't resist, the path will be blocked for the new filmmakers and therefore in the eyes of the next generation we will be responsible. There is no other way.

The confidence the major Iranian filmmakers show in defiance of censorship is further enhanced by not having to depend on Iranian sources financially. Since the mid

1990s, some Iranian filmmakers have been involved in co-productions, using funds from countries such as France, Switzerland, Canada and Italy. In most cases, in return for their 50 per cent investment in a film, the foreign investors take 100 per cent of box office returns in their respective countries and 50 per cent of the ticket sales elsewhere in the world, while 100 per cent of the returns in Iran belong to the filmmaker.[18] Such funding is of course not easily available.

Iran's best-known filmmakers, such as Makhmalbaf and Kiarostami, finance their own films and subsequently sell the international distribution rights to foreign companies for between US$300,000 and US$750,000.[19] Iranian films are screened at art house cinemas across the world, with some films such as *The White Balloon* (1995) and *Kandahar* (2001) doing well at the box office.[20] As a result of this transnational investment in art cinema in Iran, some directors have become independent of Iranian financial support and hence, to a degree, of the political control of the Islamic Republic.

### 'Film-e sefareshi' (film to order) and nationalism

Aspiring to the heights of top Iranian directors, many hopeful filmmakers have attempted to make films aimed at international festivals. This has led to a large number of films that emulate elements of Kiarostami's cinema. In Iran, disparaging labels such as *film-e sefareshi* (film to order) have been used for such films. Others refer to them as *film-e jashvareh'i* (festival film), a label they use with the same level of disapproval. Some claim that at times festivals have 'ordered' a certain type of film to be made in Iran. For example, the filmmaker Hatamikia told me:

> Once when I was editing a film, a filmmaker [whose name he asked me to omit] was editing his documentary in the room next door. Then he took his documentary to Cannes and he was told to go back and remake it as a *mostanad-e dastani* (literally narrative-documentary). He came back, remade his film and took it to the festival to receive an award. It worries me to see how a foreign festival decides what a filmmaker should make.

During the course of my research, others told me stories of festivals having influenced the type of films some filmmakers made. However, it is highly unlikely that films are made to order exactly in the fashion Hatamikia claims. Nevertheless, since some filmmakers such as Majid Majidi, who are respected even in conservative circles, have worked with foreign funding, such funding is not usually taken as compromising a filmmaker.

I brought up the issue of pandering to festival tastes in my interview with the director Jafar Panahi, who told me:

> When I am making a film no one matters to me, neither Iranians nor non-Iranians. I don't care what the politicians will say either. When you are not dependent on the government, then you can say exactly what you want, or what you understand. I have one viewer and that is my conscience.

Shahbazi, another award-winning Iranian filmmaker, whose *Deep Breath* featured at Cannes 2003, also denied that his films were solely aimed at festivals, arguing that they were meant primarily for educated Iranians:

> There are many things in Iranian films which are difficult to fathom for the non-Iranian viewer and are best understood by Iranians, particularly the better educated ones. For example, there is a scene in my film where the girl says to the boy that she likes classical and blues music and asks the boy about his favourite music. The boy simply answers, 'Dariush!'; end of conversation.[21] For us, Dariush's music means a lot of things but for the non-Iranian that is just an unfamiliar name.

Indeed, as Shahbazi suggests, there are a number of elements in all such Iranian films which are much easier to understand for the more educated Iranians. At the same time, this does not diminish festivals' interest in Iranian films. Lack of understanding on the part of viewers may be (mis-)interpreted as 'ambiguity in art', which may increase a film's appeal.

Making films with festival audiences in mind is not exclusive to Iranian art cinema; it is common among filmmakers who want to transcend the limited local market for their films. This has at times led filmmakers to forgo the possibility of domestic public release by including themes and stories that they know to be highly unlikely to be shown in their country of origin.[22] Although I do not have any positive evidence of this practice among Iranian filmmakers, I do not discount its possibility. This is because filmmakers are aware of the extent of the black market in Iran and know that their film will reach the domestic market on bootleg videos and eventually be seen. Panahi and Makhmalbaf talked to me with obvious pleasure about how their banned films have been seen by many Iranians.

As mentioned in Chapter 3, the circulation of banned films on illegal video CDs (or VCDs) and to a lesser degree DVDs defies state control and hence renders Iranian cinema closer to radical media for remaining outside the channels of distribution controlled by the state or commercial interests. The unofficial black market in VCDs is not regulated by the state and of course does not benefit the filmmakers either. However, because filmmakers like Panahi, Makhmalbaf and Kiarostami do not rely on the domestic box office returns, they can afford to be less concerned about the reactions of the Iranian censors and hence be more daring in their films. As I explained earlier, these films do get distributed through the black market in VCDs.

One of the allegations against these films is that they show 'backwardness, poverty and negative images of Iranian society' which conform to the stereotype of the country, and that is why they are popular at festivals. For example, speaking about the ban on *The Circle,* Pezeshk, the Cinema Deputy (2001–3), said he would not allow the screening of the film because it has 'such a completely dark and humiliating perspective'.[23] Endorsing the same judgement, the director Hatamikia told me, 'when [these filmmakers] make a film in cities, they have a very dark and negative perspective like that of the [exiled] opposition to the regime'. Hatamikia's claim

*Figure 5.2*  Still from Rakhshan Bani-Etemad's *May Lady*.

is rather exaggerated, because there are many award-winning films made in the cities, such as *Children of Heaven* (Majidi 1997) and *May Lady* (Bani-Etemad 1997), that do not fit his descriptions (see Figure 5.2). Furthermore, the domestic reaction to these films shows that their makers are attuned to Iranian tastes as well. Many of these films have also been considered important in Iran. For example, Iranian cinema guilds chose *The Circle* as the best film at their annual award ceremony in 2001.[24] When I asked Panahi about the alleged 'dark images' in his films, he said:

> My latest film *Crimson Gold* is filmed mainly in a penthouse, in an apartment tower in a posh suburb of Tehran. Why aren't [the authorities] allowing this film then? Whenever the film does not comply with what they want, they stick labels to it in order to push away those filmmakers who are independent and to create restrictions for their work.

This view is not, however, shared by all. A director who asked not to be named explained:

> Talking about Iranian problems abroad is like talking about your family problems to someone outside your family. In the same way that you would not discuss your family problems outside, you should not discuss your country's problems abroad either.

When I asked him about what sort of social problems were OK to show in films, he responded, 'only those which we share with modern societies'.

The above filmmaker's attitude is consistent with the Iranian nationalist concern to appear modern. The Pahlavi regime's drive to modernize Iran has left a sediment on the middle class's collective common sense. In spite of the conservative forces' attempt at reversal of cultural trends set under the Pahlavis, they have not had much success in their mission. The middle class that has emerged under the Islamic republic acknowledge the place of an Iranian identity in the convergence point of three cultures: 'Islam, [pre-Islamic] Iran and modernity' (Soroush undated in Rajaee 1999: 224; Makhmalbaf 1997: 83). Modernity is no longer perceived as the alienating form of aping consumerist Western ways, which was rejected by intellectuals before the revolution as *gharbzadegi* (West-struckness). Rather, it is understood as the adaptation of the principles of democratic society as well as equal respect for Western intellectualism (Irfani 1996; Makhmalbaf 1997).

With the acceptability of Western ideas for the reformists and the popularity of their worldview, now the use of Western terms, or just throwing English words into one's speech, is seen as a sign of sophistication. While this would have been subject to ridicule in the 1970s and the 1980s, now the use of English words has become normalized even on the conservative controlled national TV, and it also happens in films.

In addition, post-revolutionary social changes such as the Islamization of public spaces, villages are no longer the repository of authenticity in contrast to the cities. Furthermore, unlike the 1960s and the 1970s, nowadays the urban lifestyle is taken for granted, with little nostalgia for life in the villages. In this context, it is understandable that middle-class urban Iranians want to project a modern image to the rest of the world.

Self-consciousness as a result of 'negative' representations by one's compatriots is not unique to Iranians. From my own experience of living in the West, a number of my friends from different countries have indicated their embarrassment because of the depiction of their countries or countrymen in films.[25] Since there are few films coming out of their countries, they worry that the films' representations might be taken as a true depiction of life in their countries. This is a concern that people from countries with a large film export market may not share, since unflattering portrayals in some films are off-set by other films. Furthermore, unlike the more easily accessible parts of the world, travel to countries such as Iran is, or is perceived to be, difficult, and hence people generally rely on media representations for information about them. This makes Iranians, both expatriates and those living in Iran, sensitive to such media representations.

Aware of such sensitivities, the director Bahman Farmanara explained away the lack of international acclaim for his *House on the Water* (2001) in an interview with a reformist newspaper by appealing to modernist national sentiments. He claimed that most of the Iranian films which win awards abroad show Iran as a miserable place, and his film did not win any awards since it was about an affluent Iranian doctor (Anon. 2003: 12). In an interview with me, Farmanara repeated the same argument. I then asked him about the international acclaim for his previous film *Smell of Camphor, Fragrance of Jasmine* (1999). He said:

> The reason was that that film is very intellectual since it discusses the issue of the restriction of artistic work. Also the film has a new kind of structure. There is an honesty in the main character as well that you sense on the screen.

Farmanara did not mention the fact that *Smell of Camphor, Fragrance of Jasmine* was also about the life of a wealthy Iranian. Obviously Farmanara's earlier argument could not explain 'the foreigners', i.e. Westerners'', interest in that film. As this example demonstrates, filmmakers at times appeal to nationalist sentiments to their advantage.

Another allegation against art cinema is that Iranian films are 'primitive in style' and show Iran as 'an exotic other' which allegedly non-Iranians enjoy to see. Hatamikia explains:

> The problem is that the festivals force you to see things from a certain perspective. The Western person who is sick of technology and loves the primitive wants me, the Eastern person, to create primitive work. If you show them the city, they say, 'We don't want to see that. What we want happens in the villages.' They are more comfortable with this version of the orient.

Although there is some truth to Hatamikia's claim that an element of exoticism has helped the cinema's international exposure,[26] the reasons for Hatamikia's rejection of that sort of film are mainly aesthetic. Hatamikia, like many other mainstream Iranian directors, aspires to the technical sophistication of Hollywood. Unlike other internationally prominent filmmakers who spend much time at festivals, Hatamikia had not been exposed to films from the rest of the world enough to realize that Iranian films are not the only ones which do not conform to Hollywood standards.

Another reason for hostile reactions to the international reputation of Iranian art films is that some filmmakers who are critically acclaimed in Iran have not attracted much international attention. One such filmmaker is Bahram Beyza'i.[27] A veteran of the 1960s New Wave, Beyza'i is part of the Writers' Guild whose members have often been persecuted by hardliner conservatives since the revolution. Between 1979 and 1997, Beyza'i's filmmaking career was hampered by the conservatives, but since 1997 the restrictions on him and other pre-revolution filmmakers have been lifted and his films are popular, particularly among Iranian critics. Ahmad Talebinejad, a prominent film critic, told me in an interview that Beyza'i's films were not popular at festivals because they are about Iran's 'glorious history and not misery'.

Farahmand claims that the Iranian regime has prevented Beyza'i's eminence through its contacts in festivals (2002). However, there is evidence that Beyza'i's films are in fact not popular with the festival representatives. A director who did not wish to be named told me that at the FIFF screenings of both Beyza'i's films

*The Travellers* (1992) and *Killing Rabids* (2001) most of the representatives of international festivals walked out of the hall after the first few minutes of the screenings. Obviously, most of his work is not considered 'high art' so far as the international critics are concerned. An Iranian critic, Mohammad-Kashi, suggests that films by Beyza'i and Mehrju'i (another filmmaker who is critically acclaimed in Iran), whose films have 'more interesting details about Iranian thought and civilization', are not easy for non-Iranian audiences to comprehend because they do not have any knowledge of 'the thoughts and Iranian life-style' and thus cannot understand these 'more complex films'. She suggests that, by contrast, foreigners can easily understand 'the simpler films' (Mohammad-Kashi 2000: 55). Although I agree that there are some details in Beyza'i and Mehrju'i's films that are perhaps impenetrable for Western audiences, the same applies to many films by Makhmalbaf or Kiarostami that Mohammad-Kashi considers 'simple'. Furthermore, in order to become prominent in art cinema circuits, a certain degree of cinematic freshness is required for the film to be a 'discovery'. Beyza'i's and Mehrju'i's works generally lack such elements and remain in the realm of classic narrative cinema.[28]

## Women and international success

The strong presence of women in Iranian cinema has attracted much attention to 'women's films'. Numerous seminars and international events have been organized about films which focus on women's issues. Many women filmmakers and actors have been invited to events around the world to talk about their films. These events have been an excellent opportunity for the women to exchange ideas with their Western counterparts. They also present non-Iranian (generally Western) audiences the opportunity not only to see films which depict the struggles of women for social change, but also to listen to first-hand accounts by Iranian female actors and filmmakers.

Although many 'women's films' which are shown abroad explore women's agency in the struggle against patriarchy, some films such as Panahi's *The Circle* appear to reinforce stereotypical Western perceptions of Middle Eastern women as victims. As Arora notes, such stereotypical representations are generally more easily accepted by mainstream Western audiences (1994: 303). For example, on two occasions non-Iranian friends of mine who had watched *The Circle* in London asked me whether the conditions of women in Iran were 'as bad as' those shown in that film.[29] Iranians are conscious of such reactions, which find their way to Iran either through the Iranian exiles who, since 1997, have often travelled to Iran or in reports published in the Iranian press.

How the female directors and actors are received in the West in person has also been reflected in Iran. Milani, who has regularly gone to these events, told me, 'I enjoy [my trips abroad] very much because I think they understand me very well. Unlike in Iran, when I speak in public there is no attack on me. There is much sympathy there.' The reactions are not always so complimentary. Pegah Ahangarani, a young Iranian actress who has attended a number of events, said to me that, to her disappointment, some of the questions she was asked made her think some members of the audience believed 'Iranian women are from another planet' and that Iranian women were generally weak and submissive. She added, 'Iranian women are much stronger than most Western women because in spite of difficulties they have achieved a lot.' It thus appears that at times Iranian women actors/directors on the stage are treated as exceptions that prove the rule about the situation of women in Iran.[30]

At times, in interviews journalist treat award-winning female Iranian directors as exceptions as well. One phenomenally successful Iranian woman director is Samira Makhmalbaf, Mohsen Makhmalbaf's daughter. Samira has won many international awards since her debut at Cannes with *The Apple* (1998) when she was only 18. She has also been a jury member at prestigious festivals such as Venice Film Festival in 2000. Relating an interview with her, the reporter for *The Independent* (Anon. 2003b) claimed, '[Samira] Makhmalbaf has made it absolutely acceptable for a woman to become a filmmaker in Iran.' Far from Samira being an 'exception' for her pioneering filmmaking, long before her advent on the scene a number of other Iranian women filmmakers established their reputations both nationally and internationally. None of course has a comparable international profile to Samira's.

Interviews with filmmakers abroad are published in Iran, and not always to positive reactions. For example, Homa Tavasoli, a young female journalist, told me that she disliked the fact that Westerners treat Samira as a rare exception. She explained that, although Samira was an accomplished director, so many strong-minded young Iranian women were achieving their own goals using the more limited opportunities available to them. She mentioned the example of the university entrance exam in Iran, in which, among the top five students every year, there were always more women than men.

## Reactions among cinema-goers

Before 1997, two filmmakers who were successful both at the box office and on the festival circuit were Makhmalbaf and Bani-Etemad. During this period, these two consistently made films with social commentaries, which, as Tables 5.2 and 5.3 demonstrate, were also popular at the box office.

*Table 5.2* Mohsen Makhmalbaf's films released between 1989 and 1997

| Film | Year of release | Box office ranking in the year of release in Tehran |
| --- | --- | --- |
| *The Cyclist* | 1989 | 5 |
| *Marriage of the Blessed* | 1989 | 8 |
| *Once upon a Time Cinema* | 1992 | 7 |
| *The Actor* | 1993 | 1 |
| *Salam Cinema* | 1995 | 3 |
| *Gabbeh* | 1996 | 5 |

Source: Produced by the author using box office figures in Javedani (2002: 204–68.

*Table 5.3* Rakhshan Bani-Etemad's films between 1989 and 1997

| Film | Year of release | Box office ranking in the year of release in Tehran |
|---|---|---|
| *Canary Yellow* | 1989 | 9 |
| *Foreign Money* | 1990 | 30 |
| *Narges* | 1992 | 9 |
| *The Blue Veiled* | 1995 | 2 |

Source: Produced by the author using box office figures in Javedani (2002: 204–58).

As Table 5.4 demonstrates, other internationally successful films released in the same period by Kiarostami and Panahi did not do well at the box office in Iran.

These tables suggest that international prominence alone does not entice people in Iran to see the films. From my own fieldwork experience, for any individual film most people either are unaware of the awards it has won abroad or they do not think of that as important. This is particularly the case nowadays, when the number of award-winning films is so large that the success of Iranian films at festivals is almost taken for granted. In the late 1980s and the early 1990s when I lived in Iran, such success was still a novelty. Even then, as the tables above demonstrate, a film's international acclaim did not necessarily cause people to flock to see it. In contrast to the generally apolitical films of Table 5.4, those in Tables 5.2 and 5.3, which were socially engaged films, did better in Iran.

In recent years, thanks to the aforementioned bootleg VCD economy, many art films which have either been censored or banned are widely circulating in the country. Banned films such as *The Circle* (Panahi 2000), *10* (Kiarostami 2002) and the uncensored version of *Women's Prison* (Hekmat 2002) are readily available in Iran. While the bootleg economy renders government control ineffective, it facilitates audience access to films.

## Conclusion

The global success of Iranian cinema has been implicated in the discourses of identity. Both before and after the revolution, Iranian authorities have been

*Table 5.4* Abbas Kiarostami and Jafar Panahi's films between 1989 and 1997

| Film | Filmmaker | Year of release | Box office ranking in the year of release in Tehran |
|---|---|---|---|
| *Where is the Friend's House?* | Kiarostami | 1989 | 30 |
| *Homework* | Kiarostami | 1990 | 31 |
| *Close-up* | Kiarostami | 1990 | 45 |
| *Life and Nothing More* | Kiarostami | 1992 | 41 |
| *Under the Olive Trees* | Kiarostami | 1994 | 21 |
| *The White Balloon* | Panahi | 1995 | 34 |

Source: Produced by the author using box office figures in Javedani (2002: 195–259).

sensitive to how Iran is represented in films that go outside the country. Before the revolution, the public sphere discourse about cinema saw no downside to the international success of films which showed Iran in a less than glamorous way, but since the 1990s there have been considerable self-conscious reactions to the phenomenon. The reactions can partly be attributed to social change since the revolution and to the reformists' acknowledgement of a modern aspect to contemporary Iranian identity.

Some Iranian filmmakers who previously were less willing to engage with Iranian social issues have become bolder in their films and their public statements. An example par excellence is Abbas Kiarostami, who has gone from making politically innocuous films about children, such as *Where Is the Friend's House?*, to the outspoken social critique of *10* (2002). While the opening of the political atmosphere since 1997 has played a part in this change, transnational funding has also been instrumental. As the profile of Iranian filmmakers has risen internationally, they have been able to engage with social criticism which matters to Iranians. As mentioned earlier, Naficy claims that Iranian art cinema is independent of Iranian tastes. However, the 'social films' made by Makhmalbaf and Bani-Etemad before 1997, and Kiarostami's *10* are evidence to show that at times art cinema and Iranian tastes do meet.

Critical engagement with social realities in Iran situates filmmakers in the 'national' space. Although an 'imagined reality', 'the nation' is particularly important because as Anderson puts it, it is 'the most universally legitimate value in the political life of our time' (1983: 3). Arguing for political commitment at the national level, Fanon suggests that not to do so and instead to identify with cosmopolitan humanism is 'intellectual laziness' and 'spiritual penury' (2001 [1963]: 149, 200). While I do not subscribe to Fanon's polemical stance, I believe that in making films which *only* appeal to the humanist values of the cosmopolitan elite, filmmakers drift apart from serious politics at the national level.

While the outward flow of films from Iran continues, news of the success crosses the borders in the opposite direction. As a result, when the same films are watched in Iran, they are perceived in the light of their having already been seen outside the country. Iranians do not wish to be seen as 'the primitive other' to the modern West. Nevertheless, in general, films which have critically engaged with the social realities of urban Iran have attracted Iranian cinema-goers to themselves regardless of their perception abroad.

While there is a range of ways in which the high acclaim outside the country has been framed in Iran, the phenomenon has contributed to raising the profile of Iranian cinema inside the country. Cinema has become a social institution of particular significance around which the boundaries of cultural identity are negotiated.

# 6   Conclusion

This book has shown some of the complexities of film reception in Iran and has contextualized the phenomenon in Iranian society at large. Hence the findings of the study not only contribute to film and media studies but also to ethnographic studies of Iran.

Studies of film reception generally consider the reactions to films after they are released, when audiences watch films on video or in cinemas. In this book I have highlighted how the process of reception begins earlier, when decision-makers who preside over the release of films watch the films (or read their scripts). In the USA and Britain, film is often recognized as a collective endeavour in which scriptwriters and directors as well as actors and others all have important negotiating parts (even if, in popular accounts, directors, studios or writers are privileged), and that is parallel, albeit different, to the sort of negotiation that takes place in Iran. In both cases, 'common sense' is being invoked, performed, and reformed, along with putative projections of what audiences (or, in Iran, political factions) will like or accept. In this sense, the problematic of reception begins with the submission of scripts, with the private showings of films to the various authorities to build a consensus that permits are (or are not) viable.

Through a study of Iranian cinema this book has sought to contribute to ethnographic accounts of Iranian governance (here in the field of culture, Chapter 2), of social and cultural critique (Chapter 3), of women's voices in a contested and changing arena of social justice, morality and patriarchal claims and denials (Chapter 4), and of transnational cultural politics from a domestic Iranian perspective (Chapter 5).

An important point that emerged from the research concerned the complexities of governance in the field of culture in Iran. Intricacies of the negotiations between the filmmakers and the authorities served to highlight the dynamics of cultural politics in the Islamic Republic. My research demonstrated that although there has been an attempt to create and abide by a set of regulations, a rather 'modern' approach in itself, it is 'traditional' face-to-face negotiations which rely on trust, friendship, bargaining and perseverance that determine the outcome in most cases. The interpretation of the rules is negotiated in almost every case by the regulators and filmmakers. This is also how ordinary Iranians often manage to get around restrictions in Iran. What may seem to the untrained eye from afar like a rigid system is much more fluid. At the same time, things are not as simple as 'pushing back the boundaries', a metaphor which is very often invoked in discussions of filmmakers' dealings with the limits of acceptability in Iranian cinema. For example, at the time of writing, more than four years have passed since Tabrizi's *The Lizard* was released, but no one else has made another comedy about the clergy. Boundaries are generally not so easily pushed back but are negotiated on an individual basis.

This book has examined the role of cinema at liminal moments of social/ political upheaval. According to Turner, at such moments cultural performances serve as metacommentaries on the drastic changes happening within a society and constitute attempts to pull 'meaning from the tangle of action' and to make sense of the transformations taking place (Turner 1990: 17). As my interviews with Iranian filmmakers demonstrate, they do intend their films as metacommentaries about society as a whole. The filmmakers critique the social/political circumstances of the society in subtle ways.

In spite of a filmmaker's major role as the creator of a 'cultural performance', social reflection on the liminal circumstances depends finally on the audiences. Audience interpretations in the process of engagement with films are facilitated but not dictated by the film 'texts'. My analysis of audience discourses about the films shows that the occasion of watching and discussing 'social films' constitutes audiences' reflection on the contemporary liminal period in Iran.

The role of the filmmaker is also the subject of the theory of radical/alternative media but research in this area has thus far been focused on production practices and media content generally. The political role of Iranian filmmakers is consistent with the theory of radical media as outlined by Downing (2001). However, by highlighting the audiences' cofabulation of meaning about the films, I have argued that radicalness of the politics of the media depends on the audience interpretations to a large degree. While a film's content may not appear to the researcher to be overtly political, through cofabulation audience interpretation can render it alternative or radical in respect to the hegemonic/repressive order. As I have explored, audience members at times engage in cofabulation by 'editing' films for themselves, creating their own dissenting narratives from 'social films' some elements of which they reject. Hence in their interpretation they take a film's criticism of post-revolution Iran further than the filmmaker may have intended.

Another dimension explored in this book was the audience's engagement with social/political critique. Audience assumptions about the media texts were examined along with their interpretative strategies and the enjoyment they derive from engaging with the films. The commonalities of these features among those with whom I watched and discussed the films demonstrates the possibility of generalization from my research. My informants assumed that, rather than being narratives about a set of filmic characters, the films were a critical commentary on the predicaments of Iranian society. In addition, aware of the restrictions under which films are produced, they assumed that meanings have been 'coded' into the films by filmmakers.

In their interpretative strategies, with the background of the Iranian poetic tradition of multilayered communication of meaning, audiences actively engage with film texts. Not only are they tuned into the metaphoric and symbolic content, they are also especially vigilant about instances of censorship. Any slight jump in the picture often alerts them to the censors' scissors having been at work. The complexity of such an engagement with film necessitates watching and discussing films in groups. Their often accurate speculations about censored sections, and how those sections would have contributed to the overall anti-hegemonic meaning of the film, shows that they are a very sophisticated viewing public. This culture of resistance, which largely depends on an inter-subjective understanding between filmmakers and viewers, has developed under the ideological control of the state.

The audiences' pleasures in relation to the politics of films are mainly to do with catching and sharing the anti-hegemonic 'messages' in films, whether such 'messages' are intended or not. In addition, catchphrases in films often enter popular culture and serve as pleasurable parts of everyday discourses of resistance.

This book has also sought to contribute to ethnographic accounts of gender politics in Iran. In this regard, Iranian women's engagement with film should be considered in the context of the feminist struggle for social justice and gender equality in the country. In this movement for change, filmmakers are activists whose focus on patriarchal injustice draws emotional as well as rational responses from female audience members. In the ensuing reflections on their own circumstances, women audience members see their personal experiences as part of a larger political reality of the patriarchal order. Women's collective reflection about these issues has been facilitated by the Islamization of the cinema space that has eased women's attendance in cinemas. As my research shows, contrary to Western stereotypes about Muslim women, female Iranians often assertively argue for their rights during the course of negotiations of gender that follow the watching of 'women's films'. Such counter-hegemonic performance of gender can have significant potential in relation to gender identity.

As regards the international profile of Iranian cinema, it appears that Iranians are quite sensitive to what the rest of the world thinks of their country. This is quite unlike how Iranian leaders conduct their international affairs, often behaving as if they do not care at all about the country's image in the West. Ordinary Iranians hope that festival films will counteract the negative image of the country that exists in the West. While filmmakers appear uninterested in altering the stereotypical image of the country abroad, many of them do want to engage in the national politics of culture. Assured of the global spotlight and hence of local immunity as well as international funding, Iranian filmmakers have become more daring in their engagement with social/political issues in their films. Although such films are often banned, the existence of the bootleg video economy has meant that the films are still viewed by Iranian audiences. This economy remains largely unchallenged by the authorities inside the country and invisible from the perspective of those observing from the outside.

Those who have not themselves experienced life under undemocratic regimes often wonder how others live and work under such conditions. They are imagined as either unthinkingly/fearfully toeing the official line or voicing dissidence and being persecuted. This is a gross simplification of much more complex phenomena on the ground. 'Resistance', 'compromise' and 'negotiation' constitute multidimensional political realities that must be understood in their local contexts. I hope that this book's examination of such realities in the case of Iran would foster better appreciation of the complex possibilities in other societies.

# Notes

## 1 Introduction

1 My account of the Frankfurt School is based on Hall (1982).
2 Notable exceptions are Dickey's (1993) and L. Srinivas' (2002) research on cinema audiences in South India.
3 Quoted in *Siyasatha va raveshha-ye ejra'i-ye tolid, tozi' va namayesh-e filmha-ye sine-mai-ye* 1375 obtained from the MCIG, p. 1.
4 About women's movement, see Chapter 4, section entitled, 'Changes to women's social position in contemporary Iran: an overview'.
5 This is not the only way that Iranian films are grouped. Nowadays, they also appear under the auteurs' names, such as retrospectives made up of Kiarostami's or Makhmalbaf's works at festivals.
6 Hyphenated identities such as Iranian-American are also used by many individuals.
7 Expatriate Iranians have also been prolific in filmmaking. An examination of this cinema, which Naficy (2001b) refers to as 'accented cinema', is beyond the scope of this publication. The reader is invited to consult Naficy (1993, 1999, 2001b), and Gow (2006) for in depth discussions about these films.
8 Marcus and Fischer (1986: 176) had earlier referred to this project as 'multilocale' ethnography.
9 Abu-Lughod (1991) uses the term 'halfies' to refer to indigenous ethnographers. I do not like this label because it connotes being two incomplete halves and not one whole anything. I much prefer Aguilar's metaphor.
10 Since 2004 the films in the festival have been simultaneously shown in other major cities of Iran such as Mashhad, Shiraz and Isfahan.
11 See section entitled 'A note on the economics of Iranian Cinema' in Chapter Three about the circulation of bootleg copies of films in Iran and their political significance.

## 2 State control of Iranian cinema: the shifting 'red lines'

1 Here I concentrate on the politics of Iranian cinema before the revolution. For other aspects, the reader is referred to Gaffary (1989), Naficy (1999), Parhami (1999), Golestan (1995), Issari (1989), Mehrabi (1984) and Omid (1998).
2 The Supreme Leader (*vali-ye faqih*) is an ayatollah who is the highest authority in the Islamic Republic. The post was initially taken up by Ayatollah Khomeini and, since his death, Ayatollah Khamenei has become the Supreme Leader. For a discussion of the role of the Supreme Leader see Haghayeghi (1993).
3 Quoted in an unpublished document obtained from the MCIG entitled, *Siyasatha va raveshha-ye ejra'i-ye tolid, tozi' va namayesh-e filmha-ye sinemai-ye* 1375, p. 1.
4 For example, if a character was robbing a bank in a film, through dubbing his motives would be made into wanting to fund a revolutionary movement.

5   Shari'ati was a religious intellectual and the leading non-clerical ideologue of the revolution. He and others used Hoseiniyeh Ershad as a hub of political opposition to the Shah's regime.

6   The only film that *Ayat Film* produced before the revolution was buried in the ground for fear of SAVAK (the Shah's brutal secret police) and was ruined as a result.

7   The number of categories changed from four (A, B, C, D) in the first year to three (A, B, C) two years later.

8   It is important to note that until 1997 films were allocated to cinemas by the MCIG. See below, section entitled 'Cinema after 1997', for the post-1997 changes.

9   Quoted in an unpublished document obtained from the MCIG, entitled, *Siyasatha va raveshha-ye ejra'i-ye tolid, tozi' va namayesh-e filmha-ye sinemai-ye* 1375, p. 4.

10  The authorities have referred to these films using different labels. *Sinema-ye eslami* or Islamic cinema (Avini 2000: 156–57), *Sinema-ye dini* or 'religious cinema' (Mirsalim 1997: 34), *Sinema-ye Ma'nagara* or 'meaning-driven cinema' (http://www.fcf.ir/farsi/home.asp?dbname = cultural_mana, accessed on 20.4.2006). The meaning and the boundaries of these terms have never been clear and are subject to debates. About these debates the reader is invited to consult *Gozaresh-e farabi*, No. 1, 1997 and Anon. 2001a. The two major types of films which are concerned with religion are explored below.

11  The section later changed its name to *Nezarat va arzeshyabi* (Supervision and evaluation).

12  The chapter does not include all the clauses in the code. For the full list see Nuri (1996).

13  This relaxation of censorship lasted for a short while only. See below about the period after 1992.

14  A similar situation exists in Persian poetry, in which, because of the art of ambiguity (*iham*) it is not clear whether the poet is writing about earthly or divine love.

15  Ahmadinejad has installed a number of officials with military background who do not belong to any of the factions. However, like those from the conservative factions, when it comes to matters of culture, they have a narrow point of view (see section entitled 'Ahmadinejad's presidency and cinema' below).

16  Ayatollah Jannati, head of the Guardian Council and a leading conservative figure, says in 1997 that after many years his favourite film is still Makhmalbaf's *Nasuh's Repentence* (1983) for its depiction of the afterlife (Jannati 1997: 43).

17  See Chapter 5 for further comments by Kasehsaz about how the censorship of *Women's Prison* was framed in Iran.

18  In real life, there has been much resistance by women against the impositions of standards of modesty by Iranian authorities. This has included resistance both to strict adherence to the dress code as well as to the limitations on interaction with the opposite sex in public. See for example Moghissi (1996).

19  A head to toe cloak.

20  See Naficy (1994) for an excellent examination of veiling and its representation in Iranian cinema.

21  See Chapter 4 for a summary of the plot of *Two Women* and the transcript of my interview with the filmmaker.

22  Unpublished document obtained from the MCIG, entitled, *Siyasatha va raveshha-ye ejra'i-ye tolid, tozi' va namayesh-e filmha-ye sinemai-ye* 1375.

23  *Basij* is a paramilitary force founded by Ayatollah Khomeini in 1979. *Basijis,* or members of *Basij,* have been entitled to many benefits such as easy entry into the universities as well as numerous subsidies and quotas for themselves and their families. See section entitled 'Discussion' in relation to *Glass Agency* (in Chapter 3).

24  Both Makhmalbaf and Beyza'i returned to Iran after a short while.

25  As Dad and others at the MCIG told me, the statistics the MCIG uses for planning are mainly from the city of Tehran. Local branches of the MCIG look after the rest of Iran. However, there is little co-ordination and planning at the national level.

26  Fardin was one of the stars of pre-revolution cinema who took on lumpen roles.

27 Unpublished document obtained from the MCIG, entitled, *Siyasatha va raveshha-ye ejra'i-ye tolid, tozi' va namayesh-e filmha-ye sinemai-ye* 1379, p. 2.

28 Unpublished document obtained from the MCIG, entitled, *Siyasatha va raveshha-ye ejra'i-ye tolid, tozi' va namayesh-e filmha-ye sinemai-ye* 1379, p. 5.

29 During the five-year period under Dad, many filmmakers who previously made Sacred Defence films abandoned the genre. This was partly due to the lack of funding from the MCIG. In addition, since much attention was paid to *Saving Private Ryan* (Spielberg 1998) in the Iranian press and cinema circles, many decided that what was lacking from the genre was big budgets, technical sophistication and Hollywood-style spectacle. The debate led to the making of the spectacular *Duel* (Darvish 2004) as the Iranian answer to Spielberg's film. The film's cinematic achievement has been praised in Iran.

30 http://www.ketabnews.com/detail-2845-fa-1.html (accessed 26 January 2008).

## 3 'Social films'

1 A member of the paramilitary force called *Basij*, which was founded by Ayatollah Khomeini in 1979.

2 Below is a brief discussion of Makhmalbaf's contribution to Iranian cinema. For an in-depth discussion of Mohsen Makhmalbaf's cinema see Ridgeon (2000), Egan (2005) and Dabashi (2001, 2002, 2007).

3 See section on '*Filmha-ye dini*' or 'Religious films' in Chapter 2.

4 For discussion of the novel see Dabashi (2002).

5 While less than 20 per cent of the population live in Tehran, they generally account for almost half the national box office receipts. In addition, the MCIG's plans for the development of cinema have been based almost entirely on Tehran at the expense of the rest of the country. Dad, the former Cinema Deputy at the MCIG, tried to address this issue, but had little success according to himself. Tahmasebi says that now other major urban centres, such as Mashhad, Isfahan and Shiraz, are taken into account to a degree. The screening of the FIFF films in these cities at the same time as Tehran since 2004 is a sign that the MCIG is taking steps to implement such a change.

6 See also in this chapter for details about the censorship of *House on the Water* because of a sneering reference to a saying by Khomeini, which at the time was a catchphrase.

7 This is not to suggest that the apparent police intrusion and the behind-the-scenes sequence is necessarily documentary footage.

8 'Ali, Prophet Mohammad's son-in-law, is believed to have been dedicated to the achievement of social justice. He and his wife Fatima are believed to have lived a humble life.

9 Contrasting the 'traditional' with the 'organic' intellectual, Gramsci (1971) saw the former as seeking to maintain the status-quo of the existing hegemonic power relations, while the 'organic' intellectual rise up from the ranks of the subaltern classes in order to act as a mouthpiece for their concerns and empower them with a voice in the political movement.

10 As mentioned earlier, only relevant sections of interviews and group discussions are quoted in this book. Often my discussions with the respondents were wide ranging and beyond the scope of this book.

11 Like Khatami, Musavi and Beheshti are part of the modern left who later came to be known as the reformists.

12 So much so that later, when Makhmalbaf claimed that his film *Gabbeh* (1996) was not a metaphoric film, the censors would not believe him. See Ditmars (1996: 11).

13 The public broadcasters and the press, with the exception of the few remaining reformist publications, still do the same.

14 My interview with Dad.

15 My interview with Hatamikia.

16  Saffarian (1998: 18–19), using detailed comparison between the form and narrative of the two films, demonstrates how Hatamikia has adapted the Hollywood film to the Iranian context.

17  The audience data presented about this film are from several informal interviews and two group discussions.

18  The agency manager saying to Kazem, 'Did you ask for my permission for those eight years of killing?'

19  The vocabulary Saeed and Mehrdad use is informed by the reformist discourse which has circulated through the press and in the reformist speeches. I cannot verify whether Saeed and Mehrdad thought of the film in these terms when they first saw it. This is a shortcoming of working with people's recollections about a film they had seen many years earlier. Nevertheless, almost everyone I talked to in relation to *Glass Agency* commented that they found the film unique for the way many different political perspectives were voiced in it.

20  Two of the actors in the film, Habib Reza'i (Abbas in the film), and Reza Kianian (Salahshur), confirmed the director's statement that when the film was being made they were not sure whether it would be completed or shown at all.

21  As already mentioned, *Javanmard* (adjective, noun) is an ideal Iranian character type embodying selfless courage and generosity (Adelkhah 1999: 4, 6–7). *Javanmardi* (noun) means being a *javanmard*.

22  *Hambastegi*, No. 232, p. 4.

23  In this summary the plot appears disjointed, it reflects the fact that the film is a collection of inter-related sub-plots.

24  A six or seven year-old blonde girl in a white dress with wings on her back. Later in the film she is refered to as 'an angel'.

25  See below for the censored sections of the film.

26  At the time, the MCIG did not have the figures for the rest of Iran.

27  See Chapter 4 about the restrictions relating to seating and its effect on women's access to cinemas.

28  Internal surveys by the MCIG also concurred with my findings in this regard. Tahmasebi told me that surveys conducted by the MCIG show that people generally go to films because of what they hear about them from others. The surveys are not published and Tahmasebi did not show me the results.

29  This is not to suggest that dissident clerics are treated any less harshly. Abdollah Nuri, Yousef Eshkevari and Mosen Kadivar have all served lengthy jail terms as prisoners of conscience.

30  See note 21 above.

31  The discussion took place on a walk and then in a car, which prevented me from audio taping.

32  This is not to claim that Makhmalbaf does not have a sense of humour. His *Once upon a Time Cinema* (1992) and *A Moment of Innocence* (1996) are particularly funny in parts.

33  According to screening regulations of the time a film would be taken off the screen when ticket sales would fall below a minimum limit. When *The Lizard* was taken off this obviously was not the case.

34  Since DVDs require rather up-to-date PCs to run, they are not so common as VCDs which run on very basic PCs and VCD players.

## 4  'Women's films'

1  Naficy in Tapper (2002) makes too sharp a distinction between the politics of 'art cinema' and other films which he groups together as 'populist cinema', claiming that the latter 'affirms post-revolutionary Islamic values more fully', while the former 'engages with those values'; as I have shown so far, the reality is more complex than this dichotomy allows.

2 The theories discussed here have already been considered in some detail in Chapter 1.

3 For detailed discussion of women's movements see Paidar (1995).

4 About the involvement of Manijeh Hekmat and Shirin Ebadi in the movement see the following webpages (accessed on 20 August 2008): http://www.advarnews.us/womenarticle/print/6814.aspx and http://www.we-change.org/spip.php?article2170

5 A head to toe cloak.

6 The only woman filmmaker among these intellectuals was the poet Forough Farrokhzad; but, in spite of the fact that most of her poems concern women, her only film was the documentary *The House is Black* (1964), in which gender was not an issue.

7 Fischer (1984: 178) mentions similar behaviour among cinema-goers in Yazd in 1969 whereby elite women would only feel safe to go to the cinema protected by their menfolk.

8 For my reasons to choose these films see 'methodology' in Chapter 1.

9 http://news.gooya.com/2003/05/31/3105-h-39.php (accessed on 21 June 2003).

10 Milani's comments at the press conference following the screening of *Fifth Reaction* at the FIFF.

11 For female bonding in *Thelma and Louise* see Macdonald (1995: 159–60).

12 For Bani-Etemad's films, see Naficy (2001) and Whitaker (1999).

13 This public act would have shamed Haji in his neighbourhood.

14 This division does not exist in cinemas in the well-off areas of northern Tehran.

15 See Chapter 1 for my discussion of Ang (1990).

16 For example, *10* which I discuss on later in this chapter.

17 Milani exempted Mohsen Makhmalbaf, who she thought was genuine in his commitment to women's causes.

18 The interview lasted more than two hours and has been shortened here.

19 See the group discussion earlier in this chapter.

20 For Kiarostami, one of the main advantages of DV cameras is that they help with more 'natural' acting by non-professional actors. This is because the actors feel less self-conscious in front of small DV cameras and small (or, in the case of *10*, absent) film crews. Kiarostami made the comments in a session titled, 'Abbas Kiarostami and Seifollah Samadian in conversation with Geoff Andrew', on 30 January 2004 at Victoria and Albert Museum in London.

21 Kiarostami explained that this was because he did not want to show women unnaturally veiled at home. Although in real life women would not do so, in film the regulations restrain realistic depiction.

22 A few months later, I heard that the film was available in Iran both on VCD and on high quality DVD.

23 For the 'traditionalist' discourse of gender see Mir-Hosseini (1999: 21–79).

24 Mahsa thus interpreted a similar comment by Mania to Amin, who had complained about having to eat leftovers for dinner. Mania said, 'It is good that everything is summed up in one's stomach.'

25 Mahsa is referring to the spiritual quest for liberation through philosophical perfection which Moslem men and women are supposed to embark on in their lives.

26 In *Killing Rabids* the female protagonist is raped by two men in an off-the-camera incident. In *Women's Prison* the attempted rape of a young woman by a prison guard is implied. The women who made the comment to me did not, however, refer to these specific parts of the two films.

27 This sequence has been interpreted in the West as a significant transgression in Iranian cinema (see for example Andrew 2005: 74). However, the image of a woman's shaved head was quite tame by Iranian standards, having been shown in a number of films such as *Lead* (1989 Kimiya'i), *Marriage of the Blessed* (1989) and *Daughters of the Sun* (Shahriyar 2000). In spite of the dramatic impact of this particular scene in *10*, it is not a major transgressive move.

**5  Transnational circulation and national perceptions: art films in the Iranian context**

1  An earlier version of this chapter was published in the *British Journal of Middle Eastern Studies,* entitled 'Iranian intellectuals and contact with the West: the case of Iranian cinema', 34(3): 375–98.

2  According to Attebba'i each 'appearance' signifies a screening or run of an Iranian film (feature, short or documentary) at a cinematheque, cinema, film week or festival outside Iran. If a film has a run at a cinema, being screened several times a day, this counts as just one appearance.

3  As Omid mentions, some critics did not like the slow pace of that film.

4  The book which I refer to is Atebba'i (2004a), *25 sal sinema-ye Iran: javayez va hozur-e beinolmelali.*

5  I discuss below the reasons for the proliferation of films about children among award winning films.

6  The only festival to which the MCIG sends a film of its choosing is the Academy Awards.

7  Unpublished document obtained from the MCIG, entitled, *Siyasatha va raveshha-ye ejra'i-ye tolid, tozi' va namayesh-e filmha-ye sinemai-ye 1379,* p. 1.

8  This was repeated in 2003 when Heydarian, the Cinema Deputy at the time, praised Samira Makhmalbaf for her success at the festival but he did not mention Jafar Panahi who had also won an award at Cannes that year. See below, section entitled 'Art cinema filmmakers', regarding the case of Panahi's (2003) *Crimson Gold.*

9  In 1381 (~2002) and 1382 (~2003) there were 74 and 93 appearances of Iranian films in the USA respectively (Atebba'i 2004b: 73; 2005: 68).

10  There are also foreign 'art films', which I attended at the 2003 festival, including *Rabbit Proof Fence* (Noyce 2002), *The Son* (Dardenne 2002) and *Bowling for Colombine* (Moore 2002). *Bowling for Colombine* was later on general release in Tehran (see Figure 1.1 in Chapter 1).

11  According to Atebba'i, Farabi gives pocket money to the directors for their trips to festivals abroad (interview with the author).

12  As Makhmalbaf's comment shows, like the MCIG authorities, he is also focused on the cinema-goers in Tehran, disregarding the rest of the country. This is partly to do with the fact that often art films do not get much exposure in the rest of Iran. Even in Mashhad, Iran's second largest city, most art films are not screened in cinemas and are only available on video. Another factor is that, as mentioned in Chapter 3, it is difficult for the filmmakers to retrieve the box office takings from outside the capital.

13  According to Atebba'i (2004b: 72), of the films exhibited outside Iran in 2002, *Women's Prison* ranked second with 28 international appearances while the first had 30 appearances. The film also won two awards.

14  Vosuqi, who was the most acclaimed Iranian actor by the critics and among Iranian cinema-goers, left Iran after the revolution and settled in the USA. In spite of having been acknowledged for his talent internationally before the revolution, his career has not picked up outside Iran since his departure.

15  This, however, is not true. For example, in Cannes 2005 where he was the head of the jury for Camera d'or, *One Night* (Karimi 2005), the only Iranian film in competition, did not win.

16  My interview with Hamed Sarrafzadeh, a film critic.

17  Seyfollah Dad, the Cinema Deputy at the MCIG, told me that he banned the film because he feared that it would be used by the conservatives to launch another attack on Mohajerani, the already embattled Minister of Culture and Islamic Guidance (MCIG). Dad said that since he wanted to make sure he was making the right decision in banning the film, he showed the film to Mohajerani and about 30 reformist MPs. According to Dad, apart from Behruz Afkhami, who is also a filmmaker, everyone including

Mohajerani agreed that the film should be censored or banned for political expediency. When he approached Panahi to agree to the censoring of his film, particularly a long sequence at the end of the film showing a prostitute, Panahi flatly declined.

18  These figures, confirmed by the MCIG's Tahmasebi, were provided by Atebba'i, an ex-Farabi official who has worked on co-productions including Panahi's *The Circle*.

19  Estimates from Atebba'i and confirmed by Tahmasebi. They did not have the exact figures, which they said would be kept secret by the filmmakers for taxation purposes.

20  See my interviews with the directors Panahi and Makhmalbaf.

21  Dariush is a very popular singer who migrated after the revolution to the USA, where he has continued his career.

22  Regarding post-Tiananmen era Chinese cinema see Lu (2004: 131).

23  Quoted in Heydarzadeh (2003: 75). Banning films on such an excuse is not unique to Iran. In China, for example, *Beijing Bicycle* (Xioshuai 2001) was banned for portraying the Chinese capital as a 'grey, dirty and disorderly place' (Lin 2002: 261).

24  Because of pressure from the MCIG, at the award ceremony the winner of the Best Film category was not announced. Panahi, who was present at the ceremony, had to wait until after the ceremony to receive his award (Heydarzadeh 2003: 75).

25  Some examples are *Jamón, Jamón* (Spain, 1992), *And Your Mother Too* (Mexico, 2001) and *City of God* (Brazil, 2002). With the first two films, my friends insisted that the portrayal of their countrymen was not typical of how things actually are in their respective countries. In the case of the third film, my friend insisted that such films help strengthen Brazil's already existing reputation in the West as a violent society.

26  Mulvey agrees with this point, but she adds, 'This exoticism was there for, say, a British audience encountering Antonioni or Godard in the 1960s, and is certainly not exclusive to "third cinema"' (2002: 257).

27  The only post-revolution film by Beyza'i to have been received well critically outside Iran has been *Bashu, the Little Stranger* (1985).

28  There are exceptions in the works of both directors, such as Mehrju'i's *Bemani* (2002) and Beyza'i's *The Crow* (1978) which have been lauded internationally.

29  Although *The Circle* (2000) was about underclass women, the opening sequence, which shows a grandmother's dismay and consternation at the birth of her daughter's baby girl, reinforces the perception that the film is trying to tell the story of Iranian women as a whole. Many critics have had similar reactions to the film. Cheshire (2001) quotes a *Film Comment* reviewer of *The Circle* who claimed that in Iran, 'little has changed there since Alexander the Great', showing the age-old biases that Panahi's film has flattered.

30  This of course does not cover the range of responses at such events outside Iran. At the events I have attended myself, the questions asked by non-Iranian audience members usually showed a deeper appreciation for Iranian women.

# Bibliography

Abrahamian, E. (1982) *Iran: between two revolutions,* Princeton: Princeton University Press.

Abu-Lughod, L. (1991) 'Writing against culture', in R. Fox (ed.), *Recapturing anthropology,* New Mexico: School of American Research Press.

—— (2000) 'Locating ethnography', *Ethnography,* 1 (2): 261–67.

Adelkhah, F. (1999) *Being Modern in Iran,* trans. J. Derrick, Paris: Hurst and company.

Aguilar, J. (1981) 'Introduction', in D. Messerschmidt (ed.), *Anthropologists at home in North America: methods and issues in the study of one's own society,* Cambridge: Cambridge University Press.

Akrami, J. (1987) 'The blighted spring: Iranian political cinema in the 1970s', in J. Downing (ed.), *Film and politics in the Third World,* New York: Autonomedia.

Al-e Ahmad, J. (1982) *West-Struckness,* trans. J. Green and A. 'Alizadeh, Lexington: Mazda.

Algar, H. (1981) *Islam and revolution: writings and declarations of Imam Khomeini,* London: Routledge & Kegan Paul.

'Alipur, L. (2003) 'Mosahebeh ba bahman-e farmanara kargardan-e film-e khaneh-ye ru-ye ab: kalam-e khoda ra ham sansur mikonand!', *Yas-e No,* 36: 5.

Althusser, L. (1971) *Lenin and philosophy and other essays,* London: New Left Books.

Aminzade, R. and McAdam D. (2001) 'Emotions and contentious politics', in R. Aminzade, et al. (eds), *Silence and voice in the study of contentious politics,* Cambridge: Cambridge University Press.

Anderson, B. (1983) *Imagined communities: reflections on the origin and spread of nationalism,* London: Verso.

Andrew, G. (2005) *10,* London: BFI Publishing.

Ang, I. (1990) 'Melodramatic identifications: television and women's fantasy', in M. Brown (ed.), *Television and women's culture: the politics of the popular,* London: Sage.

—— (1996) *Living room wars: rethinking media audience for a postmodern world,* London: Routledge.

Anon. (1991) 'Cheshmandaz-e Yek Bahs', *Mahnameh-ye sinema'i-ye film,* 108: 86–94.

—— (1998) 'Goft-e-gu ba Mohammad Mehdi Do'adgu dar bareh-ye seyr-e darejeh-bandi-ye keyfi-ye film-ha az aghaz ta emruz', *Mahnameh-ye sinema'i-ye film,* 223: 52–57.

—— (2001a) *Sinema, din, Iran: sinema-ye dini az negah-e sinema-garan,* Tehran: Sherkat-e entesharat-e sureh mehr.

—— (2001b) http://www.payvand.com/news/01/oct/1015.html (accessed 10 December 2001).

—— (2002) '*Modir-e omure resane'i setad-e amr-e be ma'ruf va nah-ye az monkar*', *Hayat-e No*, 791: 12.

—— (2003a) 'Bahman-e Farmanara: "khane-ei ruye ab" tasviri az jame-e ra neshan mida-had', 905: 12.

—— (2003b) 'Samira Makhmalbaf: like father like daughter', *The Independent*, 26 October 2003.

—— (2005) 'Ekran-e sal: sinema-ye Iran 82', *Mahnameh-ye sinema'i-ye film*, 328: 297–379.

Ansari, A. (2006) *Iran, Islam and democracy: the politics of managing change*, London: Royal Institute of International Affairs.

Ansari, S. (2002) 'Introduction', in S. Ansari and V. Martin (eds), *Women, religion and culture in Iran*, Surry: Curzon Press.

Appadurai, A. (1991) 'Global ethnoscopes: notes and queries for a transnational anthropology', in R. Fox (ed.), *Recapturing anthropology: working in the present*, Santa Fe: School of American Research Press.

Arato, A. and Cohen, J. (1992) *Civil society and political theory*, Cambridge, MA: MIT Press.

Arora, P. (1994) 'The production of third world subjects for first world consumption: *Salaam Bombay* and Parama', in D. Carson et al. (eds), *Multiple voices in feminist film criticism*, London: University of Minnesota Press.

Atebba'i, M. (2003) 'Az eftekhar ta baznegari: hozur-e beinolmelali-ye cinema-ye novin-e Iran', *San'at-e Sinema*, 9: 78.

—— (2004a) *25 sal sinema-ye Iran: javayez va hozur-e beinolmelali*, Tehran: Entesharat-e bonyad-e sinema'i-ye farabi.

—— (2004b) 'Hozur-e beinolmelali-ye sinema-ye, Iran dar sal-e 1381', *Mahnameh-ye sinema'i-ye film*, 312: 73–75.

—— (2005) 'Negahi be hozurha-ye beinolmelali-ye sinema-ye Iran', *Mahnameh-ye Sinema'i-ye Film*, 328: 67–68.

Atton, C. (2002) *Alternative media*, London: Sage Publications.

Avila, R. (2001) 'The unvanquished', http://www.sfbg.com/AandE/sffilm/filma.html, (accessed 25 April 2005).

Avini, M. (2000) *Ayeneh-ye jadu: maqalat-e sinema'i*, Tehran: Nashr-e Saqi.

—— (2002) *Ayeneh-ye jadu: naqdha-ye sinema'i*, Tehran: Nashr-e Saqi.

Azmoudeh, A. (2008) http://www.bbc.co.uk/persian/arts/story/2008/01/080124_v-aa-fajr-film-names.shtml (accessed 25 January 2008).

Babagoli, M. (2003) 'Sinema-ye ba'd az enqelab: sal shomar 1361–80', in *San'at-e Sinema*, 9: 12–26.

Baharlu, A. (2000) *Abbas Kiarostami*, Tehran: Nowruz-e honar.

—— (2002) *Sad chehreh-ye sinema-ye Iran*, Tehran: Nashr-e qatreh.

Bakhash, S. (1984) *The Reign of the Ayatollahs: Iran and the Islamic Revolution*, New York: Basic Books.

Baktiari, B. (1996) *Parliamentary politics in revolutionary Iran: the institutionalization of factional politics*, Gainsville: University of Florida Press.

Barker, M. and Brooks K. (1998) *Knowing audiences: Judge Dredd, its friends, fans, and foes*, Luton: University of Luton Press.

Behnoud, M. (1998) 'Abbas-e azhans-e shish'i', *Mahnameh-ye sinema'i-ye film*, 223: 14.

Bennett, T. (1983) 'The Bond phenomenon: theorising a popular hero', *Southern Review*, 16 (2): 195–225.

Bhabha, H. (1990) 'The third space', in J. Rutherford (ed.), *Identity: community, culture and distance*, London: Laurence and Wishart.

Bird, S.E. (2003) *The audience in everyday life: living in a media world*, London: Routledge.

Bobo, J. (1988) *Black women as cultural readers*, New York: Columbia University Press.

—— (1995) 'The color purple: black women as cultural readers', in D. Pribram (ed.), *Female spectators: looking at film and television*, London: Verso.

Brecht, B. (1967) *Gesammelte Werke*, Frankfurt am Main: Suhrkamp.

Brunsdon, C. and Morley D. (1978) *Nationwide*, London: British Film Institute.

Butler, J. (1990) *Gender trouble: feminism and the subversion of identity*, London: Routledge.

Cheah, P. (1998) 'Introduction part II: the cosmopolitan today', in P. Cheah and B. Robbins (eds), *Cosmopolitics: thinking and feeling beyond the nation*, Minneapolis: University of Minnesota Press.

Chelkowski, P. (ed.) (1979) *Ta'ziyeh: ritual and drama in Iran*, New York: New York University Press.

Cheshire, G. (2001) 'Iran's high-water mark the not-so-New Wave', http://www.villagevoice.com/film/0116,cheshire,23942,20.html (accessed 20 April 2003).

Clifford, J. (1986) 'Introduction: partial truths', in J. Clifford and G. Marcus (eds), *Writing culture: the poetics and politics of ethnography*, London: University of California Press.

Cook, D. (1981) *A history of narrative film*, New York: Norton.

Corner, W. (1991) 'Meaning, genre and context: the problematics of public knowledge in the new audience studies', in J. Curran and M. Gurevitch (eds), *Mass media and society*, London: Methuen.

Counihan, M. (1972) 'Orthodoxies, revisionism and guerrilla warfare in mass communication research', CCCS mimeo, University of Birmingham.

Cox, L. (1997) 'Towards a sociology of counter cultures?', in E. McKenna and R. O'Sullivan (eds), *Ireland: emerging perspectives*, Belfast: QUB Dept. of Sociology and Social Policy.

Curran, J. (1990) 'The crisis of opposition, a reprisal', in B. Pimlott et al. (eds), *The alternative*, London: W.H. Allen.

Dabashi, H. (1995) 'Re-reading reality: Kiarostami's through the olive trees and the cultural politics of a postrevolutionary aesthetics', *Critique*, 7: 63–89.

—— (1998) 'Body-less faces: mutilating modernity and abstracting women in an "Islamic cinema"', *Visual Anthropology*, 10 (2/4): 361–80.

—— (2001) *Close up: Iranian cinema, past, present and future*, London: Verso.

—— (2002) 'Dead certainties: the early Makhmalbaf', in R. Tapper (ed.), *The new Iranian cinema: politics, representation and identity*, London: I.B. Tauris.

—— (2007) *Makhmalbaf at large: the making of a rebel filmmaker,* London: I.B.Tauris.

Dad, B. (1998) *Sad ruz ba khatami*, Tehran: Entesharat-e vezarat-e ershad va farhang-e eslami.

Dariush, H. (1964) 'Shab-e quzi', *Honar va sinema,* 9: 80.

Devictor, A. (2002) 'Classic tools, original goals: cinema and public policy in the Islamic Republic of Iran (1979–97)', in R. Tapper (ed.), *The new Iranian cinema: politics, representation and identity*, London: I.B. Tauris.

Dickey. S. (1993) *Cinema and the urban poor in south India*, Cambridge: Cambridge University Press.

Ditmars, H. (1996) 'From the top of the hill', *Sight and Sound*, 6 (12):10–14.

Dorostkar, R. (2000) 'Mojha va jarayanha-ye asli-ye sinema-ye haftad saleh-ye Iran', *Faslnameh-ye sinema'i-ye farabi,* 10 (37): 7–42.

Dorostkar, R. and 'Aqili S. (2002) *Bahman-e Farmanara: zendegi va asar*, Tehran: Nashr-e qatreh.

Dowlatkhah, P. (2008) http://www.bbc.co.uk/persian/arts/story/2008/04/080412_an-pd-harandi.shtml (accessed 8 June 2008).

Downing, J. (1984) *Radical media: the political the political experience of alternative communication*, Boston, MA: South End Press.

—— (2001) *Radical media: rebellious communication and social movements*, London: Sage Publications.

—— (2003) 'Audiences and readers of alternative media: the absent lure of the virtually unknown', *Media, culture and society*, 25 (5): 625–45.

Dyer, R. (1986) *Heavenly bodies: film stars and society*, New York: St. Martin's Press.

Egan, E. (2005) *Films of Makhmalbaf: cinema politics and culture in Iran*, Washington, DC: Mage Publishers.

Emerson, R. and Shaw L. (1995) *Writing ethnographic fieldnotes*, Chicago: University of Chicago Press.

Fanon, F. (2001) *The wretched of the earth*, trans. C. Farrington, London: Penguin.

Farahmand, A. (2002) 'Perspectives on the recent (international acclaim of) Iranian cinema', in R. Tapper (ed.), *The new Iranian cinema: politics, representation and identity*, London: I.B. Tauris.

Farmanara, B. (2002) 'Khaneh-ye ru-ye ab gereftar-e moluk altavayefi-ye farhangi ast', *Hayat-e No*, 803: 12.

Ferasati, M. (1989) 'Ba siahi be jang-e siyahi', *Sorush*, 11 (472): 42–44.

Fischer, M. (1984) 'Towards a Third World poetics: seeing through short stories and films in the Iranian culture area', *Knowledge and society*, 5: 171–241.

—— (2004) *Mute dreams, blind owls, and dispersed knowledges: Persian poesis in the transnational circuitry*, Durham: Duke University Press.

Fish, S. (1980) *Is there a text in this class?: the authority of interpretive communities*, Cambridge, MA: Harvard University Press.

Fiske, J. (1989) *Television culture*, London: Routledge.

Foucault, M. (1981) *The history of sexuality. Volume 1: an introduction*, Harmondsworth: Penguin.

Fox, R. and Starn O. (1997) 'Introduction', in R. Fox and O. Starn (eds), *Between resistance and revolution*, London: Rutgers University Press.

Fraser, N. (1992) 'Rethinking public sphere: a contribution to the critique of actually existing democracy', in C. Calhoun (ed.), *Habermas and the public sphere*, Cambridge, MA: MIT Press.

Gaffary, F. (1989) 'Coup d'oeil sur les 35 premières années du cinéma en Iran', in Y. Richard (ed.), *Entre l'Iran et l'Occident*, Paris: Maisons des Sciences de l'Homme.

Gerami, S. (1996) *Women and Fundamentalism: Islam and Christianity*, New York: Garland Publishing.

Getino, O. (1986) 'Some notes on the concept of a "Third Cinema"', in T. Barnard (ed.), *Argentine cinema*, Toronto: Nightwood Editions.

Ghaffuri-Azar, B. (2003) '*Sorkh va siyah: janjalha va hashiyehha-ye sal-e 1381*', *Mahnameh-ye sinema'i-ye film*, 312: 58–61.

Ghazian, H. (2002) 'The crisis in the Iranian film industry and the role of government', in R. Tapper (ed.), *The new Iranian cinema: politics, representation and identity*, London: I.B. Tauris.

Golestan, S. (1995) *Fanus-e khiyal: sargozasht-e sinema-ye Iran az aghaz ta piruzi-e enqelab-e Islami*, Tehran: Entesharat-e kavir.

Golmakani, H. (1992) 'New times, same problems', *Index on censorship*, 21 (3): 19–22.

Gow, C. (2006) *Iranian Cinema in long shot*, unpublished thesis, University of Warwick.

Gramsci, A. (1971) *Antonio Gramsci: selections from political writings (1921–1926)*, trans. and eds Q. Hoare and G. Nowell-Smith, London: Lawrence and Wishart.

Habermas, J. (1989) *The structural transformation of the public sphere: an inquiry into a category of bourgeois society*, translated by T. Burger with the assistance of F. Lawrence, Cambridge, MA.: MIT Press.

Haghayeghi, M. (1993) 'Politics and ideology in theIslamic republic of Iran', Middle Eastern Studies, 29(1): 36–52.

Hall, S. (1973) 'Encoding and decoding the TV message', CCCS mimeo, University of Birmingham.

—— (1980) 'Encoding/decoding', in S. Hall (ed.), *Culture, media, language: working papers in cultural studies, 1972–79*, London: Hutchinson.

—— (1982) 'The rediscovery of ideology: the return of the repressed in media studies', in M. Gurevich, et al. (eds), *Culture society and the media*, London: Methuen.

—— (1989) 'Reflections upon the encoding/decoding model: an interview with Stuart Hall', in Cruz and Lewis (eds), *Viewing, reading, listening: audiences and cultural reception*, Boulder, CO: Westview.

—— (1996) 'The problem of ideology, Marxism without guarantees', in D. Morley and C. Kuan-Hsing (eds), *Stuart Hall: critical dialogues in cultural studies*, London: Routledge.

Hanisch, C. (1978) 'The personal is political', in Redstockings of the Women's Liberation Movement (eds), *Feminist revolution,* New York: Random House.

Hartley, J. (2002) *Communication, cultural studies, media studies: the key concepts*, London: Routledge.

Hatamikia, E. (1991) 'Sinemgaran-e irani va hozur-e beinolmelali', *Faslnameh-ye sinema'i-ye farabi*, 3(2): 169–71.

Heydarzadeh, A. (2003) 'Janjalha-ye namayesh-e film dar sal-e 80: nimeh-ye penhan-e bacheha-ye bad-e sinema-ye 1380', *Mahnameh-ye sinema'i-ye film*, 296 (sup, Bahman 1381).

Higgins, P. and Ghaffari, P. (1994) 'Women's education in the Islamic Republic of Iran', in M. Afkhami and E. Friedl (eds), *In the eye of the storm: women in post-revolutionary Iran*, Syracuse: Syracuse University Press.

Hojjati, M. (2003) 'Honarmandani az yek dowran-e separi shodeh', *Yas-e no,* 11: 7.

Honarkar, H. (2005) http://www.bbc.co.uk/persian/arts/story/2005/12/051221_pm-hh-fall-review.shtml (accessed 5 March 2006).

Hosseini, G. and Khani M. (1989) 'Arusi-ye khuban, jang va basij', *Resalat*, No. 973.

Inness, S. (2004) '"Boxing gloves and bustiers": new images of tough women', in S. Inness (ed.), *Action chicks: new images of tough women in popular culture*, New York: Palgrave Macmillan.

Irfani, S. (1996) 'New discourses and modernity in post-revolutionary Iran', *The American journal of Islamic social sciences*, 13(1): 13–27.

Issa, R. and Whitaker, S. (eds) (1999) *Life and art: the new Iranian cinema*, London: National Film Theatre.

Issari, M. (1989) *Cinema in Iran 1900–1979*, London: Scarecrow.

Jannati, A. (1997) 'Sinema az nazar-e feqahat', *Gozaresh-e farabi*, 1: 42–44.

Javedani, H. (2002) *Sal-shomar-e tarikh-e sinema-ye Iran: tir-e 1279-shahrivar-e 1379*, Tehran: Nashr-e Qatreh.

Jenkins, H. (2000) 'Reception theory and audience research: the mystery of the vampire's kiss', in C. Gledhill and L. Williams (eds), *Reinventing film studies*, London: Arnold.

Keddie, N. (2004) *Modern Iran: roots and results of revolution*, London: Yale University Press.

Khiabany, G. and Sreberny, A. (2004) 'The women's press in Iran: engendering the public sphere', in N. Sakr (ed.), *Women and media in the Middle East*, London: I.B. Tauris.

Laclau, E. (1990) *New reflections on the revolution of our time*, London: Verso.

Laclau, E. and Mouffe, C. (1985) *Hegemony and socialist strategy: towards a radical democratic politics*, trans. by W. Moore and P. Cammak, London: Verso.

Lahiji, S. (2002) 'Chaste dolls succeed unchaste dolls: women in Iranian cinema since 1979', in R. Tapper (ed.), *The new Iranian cinema: politics, representation and identity*, London: I.B. Tauris.

Lewis, J. (1991) *The ideological octopus*. London: Routledge.

Lin, X. (2002) 'New Chinese cinema of the "Sixth Generation" a distant cry of forsaken children', *Third text*, 16 (3): 261–84.

Lindhof, T. (1995) *Qualitative communication research methods*, Thousand Oaks: Sage.

Linnekin, J. and Poyer, L. (1990) 'Introduction', in J.S. Linnekin and L. Poyer (eds), *Ethnicity in the pacific*, Honolulu: University of Hawaii Press.

Livingstone, S. (1998) 'Audience research at crossroads: the "implied audience" in media and cultural theory', *European journal of cultural studies*, 1 (2): 193–217.

Lu, S. (2004) 'National cinema, cultural critique, transnational capital: the films of Zhang Yimou', in S. Lu and E. Yeh (eds), *Chinese-language film: historiography, poetics, politics*, Honolulu: University of Hawaii Press.

Macdonald, M. (1995) *Representing women: myths of femininity in the popular media*, New York: Arnold.

Makhmalbaf, M. (1986) *Crystal Garden/Bagh-e bolur*, Tehran: Nashr-e Ney.

—— (1997) *Zendegi rang ast,* Tehran: Nashr-e ney.

Marcus, G. (1994) 'On ideologies of reflexivity in contemporary efforts to remake the human sciences', *Poetics today*, 15 (3): 383–404.

—— (1998) *Ethnography through thick and thin*, Princeton: Princeton University Press.

Marcus G. and Fischer, M. (1986) *Anthropology as cultural critique: an experimental moment in the human sciences*, 2nd edn, Chicago: University of Chicago Press.

Marks, L. (2000) *The skin of the film: intercultural cinema, embodiment and the senses*, London: Duke University Press.

Marx, C. with Engels, F. (1998) *German ideology*, New York: Prometheus Books.

Marx, K. (1845) 'Theses on Feuerbach', in *Collected works, Vol. 5*, New York: International Publishers.

Mazra'eh, H. (2001) *Fereshteha-ye sukhteh: naqd va barresi-ye sinema-ye tahmineh milani*, Tehran: Nashr-e varjand.

McArthur, C. (1994) 'The cultural necessity of a poor Celtic cinema', in J. Hill et al. (eds), *Border crossing: film in Ireland, Britain and Europe*, Belfast: Institute of Irish Studies.

Mehrabi, M. (1984) *Tarikh-i sinima-yi Iran: az aghaz ta sal-i 1357*, Tehran: Entesharat-e film.

Melucci, A. (1995) 'The new social movements revisited: reflections on a sociological misunderstanding', in L. Maheu (ed.), *Social movements and social classes: the future of collective action*, London: Sage.

Merton, R.K. (1946) *Mass persuasion*, New York: Free Press.

Milani, M. (1994) *The making of Iran's Islamic revolution: from anarchy to Islamic Republic*, Oxford: Westview Press.

Milani, T. (2001) *Nimeh-ye penhan*, Tehran: Tofiqafarin.

Millet, K. (1982) *Going to Iran*, New York: Coward, McCann and Georghegan.

—— (1999) *Islam and gender: the religious debate in contemporary Iran*, Princeton: Princeton University Press.

Mir-Hosseini, Z. (2000) 'Feminist movements in the Islamic Republic', http://www.hamta.co.uk/feminist.htm (accessed 2 July 2000).

—— (2002) 'Negotiating the politics of gender in Iran: an ethnography of a documentary', in R. Tapper (ed.), *The new Iranian cinema: politics, representation and identity*, London: I.B. Tauris.

—— (2003) 'The construction of gender in Islamic legal thought and strategies for reform', *Hawwa*, 1 (1): 1 – 28.

Mirsalim, M. (1997) 'Fonun-e dastansari dar qor'an', *Gozaresh-e farabi,* 1: 34–38.

Mo'tamedi, A. (2000) 'Sangha'i ke partab nashod', *Mahnameh-ye sinema'i-ye film*, 264: 16.

Moghadam, V. (2002) 'Islamic feminism and its discontents: towards resolution of the debate', *Signs: Journal of women in culture and society*, 27 (4): 1135–71.

Moghissi, H. (1996) 'Public life and women's resistance', in S. Rahnama and S. Behrad (eds), *Iran after the revolution: crisis of an Islamic state*, London: I.B. Tauris.

—— (1997) 'Populist feminism and Islamic feminism: a critique of neo-conservative tendencies among Iranian academic feminists', *Kankash*, 13: 57–95.

Mohajerani, A. (1999) *Estizah*, Tehran: Entesharat-e Etela'at.

Mohammad-Kashi, S. (2000) 'Barresi-ye elal va avamel-e movaffaqiyat-e sinema-ye Iran dar qarb', *Faslnameh-ye sinema'i-ye farabi*, 10 (3): 51–70.

Morley, D. (1980a) *The Nationwide audience*, London: BFI Publishing.

—— (1980b) 'Texts, readers, subjects', in S. Hall et al. (eds), *Culture, media, language: working papers in cultural studies 1972–79*, London: Routledge.

—— (1997) 'Theoretical orthodoxies: textualism, constructivism an the new ethnography', in M. Ferguson and P. Golding (eds), *Cultural studies in question*, London: Sage.

Morley, D. and Brunsdon, C. (1999) *The Nationwide television studies*, London: Routledge.

Moslem, M. (2002) *Factional politics in post-Khomeini Iran*, Syracuse: Syracuse University Press.

Mueller, R. (1989) *Bertolt Brecht and the theory of media*, Lincoln: University of Nebraska Press.

Mulvey, L. (1987) 'Notes on Sirk and Melodrama', in C. Gledhill (ed.), *Home is where the heart is: studies in melodrama and the women's film*, London: BFI Publishing.

—— (1998) 'Kiarostami's Uncertainty Principle', *Sight and Sound*, 8 (6): 24–27.

—— (2002) 'Afterword', in R. Tapper (ed.), *The new Iranian cinema: politics, representation and identity*, London: I.B. Tauris.

Naficy, H. (1993) *The making of exiled cultures: Iranian television in Los Angeles*, London: University of Minnesota Press.

—— (1994) 'Veiled vision/powerful presences: women in post-revolutionary Iranian cinema', in M. Afkhami and E. Friedl (eds), *In the eye of the storm: women in post-revolutionary Iran*, Syracuse: Syracuse University Press.

—— (1999) 'Iranian cinema', in R. Issa and S. Whitaker (eds), *Life and art: the new Iranian cinema*, London: National Film Theatre.

—— (2001a) 'Veiled voice and vision in Iranian cinema: the evolution of Rakhshan Banietemad's films', in M. Pomerance (ed.), *Ladies and gentlemen, boys and girls: gender in film at the end of the 20th century*, New York: State University of New York Press.

—— (2001b) *An accented cinema: exilic and diasporic filmmaking*, Princeton: Princeton University Press.

—— (2002) 'Islamizing film culture in Iran: a post-Khatami update', in R. Tapper (ed.), *The new Iranian cinema: politics, representation and identity*, London: I.B. Tauris.

Najmabadi, A. (1999) 'Reading for gender through Qajar paintings', in L. Diba (ed.), *Royal Persian paintings: the Qajar epoch, 1785–1925*, London: I.B. Tauris.

Nakane, C. (1983) 'The effects of cultural tradition on anthropologists', in H. Fahim (ed.), *Indigenous anthropology in non-Western countries*, Durham: Carolina Academic Press.

Nuri, A. (ed.) (1996) *Majmu'e-ye qavanin va moqarrarat-e vezarate farhang va ershad-e eslami va sazemanha-ye vabasteh*, Tehran: Daftar-e hoquqi-ye vezarate farhang va ershad-e eslami.

O'Sullivan, T. (1994) 'Alternative media', in T. O'Sullivan et al. (eds), *Key concepts in communication and cultural studies,* London: Routledge, p.10.

Omid, J. (1998) *Tarikh-e sinema-ye Iran 1900–1978*, Tehran: Entesharat-e rowzaneh.

Paidar, P. (1995) *Women and the political process in twentieth-century Iran*, Cambridge: Cambridge University Press.

Parhami, S. (1999) 'Iranian cinema: before the revolution', http://www.horschamp.qc.ca/new_offscreen/preiran.html (accessed 3 April 2002).

Potter, J. and Wetherell, M. (1987) *Discourse and social psychology: beyond attitudes and behaviour*, London: Sage.

Qaderi, A. (2003) 'Negahi be vakonesh-e panjom: janjal az hame chiz mohemtar ast?', *Jashvareh: ruznameh-yeb istoyekomin jashvareh-ye beinolmelali-ye film-e fajr*, 7: 7.

Rahimieh, N. (2002) 'Marking gender and difference in the myth of the nation: bashu, a post-revolutionary Iranian Film', in R. Tapper (ed.), *The new Iranian cinema: politics, representation and identity*, London: I.B. Tauris.

Rajaee, F. (1999) 'A thermidor of "Islamic Yuppies"?: conflict and compromise in Iran's politics', *Middle East Journal*, 53 (2): 217–31.

Ridgeon, L. (2000) *Makhmalbaf's broken mirror: the socio-political significance of modern Iranian cinema*, Durham: University of Durham, Centre for Middle Eastern and Islamic Studies.

Rohani, O. (2000) 'Introduction to an analytical history of Iranian cinema (1929–78): from roots to clichés', *Tavoos,* 5 & 6, Autumn 2000 & Winter 2001.

Roseneil, S. and Seymoure, J. (1999) 'Practising identities: power and resistance', in S. Roseneil and J. Seymoure (eds), *Practising identities: power and resistance*, Basingstoke: Macmillan Press.

Sadr, H. (1999) 'Hich herfeh'i mesl-e herfeh-ye namaiesh nist', *Mahnameh-ye sinema'i-ye film*, 236: 12–13.

—— (2002a) 'Children in contemporary Iranian cinema: when we were children . . .', in R. Tapper (ed.), *The new Iranian cinema: politics, representation and identity*, London: I.B. Tauris.

—— (2002b) *Tarikh-e siasi-ye sinema-ye Iran*,Tehran: Ney Publishing House.

Saeed-Vafa, M. and Rosenbaum, J. (2003) *Abbas Kiarostami,* Urbana, IL: University of Illinois Press.

Saffarian, N. (1998) 'Azhans-e shishe'i mokhalef-e jame'eh-ye madani nist', *Mahnameh-ye sinema'i-ye film*, 223.

Sarachild, K. (1978) 'Consciousness-raising: a radical weapon', in Redstockings of the Women's Liberation Movement (eds), *Feminist revolution*, New York: Random House.

Sayyad, P. (1996) 'The cinema of the Islamic Republic of Iran', *Iran Nameh*, 4 (3), reproduced in http://www.fis-irn.org/cinema.htm (accessed 9 March 2000).

Scholte, B. (1972) 'Towards reflexive and critical anthropology', in D. Hymes (ed.), *Reinventing anthropology*, New York: Pantheon Books.

Scott, J. (1985) *Weapons of the weak: everyday forms of peasant resistance*, London: Yale University Press.

Sharabi, H. (1988) *Neopatriarchy: a theory of distorted change in Arab society*, New York: Oxford University Press.

Shari'ati, A. (1979) *Majmu'eh-ye asar*, Tehran: Husseinieh-ye Ershad Press.

Siavoshi, S. 1997. 'Cultural policies and the Islamic Republic: cinema and book publication', *International Journal of Middle East Studies*, Vol. 29, No. 4, pp. 1482–84.

Skeggs, B. (1997) *Formations of class and gender: becoming respectable*, London: Sage.

Solanas, F. and Getino, O. (1976) 'Towards a Third Cinema', in B. Nichols (ed.), *Movies and methods, volume I,* Berkeley and Los Angeles: University of California Press.

Sreberny, A. (2000) 'Media and diasporic consciousness: an exploration among Iranians in London', In S. Cottle (ed.), *Ethnic minorities and the media*, Philadelphia: Open University Press.

—— (2002) 'Globalization and me: thinking at the boundary', in J. Chan and B. McIntyre (eds), *In search of boundaries: communication, nation-states and cultural identities*, London: Ablex Publishing.

Sreberny, A. and Zoonen, L. (2000) 'Gender, politics and communication: an introduction', in A. Sreberny and L. Zoonen (eds), *Gender, politics and communication*, Cresskill, NJ: Hampton Press.

Sreberny-Mohammadi, A. and Mohammadi, A. (1994) *Small media, big revolution: communication, culture, and the Iranian revolution,* Minneapolis: University of Minnesota Press.

Srinivas, L. (2002) 'The active audience: spectatorship, social relations and the experience of cinema in India', *Media, Culture and Society*, 24 (1): 155–73.

Srinivas, M. (1966) *Social change in modern India*, Los Angeles: University of California Press.

Stacey, J. (1994) *Star gazing: Hollywood cinema and female spectatorship*, London: Routledge.

—— (1999) 'Feminine fascinations: forms of identification in star-audience relations', in S. Thornham (ed.), *Feminist film theory: a reader*, Edinburgh: Edinburgh University Press.

Staiger, J. (2000) *Perverse spectators: the practices of film reception*, New York: New York University Press.

Stam, R. (2000) *Films theory: an introduction*, London: Blackwell.

Stephenson, J.B. and Greer, L.S. (1981) 'Ethnographers in their own cultures: two Appalachian cases', *Human organization*, 40 (2): 123–30.

Stokes, G. (1997) 'Introduction', in G. Stokes (ed.), *The politics of identity in Australia*, Cambridge: Cambridge University Press.

Tabe'-Mohammadi, S. (2000) 'Goft-e gui ba Abbas Kiarostami: hargez film-e siasi nakhaham sakht', *Mahnameh-ye sinema'i-ye film*, 245: 42–44.

Talebinejad, A. (1998) *Dar hozur-e sinema: tarikh-e tahlili-ye sinema-ye ba'd az enqelab*, Tehran: Farabi Cinema Foundation Publications.

Tapper, R. (2002) 'Introduction', in R. Tapper (ed.), *The new Iranian cinema: politics, representation and identity*, London: I.B. Tauris.

Taraqijah, M. (1989) 'Arusi-ye khuban va edalat-e ejtema'i', *Sorush*, 11 (472): 37–39.

Turner, V. (1984) 'Liminality and the performance genre', in J. MacAloon (ed.), *Rite, drama, festival, spectacle*, Philadelphia: Institute of Study of Human Issues.

—— (1986) *The anthropology of performance*, New York: PAJ Publications.

—— (1990) 'Are there universals of performance in myth, ritual and drama?', in R. Schechner and W. Appel (eds), *By means of performance: intercultural studies of theatre and ritual*, Cambridge: Cambridge University Press.

Walkerdine, V. (1999) 'Video replay: families, films and fantasies', in S. Thornham (ed.), *Feminist film theory: a reader*, Edinburgh: Edinburgh University Press.

Watson, G. (1987) 'Make me reflexive – but not yet: strategies for managing essentials reflexivity in ethnographic discourse', *Journal of anthropological research*, 43 (1): 29–41.

Weston, K. (1997) 'The virtual anthropologist', in A. Gupta and J. Ferguson (eds), *Anthropological locations*, Berkeley: University of California Press.

Whitaker, S. (1999) 'Rakhshan Bani-Etemad', in R. Issa and S. Whitaker (eds), *Life and art: the new Iranian cinema*, London: National Film Theatre.

Willemen, P. (1989) 'The Third Cinema question: notes and reflections', in J. Pines and P. Willemen (eds), *Questions of Third Cinema*, London: BFI Publishing.

Williams, R. (1976) *Keywords: a vocabulary of culture and society*, London: Fontana Press.

Zeydabadi-Nejad, S. (2007) 'Iranian intellectuals and contact with the West: the case of Iranian cinema', *British Journal of Middle Eastern Studies*, 34 (3): 375–98.

—— (Forthcoming) '10: women in Kiarostami's cinema', in R. Tapper and L. Mulvey (eds), *Beyond the veil, behind the lens: women in Iranian cinema*.

Zoonen, L. (1994) *Feminist media studies*, London: Sage.

# Filmography

—— *10* (Abbas Kiarostami, 2002, Iran/France/USA)
—— *20 Fingers/Bist angosht* (Mania Akbari, 2004, Iran)
—— *ABC Africa* (Abbas Kiarostami, 2001, Uganda/Iran)
—— *Abjad* (Abolfazl Jalili, 2003, Iran/France)
—— *And Your Mother Too/Y tu mamá también* (Alfonso Cuaron, 2001, Mexico)
—— *Apple, The/Sib* (Samira Makhmalbaf, 1998, Iran/France)
—— *Ashamed/Sharmsar* (Esmail Kushan, 1950, Iran)
—— *At Five in the Afternoon/Panj-e asr* (Samira Makhmalbaf, 2003, Iran/France)
—— *Barzakhiha* (Iraj Qaderi, 1982, Iran)
—— *Bashu, the Little Stranger/Bashu, Gharibeh-ye Kuchak* (Bahram Beyza'i, 1985, Iran)
—— *Battle of Algiers/La Battaglia di Algeri* (Gillo Pontecorvo, 1966, Algeria/Italy)
—— *Beijing Bicycle/Shiqi sui de dan che* (Xioshuai Wang, 2001, Taiwan/China)
—— *Bemani* (Dariush Mehrju'i, 2002, Iran)
—— *Bowling for Colombine* (Michael Moore, 2002, USA)
—— *Brick and the Mirror, The/Khest-va Ayeneh* (Ebrahim Golestan, 1965, Iran)
—— *Children of Divorce/Bacheh-ye talaq* (Tahmineh Milani, 1989, Iran)
—— *Children of Heaven/Bachehha-ye aseman* (Majid Majidi, 1997, Iran)
—— *Circle, The/Dayereh* (Jafar Panahi, 2000, Iran/Switzerland/Italy)
—— *City of God/Cidade de Deus* (Fernando Meirelles and Katia Lund, 2002, Brazil/France/USA)
—— *Close-up/Nama-ye Nazdik* (Abbas Kiarostami, 1990, Iran)
—— *Colour of Paradise, The/Rang-e Khoda* (Majid Majidi, 1999, Iran)
—— *Colour of Pomegranate, The/Sayat Nova* (Sergei Parajanov, 1968, Soviet Union)
—— *Cow, The/Gav* (Dariush Mehrju'i, 1969, Iran).
—— *Crimson Gold/Tala-ye sorkh* (Jafar Panahi, 2003, Iran)
—— *Croesus' Treasure/Ganj-e Qarun* (Siamak Yasemi, 1965, Iran)
—— *Crow, The/Kalagh* (Bahram Beyza'i, 1978, Iran)
—— *Cyclist, The/Baisikelran* (Mohsen Makhmalbaf, 1989, Iran)
—— *Daughters of the Sun* (Maryam Shahriyar, 2000, Iran).
—— *Dead Wave/Moj-e mordeh* (Ebrahim Hatamikia, 2001, Iran)
—— *Deep Breath/Nafas-e Amiq* (Parviz Shahbazi, 2003, Iran)
—— *Dog Day Afternoon* (Sidney Lumet, 1975, USA)
—— *Duel* (Ahmad-Reza Darvish, 2004, Iran)
—— *Fifth Reaction/Vakonesh-e panjom* (Tahmineh Milani, 2003, Iran)
—— *From Karkheh to Rhine/Az karkheh ta rain* (Ebrahim Hatamikia, 1993, Iran)
—— *Gabbeh* (Mohsen Makhmalbaf, 1996, Iran/France)

—— *Ghost* (Jerry Zuker, 1990, USA)

—— *Glass Agency/Azhans-e shisheh'i* (Ebrahim Hatamikia, 1997, Iran)

—— *Golnesa* (Serzh Azarian, 1953, Iran)

—— *Haj Aqa, the Cinema Actor/Haj aqa aktor-e sinema* (Avans Oganians, 1933, Iran)

—— *Harmonica/Sazdahani* (Amir Naderi, 1974, Iran)

—— *Hemlock/Shokaran* (Behruz Afkhami, 2000, Iran)

—— *Hidden Half, The/Nimeh-ye penhan* (Tahmineh Milani, 2001, Iran)

—— *House is Black, The/Khaneh Siah Ast* (Farough Farrokhzad, 1963, Iran)

—— *House on the Water/Khaneh'i ru-ye ab* (Bahman Farmanara, 2001, Iran)

—— *Identity/Hoviat* (Ebrahim Hatamikia, 1986, Iran)

—— *In the Alleys of Love/Dar kucheh-ha-ye eshq* (Khosrow Sina'i, 1992, Iran)

—— *In the Slaughterhouse of Love/Dar maslakh-e eshq* (Kamal Tabrizi, 1988, Iran)

—— *Jamón, Jamón* (Bigas Luna, 1992, Spain)

—— *Kandahar/Safar-e Qandehar* (Mohsen Makhmalbaf, 2001, Iran/France)

—— *Keeper: the Legend of Omar Khayam, The* (Kayvan Mashayekh, 2005, USA)

—— *Killing Rabids/Sag Koshi* (Bahram Beiza'i, 2001, Iran/France)

—— *Lead/Sorb* (Mas'ud Kimiya'i, 1989, Iran)

—— *Leili is with Me/Leili ba man ast* (Kamal Tabrizi, 1996, Iran)

—— *Letters of the Wind/Nameha-ye bad* (Alireza Amini, 2002, Iran)

—— *Life and Nothing More* aka *And Life Goes On . . . /Zendegi va digar hich* (Abbas Kiarostami, 1991, Iran)

—— *Lizard, The/Marmulak* (Kamal Tabrizi, 2004, Iran)

—— *Lor Girl, The/Dokhtar-e lor* (Ardeshir Irani, 1933, Iran/India)

—— *Marriage of the Blessed/Arusi-ye khuban* (Mohsen Makhmalbaf, 1989, Iran)

—— *Martyrdom Seekers/Shahadat talaban* (Kamal Tabrizi, 1980, Iran)

—— *Matrimony of the Good/Vasl-e nikan* (Ebrahim Hatamikia, 1992, Iran)

—— *May Lady/Banu-ye ordibehesht* (Rakhshan Bani-Etemad, 1997, Iran)

—— *Mix, The/Miks* (Dariush Mehrju'i, 2000, Iran)

—— *Mojahid's Call/Faryad-e mojahed* (Mehdi Ma'danian, 1980, Iran)

—— *Moment of Innocence, A/Nun-o-goldun* (Mohsen Makhmalbaf, 1996, Iran/France)

—— *Mongols, The/Mogholha* (Parviz Kimiavi, 1973, Iran)

—— *Mrs Ahou's Husband/Shohar-e Ahu Khanum* (Davud Mollapur, 1968, Iran)

—— *Narges* (Rakhshan Bani-Etemad, 1992, Iran)

—— *Nasuh's Repentence/Tobeh-ye nasuh* (Mohsen Makhmalbaf, 1983, Iran)

—— *Night Never Ends, The/Dar emtedad-e shab* (Parviz Sayyad, 1977, Iran)

—— *Night of the Hunchback/Shab-e quzi* (Farrokh Ghaffari, 1964, Iran)

—— *Nights of Zayandehrud/Shabha-ye Zayandehrud* (Mohsen Makhmalbaf, 1991, Iran)

—— *Offside/Afsaid* (Jafar Panahi, 2006, Iran)

—— *Once upon a Time Cinema/Naseroddin shah aktor-e sinema* (Mohsen Makhmalbaf, 1992, Iran)

—— *One Night/Yek shab* (Niki Karimi, 2005, Iran)

—— *Passage/Obur* (Kamal Tabrizi, 1988, Iran)

—— *Peddler, The/Dastforush* (Mohsen Makhmalbaf, 1986, Iran)

—— *Prince Ehtejab/Shazdeh Etehjab* (Bahman Farmanara, 1974, Iran)

—— *Qamar Khanom's House/Khane-ye qamar khanom* (Bahman Farmanara, 1972, Iran)

—— *Qeysar* (Mas'ud Kimia'i, 1969, Iran)

—— *Rabbit Proof Fence* (Phillip Noyce, 2002, Australia)

—— *Realm of Lovers/Diyar-e asheqan* (Hasan Karbakhsh, 1984, Iran)

—— *Red/Qermez* (Ferydun Jeyrani, 1999, Iran)

—— *Report, The/Gozaresh* (Abbas Kiarostami, 1977, Iran)

—— *Runner, The/Davandeh* (Amir Naderi, 1985, Iran)

—— *Salam Cinema/Salam Sinema* (Mohsen Makhmalbaf, 1995, Iran)

—— *Saving Private Ryan* (Steven Spielberg, 1998, USA)

—— *Sentry/Didehban* (Ebrahim Hatamikia, 1989, Iran)

—— *Shelterless/Bipanah* (Ahmad Fahmi, 1953, Iran)

—— *Simple Event, A/Yek Ettefaq-e Sadeh* (Sohrab Shahid Sales, 1973, Iran)

—— *Smell of Camphor, Scent of Jasmine/Bu-ye kafur, atr-e yas* (Bahman Farmanara, 1999, Iran)

—— *Snowman/Adambarfi* (Davud Mirbaqeri, 1995, Iran)

—— *Son, The/Le Fils* (Jean-Pierre Dardenne, 2002, Belgium/France)

—— *South/Sur* (Fernando Solanas, 1988, Argentina/France)

—— *South of The City/Jonub-e Shahr* (Farrokh Gaffary, 1958, Iran)

—— *Still Life/Tabi'at-e Bijan* (Sohrab Shahid Saless, 1974, Iran)

—— *Tall Shadows of Wind/Sayeha-ye boland-e bad* (Bahman Farmanara, 1978, Iran)

—— *Taste of Cherry/Ta'm-e Gilas* (Abbas Kiarostami, 1997, Iran/France)

—— *Thelma and Louise* (Ridley Scott, 1991, USA)

—— *Through the Olive Trees/Zir-e Derakhtan Zeytun* (Abbas Kiarostami, 1994, Iran/France)

—— *Time of Love/Nobat-e asheqi* (Mohsen Makhmalbaf, 1991, Iran/Turkey)

—— *Travellers, The/Mosaferan* (Bahram Beyza'i, 1992, Iran)

—— *Tutia* (Iraj Qaderi, 1999, Iran)

—— *Two Sightless Eyes/Do cheshm-e bisu* (Mohsen Makhmalbaf, 1984, Iran)

—— *Two Women/Do Zan* (Tahmineh Milani, 1999, Iran)

—— *Under the Moonlight/Zir-e nur-e mah* (Seyyed Reza Mir-karimi, 2001, Iran)

—— *Under the Skin of City/Zir-e oost-e shar* (Rakhsan Bani-Etemad, 2001, Iran)

—— *Water, Wind and Dust/Ab, khak va bad* (Amir Naderi, 1988, Iran)

—— *What's New?/Digeh che khabar?* (Tahmineh Milani, 1992, Iran)

—— *Where Is the Friend's House?/Khaneh-ye dust kojast?* (Abbas Kiarostami, 1987, Iran)

—— *White Balloon, The/Badkonak-e sefid* (Jafar Panahi, 1995, Iran)

—— *Wind Will Carry Us, The/Bad ma ra khahad bord* (Abbas Kiarostami, 1999, Iran/France)

—— *Women's Prison/Zedan-e zanan* (Manijeh Hekmat, 2002, Iran)

—— *Z* (Costas Gavras, 1969, Algeria/France)

# Index

*10* (Kiarostami) 16, 52, 104, 125–36,
150–51, 159, 160
*20 Fingers* (Akbari) 135, 136

*ABC Africa* (Kiarostami) 125
*Abjad* (Jalili) 148
Afkhami, Behruz 41, 51, 103
Afshari, A. 111
Ahangarani, Pegah 157–8
Ahmadinejad, Mahmoud 53
Akbari, Mania 135–6
Akhavan-Sales, Mehdi 33
'Alipur, L. 82
allegory 10–11, 30
alternative cinema 32–4, 139–42
alternative media *see* radical media
Althusser, L. 7, 8, 35
Aminzade, R. 64, 119
Andrew, Geoff 127–8, 136
Ang, I. 16, 104, 116, 137
Ansari, S. 105
Anvar, Fakhred-Din 37, 39–40, 48
Appadurai, A. 21
*The Apple* (Makhmalbaf) 158
Arato, A. 10
Art Centre of the Islamic Propaganda
Organization 38–40, 43, 58
art films *see* festival films
Association of Moslem Writers and Artists
68
Atebba'i, M. 138, 141, 142, 144, 170
Atton, C. 10, 15, 55, 89, 100
audience: concepts of 19–20; engagement
2, 162–3
Avini, M. 42, 146
*Azadi* cinema 147
Azmoudeh, A. 53

'backwardness', representations of 33–4,
138, 140, 153–7
Bahonar, Mohammad-Javed 36
Bani-Etemad, Rakhshan 109, 124, 158–9
Bani-Sadr, A. 36
*Barzakhiha* (Qaderi) 36
Barzargan, Mehdi 36
*Bashu, the Little Stranger* (Beyza'i) 109,
136, 142
*basij* 62, 166
*basiji* 58, 61, 62, 69, 70–73, 97
*batin* 11
Beheshti, Seyed Mohammad 37, 39–40,
42, 43–4, 48, 68, 142–3
Behnoud, M. 73
Bennett, T. 5
Beyza'i, Bahram 41, 49, 50, 79, 136,
156–7
Bhabha, H. 10
Bird, S.E. 20
black market 101–2, 153, 163
*The Blind Owl* (Hedayat) 33
bootlegs *see* black market
box office statistics 60, 72, 86, 114, 158–9
Brecht, Bertolt 11, 88–9
*The Brick and the Mirror* (Golestan) 33
Brunsdon, Charlotte 4, 19
Butler, J. 16, 18, 104, 134, 137

Cannes Film Festival 125, 141, 144, 148,
153, 158
catchphrases 73, 74, 76, 85
censorship: of *10*, 125; audience
awareness of 11–12, 88, 95, 163; based
on law suits 47; based on moral issues
45–7; based on political expediency
43–5; based on taste 47; censorship
codes 40–41, 48–9; changes under Dad
50–51; and creation of publicity 89, 91;
of festival films 147–9, 151; of *Fifth*

censorship (*cont.*):
  *Reaction* 120–21; filmmakers'
    negotiation with 14, 79, 99, 124;
    filmmakers' strategies to avoid 6, 30,
    67–8; of *Glass Agency* 74; of *House on
    the Water* 84–5; of *The Lizard* 96–8; of
    New Wave films 33–4; *see also nezarat*;
    state control
censorship codes 40–41, 48–9
Centre for Intellectual Development of
  Children and Adolescents 125, 145
*chador* 46, 108
characters, identification with 104, 116,
  131, 137
Cheah, P. 17
children, films about 125, 145–6
*Children of Divorce* (Milani) 111
*Children of Heaven* (Majidi) 154
cinema: economics of 100–102; and
  gender 15–17, 104–10; Neorealist 14;
  perceived threat to morals 34–5, 143–4;
  and resistance 14–15; Third 14–15
Cinema Booklet 38
cinema guilds 51
cinema law 51
cinema of reform 50
Cinema Qods *35*
cinemas: attacks on 89, 110: closures and
  burnings 35, 36; women's use of 86,
  105, 109, 116, 137
*The Circle* (Panahi) 52, 144, *148*, 151,
  153–4, 157, 159
clergy: opposition to cinema 34–5;
  representations of 90–100
*Close Up* (Kiarostami) 125
code *see* censorship code
cofabulation 11–12, 88–9, 103, 162
Cohen, J. 10
*The Colour of Pomegranate* (Parajanov)
  40
consciousness raising 64, 105, 137
conservative movement 9, 35, 37, 44–5, 49
*The Cow* (Mehrju'i) 33–4, 139–40
*Crimson Gold* (Panahi) 148, 151, 154
*Croesus' Treasure* (Yasemi) 32
*Crystal Garden* (Makhmalbaf) 58
custody laws 113, 115, 122
*The Cyclist* (Makhmalbaf) 60, 66

Dabashi, H. 125
Dad, Seyfollah 49–52, 55, 70, 79, 84, 103
Dariush, H. 33
Davudi, Abolhassan 51
*Dead Wave* (Hatamikia) 74

*Deep Breath* (Shahbazi) 1, 51, 153
Dehqan, Khosrow 143
Derakhshandeh, Puran 109
Devictor, A. 30
diaspora 139
divorce 106
*Dog Day Afternoon* (Lumet) 71
Downing, J. 9–10, 13, 55, 89, 100, 162
*Duel* (Darvish) 167
DVDs 101–2, 153

Ebadi, Shirin 106, 107
Ebtekar, Ma'sumeh 106
economics of cinema 100–102
emotional engagement 64, 134, 137
Engels, Friedrich 6–7
Esfandiyari, Amir 42
ethnography 19–21, 161

Fajr International Film Festival 23, 41, 53,
  143, 146: awards at 38, 41, 73, 79, 83,
  90–91; *Fifth Reaction* at 110, 113–14;
  *Glass Agency* at 70, 72, 73, 75; *House
  on the Water* at 79, 83; *The Lizard* at
  90–91; *Marriage of the Blessed* at 56–7
Family Protection Law 106
Fanon, F. 160
Farabi Cinema Foundation 37, 42, 47,
  142–4, 146
Farahmand, A. 17, 125, 138, 144–5, 150,
  156
Fardin, Mohammad Ali 36
Farmanara, Bahman 50, 76–90, 101,
  155–6
Farrokhzad, Forough 33, 117, 168–9
feminism *see* women's issues; women's
  movement
Ferdowsi Cinema 34
festival films 2, 14–15, 17–19, 78, 163:
  audience reactions 158–9; filmmakers
  149–57; and state authorities 144–9; and
  women 157–8
field research 23–7
FIFF *see* Fajr International Film Festival
*Fifth Reaction* (Milani) 16, 104, 110–25
*film abgushti* 32
*film-e dokhtar-pesari* 110
*film-e ejtema'i see* social films
*film-e farsi* 32, 34, 36, 108
*film-e nategh-e farsi* 32
*film-e sefareshi see* film to order
*filmha-ye dini see* religious films
*filmha-ye erfani see* mystical films
*filmha-ye zananeh see* women's films

film to order 152–7
Fischer, M. 33, 140, 169
Fiske, J. 19
Frankfurt School 3
Fraser, N. 13
*From Karkheh to Rhine* (Hatamikia) 70
funding 100–102, 145, 151–2

*Gabbeh* (Makhmalbaf) 48, 167
Gaffary, Farrokh 140
Ganji, Akbar 49
gender: and cinema 15–17, 104–10, 163;
    and identity 104; performativity of 104,
    134, 137; *see also* women's issues;
    women's films
Getino, O. 14–15, 103
Ghazian, H. 30, 100
*gheyr-e khodi see* outsider filmmakers
Ghobadi, Bahman 144
*Glass Agency* (Hatamikia) 27, *69*, 69–76
global media flows 138–9
Golestan, S. 33
Golmakani, H. 36, 39
Golshiri, Hushang 79
Gorji, Monireh 106
Gramsci, A. 7–8, 9, 64, 167
Greer, L.S. 21–2

Habermas, J. 12–13
*Haj Aqa, the Cinema Actor* 108
Hall, S. 4, 8
*Hambastegi* 77
*Harmonica* (Naderi) 145
Hartley, J. 19–20
Hashemi, Faezeh 106
Hassani-Nasab, Nima 40
Hatamikia, Ebrahim 49, 57, 67–8, 69–76,
    143, 152, 153–4, 156
*Hayat-e No* 61
*hedayat* 37, 38
hegemony 8–9
*hejab* 106, 109, 135
Hekmat, Manijeh 107, 109, 121, 124,
    147
*hemayat* 37
*Hemlock* (Afkhami) 28
Heydarian, Mohammad-Mahdi 52–3, 96,
    97
*Hidden Half* (Milani) 111, 117
Hollywood films 5, 14, 32, 43, 70, 113,
    141, 156
Hosseini, G. 58, 64
*The House is Black* (Farrokhzad) 33
House of Cinema 51

*House on the Water* (Farmanara) 52,
    76–90, *78, 80, 81*, 98, 101, 155–6
*howzeh-ye honari see* Art Centre

identity: gender 104; national 17–19,
    138–9, 140, 152–7
*Identity* (Hatamikia) 70
Ideological State Apparatuses 7, 35
ideology, concepts of 6–9
Inness, S. 137
insider filmmakers 38, 60, 64, 79
insider research 21–3
Institute of Contemporary Art, London 1
international circulation *see* transnational
    circulation
international funding 101
interpretive groups 64
*In the Alleys of Love* (Sina'i) 42
*In the Slaughterhouse of Love* (Tabrizi) 90
Iran–Iraq war 2, 12, 36–7, 41, 56, 90, 106:
    criticism of 72, 73
Iranian revolution 1–2, 12, 34–5, 79
Islamic dress 34, 41, 46–7, 106; *see also*
    *chador*; *hejab*
Islamic feminists 107
Islamic Republic of Iran Broadcasting 35
Islamization 2, 6, 7, 35–7, 38, 106, 109

Jannati, Ayatollah 143
*javanmard* 150, 168
*javanmardi* 76, 150–51, 168
Jenkins, H. 4
*Jomhuri-ye Islami* 99

*Kandahar* (Makhmalbaf) 152
Kar, Mehrangiz 206
Karbaschi, Gholam-Hossein 49
Karimi, Iraj 150
Karimi, Niki 123
Kasehsaz, Habibollah 45, 46, 148
Katz, Elihu 3–4
Khamene'i, Ayatollah 38, 144
Khani, M. 58, 64
Khatami, Mohammad: election of 49,
    69–70, 76; as minister of Culture and
    Islamic Guidance 1, 37, 42, 44, 143–4;
    as president 76, 77; presidential
    candidacy 2, 65, 103
Khaz'ali, Ayatollah 94
*khodi see* insider filmmakers
Khomeini, Ayatollah: on cinema 1, 6,
    35–6, 38, 109; criticism of 60, 61; death
    of 41, 56; as leader 8, 44; quotes from
    59, 61, 84, 124

*Killing Rabids* (Beyza'i) 124, 134, 157
Kiarostami, Abbas 101, 125–36, 144, 145, 149–53, 159, 160

Laclau, E. 7, 8, 49
Lahiji, Shahla 107, 108
Larijani, Ali 47–8
law suits 47, 70
*Leili is with Me* (Tabrizi) 90, *91*, 96–7
*Letters of the Wind* (Amini) 46
*Life and Nothing More* (Kiarostami) 125
liminality 12, 55, 66, 162
*The Lizard* (Tabrizi) 43, 53, 90–100, *92, 93*, 162
*The Lor Girl* 31, 32, 108
love, representations of 42

McAdam, D. 64, 119
McArthur, C. 18
*Mahnameh see Mahnameh-ye sinema'i-ye film*
*Mahnameh-ye sinema'i-ye film* 27, 36, *57*, *69*, 72, 89, 114, 141
Majidi, Majid 152
Makarrem-Shirazi, Ayatollah 99
make-up test 46
Makhmalbaf, Mohsen 58, *65*; at the Art Centre 39; on censorship 45–6, 48, 49, 67; festival films 143, 147, 149, 158; funding 101, 153; interview with 65–9; *Marriage of the Blessed* 44, 56–69; support of Khatami 65, 103; as writer 28
Makhmalbaf, Samira 109, 144, 158
Malak-Moti'i, Nasser 36
Marcus, G. 20–21
Marks, L. 18, 138
*Marriage of the Blessed* (Makhmalbaf) 9, 27, 44, 56–69, *57*, 76
*Martyrdom Seekers* (Tabrizi) 90
Marx, Karl 6–7
Mashhad 23, 99, 109, 170
Masjed-Jame'i, Ahmad 52
*Matrimony of the Good* (Hatamikia) 70
*May Lady* (Bani-Etemad) 154, *154*
MCIG *see* Ministry of Culture and Islamic Guidance
meaning, layering of 10–11, 63–4, 103, 163
media: global flows 138–9; radical 9–11, 13, 55, 89–90, 100, 102–3, 162; research 3–5; and resistance 13–15
Mehrju'i, Dariush 89, 157
Merton, R.K. 3

Meshkini, Marziyeh 109
messages, discovery and decoding 63–4, 88, 103, 163
Milani, Tahmineh 28, 46, 101, 110–25, 157
Ministry of Culture and Islamic Guidance: controversy over films 92, 94, 98, 121, 151, 83–4; festival films 146–9; ministers and personnel 1, 5, 36, 37–41, 42, 44–5, 48–9, 51–3; policies and operation 37–41, 47, 48–9, 79
Mir-Hosseini, Z. 107, 135
Mirbaqeri, Bijan 101
Mirsalim, M. 48
*Mrs Ahou's Husband* (Mollapur) 33
*Mrs Ahu's Husband* (Afghani) 33
*The Mix* (Mehrju'i) 89
Mo'adikhah, Hojjatolislam 1, 36
Mo'tamedi, A. 72, 89
modernization 31–2, 155
modern left 44
modern right 44
Moghadam, V. 107
Moghissi, H. 107
Mohajerani, A. 1, 49, 51–2, 79, 144
Mohammad-Kashi, S. 157
Mohammadi, Hossein 41, 45, 47, 84
Mohammadi, Manuchehr 97–8
*The Mongols* (Kimiavi) 33
morality, cinema as perceived threat to 34, 143–4
Morley, David 4, 19
Mosaddeq, Mohammad 31
Mouffe, C. 8, 49
*The Mourners of Bayal* (Sa'edi) 33
Mozafferoddin Shah 31
Mulvey, L. 16, 127
Musavi, Mir-Hossein 37, 40, 44, 57, 68
mystical films 39–40, 42

Nabavi, Behzad 58
Naficy, H. 17, 38, 139, 160
*Narges* (Bani-Etemad) 109
*Nasuh's Repentance* (Makhmalbaf) 39, 58
national identity 17–19, 138–9, 140, 157
neopatriarchy 104–5, 119, 135
Neorealist cinema 14
New Poetry 11, 33
New Wave films 33–4, 77–8, 108, 139–42
*nezarat* 37, 40–41
*The Night Never Ends* (Sayyad) 79
*Night of the Hunchback* (Ghaffari) 33
*Nights of Zayandehrud* (Makhmalbaf) 28, 58, 143

Nuri, Abdollah 49

Omid, Jamal 33, 140, 170
*Once upon a Time* (Jamalzadeh) 33
outsider filmmakers 38, 79

Pahlavi, Mohammad Reza Shah 31–2
Pahlavi, Reza Shah 31
Pahlavi regime 7, 11, 31–4, 79, 106, 140,
    155
Panahi, Jafar 144, 145, 148, 151, 152,
    153–4, 159
Parajanov, Sergei 40
*Passage* (Tabrizi) 90
patriarchy 15–17, 104–5, 113, 119, 129,
    137; *see also* women's issues
*The Peddler* (Makhmalbaf) 58
Persian mystical poetry 11
Pezeshk, Mohammad-Hassan 52, 84
pluralism 74, 76, 99–100, 103
poetry 10–11: New 11, 33; Persian
    mystical 11
police 61, 70, 75
political factions 44–5, 75–6
polygamy 106, 113, 121
*Prince Ehtejab* (Farmanara) 77
propaganda: conservative 37; Islamic
    regime 38; state 31–2
public spheres, concept of 12–13, 103
publicity 89, 91

Qaderi, A. 36, 114
Qajar dynasty 31, 79
*Qamar Khanom's House* (Farmanara) 77
*Qeysar* (Kimia'i) 33
*Qods* 114

radical media 9–11, 13, 55, 89–90, 100,
    102–3, 162
Rafsanjani, Ayatollah 41–2, 44, 56
Raja'i, Mohammad-Ali 36, 58
rating system 38
*Realm of Lovers* (Karbakhsh) 142
reception studies 2, 5, 19–20, 161
reconstruction period 56
*Red* (Jeyrani) 109–10
reformist movement 2, 44–5, 49, 109–10,
    144–5; support for 9, 76–7, 83, 100, 103
relativism 73–4
religion, representations of 82, 90–100
religious films 38–40
*The Report* (Kiarostami) 79
repression 8
Repressive State Apparatuses 8

research: field 23–7; by the insider 21–3;
    media 3–5
resistance 56, 60; and cinema 14–15; and
    media 13–14
Rex Cinema 35
role models 104
Rumi 11
*The Runner* (Naderi) 142

Sa'edi, Gholam-Hossein 33
Sacred Defence films 39, 50, 52, 70, 142,
    144
Sadr, Hamid Reza 145, 149–50
Sadr-'Ameli, Rasul 101
Saffar-Harandi, Hossein 53
Saffarian, N. 73
*Salam Cinema* (Makhmalbaf) 48
Saminejad, Sediqeh 108
*Santuri* (Mehrju'i) 53
Sarachild, K. 105
SAVAK 31
Sayyad, P. 139, 150
Scott, J. 13
self-reflection 104, 116, 137
sexuality, representations of 46, 90
Shahbazi, Parviz 1, 153
Shamlu, Ahmad 33
Sharabi, H. 104–5, 135
*she'r-e no* (New Poetry) 11, 33
Sherkat, Shahla 106, 107
Shoja'nuri, 'Ali Reza 142, 144, 146
Shourjeh, Jamal 53
*A Simple Event* (Shahid-Sales) 140
*sinema-ye moslehaneh see* cinema of
    reform
*sinema-ye motefavet* 32–4, 139–42
Skeggs, B. 16, 104, 137
*Smell of Camphor, Fragrance of Jasmine*
    (Farmanara) 79, 83, 156
*Snowman* (Mirbaqeri) 28, 50
social films 3, 27–8, 55–6, 102–3;
    discussion of *Glass Agency* 69–76;
    discussion of *House on the Water*
    76–90; discussion of *The Lizard*
    90–100; discussion of *Marriage of the*
    *Blessed* 56–69; and economics
    100–102
social justice 58, 60
social movements 10
social position, women 106–7
social realism 32–3
Solanas, F. 14–15, 103
*South of the City* (Gaffary) 33
Sreberny, A. 13, 17–18, 105, 139

state control  2, 6, 30–54: 1978–1981:
34–7; 1982–1989: 37–41; 1989–1993:
41–8; 1994–1997: 48–9; 1997–present
49–53; and economics  100–102;
pre-revolution  31–4; and international
success  142–9; *see also* censorship
statistics, Dad's use of  50
Stephenson, J.B.  21–2
Stokes, G.  18
subsidies  47
*Sureh*  125
symbolism  10–11, 30

Tabrizi, Kamal  28, 90–100
Tahmasebi, Mohammad-Hassan  27, 47,
51, 94, 149
Talebinejad, Ahmad  150
Talebzadeh, Nader  144
Taleqani, 'Azam  106
*Tall Shadows of Wind* (Farmanara)  79
Tapper, Richard  32, 104
Taqva'i, Naser  50
Tarkovsky, Andrei  40
Taslimi, Susan  136
*Taste of Cherry* (Kiarostami)  125, 132,
149–50
Tavasoli, Homa  158
Tehran  10, 23, 33, 61, 77, 85, 99, 109,
146–7, 167, 170
Tehran International Film Festival  77
television  35, 61, 87, 89, 101
*Thelma and Louise* (Scott)  113
Third Cinema  14–15
*Through the Olive Trees* (Kiarostami)
125
*Time of Love* (Makhmalbaf)  28, 58, 109,
143
traditional left  44–5
traditional right  44–5
transnational circulation  6, 17–19, 138–9,
163: audience reactions  158–9; makers
of festival films  149–57; New Wave

films  139–42; and state authorities
142–9; and women  157–8
*The Traveller* (Kiarostami)  145
*The Travellers* (Beyza'i)  41, 157
Turner, Victor  12, 55, 89, 102, 162
*Two Sightless Eyes* (Makhmalbaf)  39, 58
*Two Women* (Milani)  46, 109–10, 111,
114, 119, 120, 134

*Under the Moonlight* (Mir-Karimi)  97

VCDs  101–2, 153
Venice Film Festival  144, 148
Vosuqi, Behruz  150

*What's New?* (Milani)  111
*Where Is the Friend's House?* (Kiarostami)
125, 132, 142, 145, 160
*The White Balloon* (Panahi)  152
*The Wind Will Carry Us* (Kiarostami)  125
women: involvement in cinema  107–10,
157–8; representation of  34, 40–41,
45–7, 53, 108–10; social position
106–7; use of cinema space  86, 105,
109, 116, 137
women's films  15–17, 28, 104–10, 136–7,
157–8; discussion of  *10*, 125–36;
discussion of *Fifth Reaction*  110–25
women's issues  15–17, 104–10 , 157–8,
163; *see also* women's films
women's movement  2, 105–7, 122–3
*Women's Prison* (Hekmat)  45, 118, 121,
124, 134, 147–8, 159
Writer's Guild  41, 156

*Yas-e No*  82–3
Yektapanah, Hasan  144

*zahir*  10–11
Zamm, Hojjatolislam  43, 58
Zarghami, Ezzatollah  48
Zoonen, L.  13, 15, 105